THE THERAPY EXPERIENCE

HOW HUMAN KINDNESS HEALS

ROGER KINGERLEE

PCCS Books
Ross-on-Wye

First published in 2006

PCCS BOOKS
3 Thomas Row
Alton Road
ROSS-ON-WYE
HR9 5LB
UK
Tel +44 (0)1989 763 900
contact@pccs-books.co.uk
www.pccs-books.co.uk

The Therapy Experience:
How human kindness heals

British Library Cataloguing in Publication Data.
A catalogue record for this book is available from the British Library.

ISBN 1 898059 78 0
ISBN 978 1898059 78 3

Cover design by Jill Marsh and Old Dog Graphics
Printed by Bell & Bain, Glasgow, UK

Contents

Acknowledgements

Above all, I should like to thank the people with whom I've met and worked with over the last decade, in various settings, in Oxford and Norfolk. From them I've learned about the joys that come with a change in perception.

I should also like to acknowledge the assistance of the following colleagues and friends from whom I have learned so much during the development of this book over the last five years or so in particular. Professor Malcolm Adams, for his excellent organization of the Clin. Psy. D. course at the University of East Anglia (UEA); Jackie Baker, for her excellent supervision as I began to find my feet with cognitive analytic therapy (CAT); Gillian Bowden for her psychodynamic expertise; Michael Chaskalson, for his reflections on mindfulness; Dr Mary Cubitt and Norfolk and Waveney Mental Heathcare Partnership, for their encouragement and support Mark Donovan, for his help with narrative approaches; Dr Adam Duncan, for his mindful take on life; Patricia Kingerlee, my mother, for unflagging encouragement and support; George Mak-Pearce, for listening and responding to me in the ways that he did; Penny Morgan, for her insights into working with people who have learning disabilities; Gillian Oaker, for her cognitive behavioural therapy supervision from which I learned so much; Dr. Anne Palmer, for our various and wide-ranging discussions of mindfulness-related matters, and her unstinting encouragement over the last few years; Professor Shirley Reynolds, again for her excellent organization of the UEA course; Sid Singer, for his expert advice and supervision on eye movement desensitization and reprocessing; Darren Spooner of the St Giles Clinic, for his psychological reflectoins and his belief in me; Maggie Taylor-Sanders for her editorial help and understanding at PCCS Books; Dr. Mark Westacott, for his CAT-related insights; Pete Williams for his psychodynamic reflections; and Dr. Giles Yeates, for his neuropsychological interests and expertise. Despite all this help, of course, any remaining mistakes or misunderstandings are mine.

Finally, I should like to thank my lovely wife Lucy, who encouraged me every step of the way.

Dedication

This book is for Lucy, who does it all, naturally

Have you seen the horizon lately?
Yoko Ono

Preface

> Begin afresh, afresh, afresh.
>
> Philip Larkin, 'The Trees'

Knowing Me, Knowing You

There is, I do believe, too much unnecessary psychological suffering in the world. I've written this book because I'm against such mindless suffering. This is simply what I have most experience of, both as a practising clinical psychologist and, equally importantly, as a person. It has recently been established beyond reasonable doubt that much suffering occurs because of how we, as human individuals and societies, organize ourselves.[1] What has not been convincingly explained until now is *why* we arrange ourselves in these damaging ways, and how we can improve matters and come to treat each other more respectfully. These are my subjects here. As I will show, and despite what we might automatically think, it actually feels *good* to be good to others—especially in a world where we now know that race is rubbish, since whatever our skin colour, genetically we all belong.[2] In this new world, it's good to respect each other; it's *nice* to be nice. It may really be the best we can do.

Various recent books by philosophers and other professional writers have concerned themselves with what it means to be good,[3] to live well[4] and to love;[5] but

---

1. Marmot, M. (2004). *Status Syndrome: How your social standing directly affects your health and life expectancy.* London: Bloomsbury.
2. Tettelin, H. & Parkhill, J. (2004). The use of genome annotation data and its impact on biological conclusions. *Nature Genetics 36 (10),* 1028–9.
3. E.g. Blackburn, S. (1999). *Being Good.* Oxford: Oxford University Press. Foot, P. (2002). *Natural Goodness.* Oxford: Oxford University Press. Hornby, N. (2002). *How To Be Good.* Harmondsworth: Penguin.
4. Botton, A. de (2003). *Status Anxiety.* Harmondsworth: Penguin. Comte-Sponville, A. (2001). *A Small Treatise on the Great Virtues: The uses of philosophy in everyday life.* Harmondsworth: Penguin. Murdoch, I. (1970; repr. 1996). *The Sovereignty of Good.* London: Routledge.
5. Frankfurt, H. (2003). *The Reasons of Love.* Princeton, NJ: Princeton University Press. Wynne-Tyson, E. (1962; repr. 1970). *The Philosophy of Compassion.* Fontwell: The Centaur Press.

by definition most writers spend their time writing. Some, as they themselves admit and as Sigmund Freud suggested, write to avoid involvement in life and in reality. In contrast, while I too am concerned about what it means to be good and to live well, no imagination was needed here, either from me or from the good people I've worked with. There have been difficult, fearful, painful times; we did make mistakes. We do make mistakes; and at least for a while, and like most people, we'll keep making mistakes of different kinds. We lived it.

In what follows I'll talk about psychological theory, the experiences of the people I've met (in fictionalized, imaginary form) and my own quite extensive personal experience of psychological issues. At some level or other, as a clinical psychologist I always hear the same story—more or less, and with a number of variations on a theme. Something has happened, someone's been hurt—but almost always other people have somehow done the hurting, or at least some hurting. Sometimes people I meet have been hurt so badly by other human beings that their lives—years, decades of their existences—have been effectively smashed, smashed, smashed: smashed by other people. Until others help, the person who has been hurt won't begin to feel much better; and since I myself have needlessly wasted so much time personally, and lost so many chances to be happy and to enjoy life as it passed me by, I'd like to help you and the people you care about not to do that. I have at least some qualifications that might be useful. During some parts of my life—months, sometimes even years at a time—I have voluntarily run a one-man race to be crowned The Unhappiest Man in the World. Few other people were aware of this crazy, nonsensical quest at the time; indeed, as is often (or perhaps always) so in the world of the psyche, I wasn't completely aware of it myself until others helped draw attention to it. I was making myself miserable by failing to live up to fixed standards, of whose existence I was not even aware—but that didn't stop me. I carried on regardless until, in the light of psychology and psychotherapy, I knew better. Are you, or members of your family, feeling troubled? I was, too. This book is for you.

Perhaps the best illustration of the earlier, unhappier part of my life is my experience starting at Oxford University in October 1988. I was a confused, fatherless, sensitive young man, just nineteen. With no firm sense of my own identity, I tried in vain to find out from books of literature and philosophy some pretty important questions: who I was, who I should become, how I should live. I hardly need say that the look-at-books-to-suss-out-the-meaning-of-life idea didn't really work out as planned. Many of the writers seemed to be even more miserable than me—and that was saying something.

It was 'matriculation' day, the time at the start of term when all new students, eager young things full of hope and light, troop off to the grand Sheldonian Theatre to be officially sworn into the university. Traditionally this is a day of celebration for those concerned, rightly so, and it should have been for me. I'd earned my place there through hard work, and deserved—like everyone else in life—to have some fun: but no. I struggled a great deal in those first days there, away from home for the first time. Clueless how to cook and look after myself; hopeless with women, having never by that time seen a naked one unrelated to me; and with famous (and therefore to me massively intimidating) writers like John Bayley walking around the college, I felt way out of my social depth. Or rather, I didn't feel it; I swallowed the feelings—and so while thousands of other students quaffed drinks after the ceremony, had fun and made happy fools of themselves, throwing flour around and getting it in each other's hair, I looked on from a distance, in my room. I stood there, teetotal, looking at the jollity before me and thinking, 'This is dreadful. We're not here for enjoyment.' The others went off to the bar while I, feeling very lonely but not yet having the emotional intelligence to realize it, stayed in my poky room. A little later I went on a food binge; fit to burst with secret sadness and distress and missing home badly, I consoled myself with fast food—a *lot* of fast food. By that time I see now that I was bulimic, well on course to my title as the World's Unhappiest Man. I was tortuously turned in on myself, while others were enjoying the springtime of their lives, drunk on the wine of youth and with every right to be so.

The flour in the college quad was blown away after a few days of early autumn wind; my problems, though, took longer to heal. They were a terrible waste of valuable time, yet with a little psychological understanding there was no need—there *is* no need—for this to happen.

This is because in the light of even a touch of psychological knowledge and psychotherapy, we can make valuable changes in our own lives that have clear and real benefits for ourselves and others. While our ancestors relied on an external force—God—for salvation of their souls, given modern psychological knowledge we can rely on ourselves. Our psychological destinies are now firmly in human hands: in our own and in each other's.

Now I've resolved my own psychological issues to a good degree, I try to help other people to do the same for themselves. I've long since given up the race for the title of The World's Unhappiest Man, but others, sadly for them, are still in the running for the world's worst prize—open, of course, to members of both sexes. The prize might perhaps be a lifetime's anti-depressant prescription that, as well as changing nothing much in the external form of your life, may make you feel dizzy and could have powerful genital-disabling properties. This isn't likely to be so great for us today, in a world where sex is king (well, maybe not, but there's a lot of it about).

When I reflect on my own life so far and on the experiences of the people I meet when working as a clinical psychologist, I'm struck by how much people could be helped, and how much suffering could be reduced, if we tried to change some of our basic—but most often unnoticed and unrecognized—mindless habits of living. Maybe also we need to question or even remove some of the invisible yet powerful barriers in our minds that emerge from our culture, gender and upbringing, whether these habits are 'genetic', learned, or a mixture of the two. We may never know anyway—or at least not in any way that is of much practical use to us, especially in today's world of often unbridled self-assertion, where no one single story or view can ever convey the subtlety of reality. It is a reality in which different people inhabit different bodily and psychological worlds, each person having their own feelings and creating their own meanings—and indeed their own ongoing lives—at any moment, depending on the working of many factors.

But in other, simple ways, you could be helped; I could be helped. Hey, you know what? We could *even* help each other, just by following the emotional logic and being a little more mindful of ourselves and each other—a natural ability with which almost all of us are born but not all of us make full use of. All human behaviour is psychologically explicable. Ask the right questions, and the psyche explains itself. There is no such thing as 'madness', as 'sane' people used to think:[6] just the changing feelings that we and the world we live in produce in each other. And even better, none of us *needs* to be heading for Gloom Central Station or staying there for long. It really wouldn't take much to change and, believe me, it'd make a lot of difference, especially to some people. Honestly: I see it every day.

Now, do take a seat. What seems to be the problem?

6. Phillips, N. (2005). *Going Sane.* London: Faber.

1

We Affect Each Other

Humility
Is the essential ability
Before the loved object.
Elizabeth Jennings, 'Relationships'

Why Mindful Psychotherapy? Why Mindful Life?

Every human being is born precious—yet we treat each other, and ourselves, like trash.

In this book I am going to ask the seemingly impossible: that as a species, we human beings step back from ourselves momentarily and try harder, *just a little harder,* to treat each other and ourselves more mindfully and to treat each other well. I shall claim, as a practising clinical psychologist, that there are good scientific reasons to support a certain central tenet—perhaps even *the* central tenet—of Christianity and Buddhism. Psychology and religion, as we have known for over a century, have much to offer one another.[1] Above all, though, the old-fashioned-seeming Christian ideal that we should treat others as we wish to be treated ourselves remains as true today as it has been throughout history. Now we have the scientific research to prove it. Mindful compassion[2] and forgiveness, based in psychological understanding, is called for because human imperfections inevitably intrude on our own lives and those of others. This can produce pain and suffering. Being of the flesh, we are *all* fallible; but when our lives go wrong we can, in the light of modern clinical psychology and associated fields, consciously choose to help ourselves and others back to happiness and health. In a world where all too often now, nothing is a guarantee of anything; where many

---

1. James, W. (1902; repr. 1985). *The Varieties of Religious Experience.* Harmondsworth: Penguin; Argyle, M. (2000). *Psychology and Religion: An introduction.* London: Routledge.
2. For a recent psychological summary, see Gilbert, P. (ed.). (2005). *Compassion: Conceptualizations, research and use in psychotherapy.* London: Routledge.

more older people are living isolated, vulnerable and alone, where once they were better supported; and where divorce is fast becoming the norm, families are regularly shattered and vulnerable children are left floundering emotionally, consciously helping others in various ways might be important to many people—especially to the youth. For the psychological life of people in general, and children in particular, today affects tomorrow.

We now know enough about ourselves and our human psychology to say with some confidence that all our failures are ultimately failures of love; the stories of our daily lives suggest that we live, and love, imperfectly. One reason for this imperfection is our ancient, evolutionary past. Because of our evolved need to survive, we often tend to think of ourselves in over-flattering terms.[3] Connected to this psychological survival mechanism, we also often tend to put ourselves before others. Perhaps more than ever here in the capitalist West now, we are demandingly self-assertive—and encouraged to be so. Yet while there is clear adaptive value for the single self in such behaviour, this default-mode, automatic self-privileging has the potential, especially where circumstances are hard—where certain groups of people live in stressful conditions—to be very damaging in physical and psychological terms. At such times, other people's needs may be routinely unnoticed, ignored and neglected by us. In turn, we may be unnoticed, ignored and neglected by them. To take a minor example: if I'm neglected by you in a social situation, I'm likely to feel a bit worse for a while; for a few moments, or even a few minutes, I might feel a slight sense of discomfort. Or, to take a more major example, if one powerful group of people chronically ignores the needs of another, less powerful group, the latter is likely to feel more than just miffed. In various psychological ways, they're likely to feel really bad. The ignored group might feel angry, dismissed or damaged—or even all three; and such a position can lead to more serious problems over time.

The great American psychologist and philosopher William James was one of the first people to notice this part of human behaviour, and to identify it clearly. In a talk to teachers at Harvard University in 1892 entitled 'On a certain blindness in human beings', James considered 'the blindness with which we are all afflicted in regard to the feelings of creatures and people different from ourselves'. According to James, our fallible human psyche finds it hard to understand others and connect meaningfully with them. As he says:

> We are practical beings, each of us with limited functions and duties to perform. Each is bound to feel intensely the importance of their own duties and the significance of the situations that call these forth. But this feeling is in each of us a vital secret, for sympathy with which we vainly look to others. The others are too much absorbed in their own vital secrets to take an interest in ours.

And according to James, our inevitable blindness and self-absorption often strongly affect our views of others:

3. Evans, D.E. & Cruse, P. (2004). *Emotion, Evolution, and Rationality.* Oxford: Oxford University Press. Pinker (2003). *The Blank State: The modern denial of human nature.* London: Allen Lane.

> … hence the stupidity and injustice of our opinions, so far as they deal with the significance of alien lives. Hence the falsity of our judgments, so far as they presume to decide in an absolute way on the value of other persons' conditions or ideals.[4]

In today's world, where the destructive imposition of one person's will upon another is quite common, despite all technology, James's point is apt. He himself considered it to have

> the most tremendous practical importance. It is the basis of all our tolerance, social, religious, and political. The forgetting of it lies at the root of every stupid mistake that rulers over subject-peoples make.[5]

In the light of current clinical psychological research and practice, I will agree with James; but I will take his point further. The 'forgetting' of our blindness, I shall say, affects not just our rulers and their 'subject-peoples', but virtually *all* our everyday lives, ourselves and others, in different ways. And simply being more mindful of others' needs—more aware of them—can help, whether in psychotherapy or in life.

What Happens, Matters

Just take three people: the powerless-feeling woman who, because of her abusive upbringing and mindless treatment from others, has learned to overlook her own many strengths; the powerful and successful man who, because of his own harsh upbringing and education, has learned to be blind to the emotional needs of others; and the man who, because of the abandonments and rejections he experienced as a child, has learned not to perceive how his girlfriend loves him and who, with every attempt on her part to show that love and bring them closer together, only pushes her further away. In each of these cases, the psychological issue was not simply inbuilt—whether by genes, temperament or any other possible relevant factor: it was largely or wholly acquired. We know from science that animals learn through experience.[6] Even the humble *fish,* science has shown, can learn, through just one experience, how to avoid capture in a net—and then tells its friends, too. And in the context of our human lives, given our basic, human tendencies, like the need to feel safe with our caregivers when we are growing up, *we* learn through experience. You got it. We are a most highly absorbent animal: so what we take in needs to be good.

Precisely *how* we are affected by a personal experience that we have—from our eating a handful of raisins to our being shouted at by someone—depends on various

4. James, W. (1899). On a certain blindness in human beings. In: W. James. *Talks to Teachers on Psychology: And to students on some of life's ideals.* London: Longman, Green: 229–264.
5. *ibid.*: 265–301.
6. Lieberman, D.A. (1993). *Learning: Behaviour and cognition: 2nd edn.* Pacific Grove, CA: Brooks/Cole.

issues, including the circumstances, our age and genetic background. But the essential point is that *what* happens to us—regardless of the channel by which the experience reaches us—really matters. This is true physically; if we are hit hard enough by someone, we may feel pain, a bone of ours may break, and various consequences for our health may follow before the injury heals. It is also true psychologically. While we are, by and large, highly adaptable and resilient, evolved creatures, if we are frightened by something—or someone—to a sufficient degree, then we will react with great fear; and if we are frightened to an extreme degree, we may be psychologically traumatised. When being attacked by other people, for example, even the toughest-seeming men and women, some of whom I've met, may shrivel in the face of massive anxiety. As well as in some ways being vulnerable to others we also, in turn, affect others in equal measure, even though we are apt to forget this—and even though this is often not so obvious in our daily lives. *We affect each other psychologically*. It is for this reason, if we are *truly* interested in the health of ourselves and others as part of the greater global human community and the living environment, that mindless treatment of other human beings, and ourselves, might be much less desirable than careful, kind, mindful treatment: the kind of treatment where we treat ourselves, and others with whom we share our lives, with respect.[7]

Countering these matters of blindness towards others' needs that James identified over a century ago, the deliberate practice of human love can have a powerful healing quality. Being conscious, or mindful, of how we can affect our own and each other's lives could, I will say, lead us towards different, happier, healthier ways of life. One reason for this is that—just as a wealth of evidence suggests that children's early exposure to certain types of positive and negative behaviour influences their possible range of behaviour later on—consciously behaving compassionately and mindfully towards others is often likely to have good results. It might feel odd for us to start being deliberately mindful towards, or 'good' to, others; but there are excellent reasons to try. People can change how they are and what they do.

Also, we all need each other. I recall working with, and feeling strongly moved by, a very financially poor couple who had treasured the plastic rings they had long ago exchanged as a sign of their unbroken love. Then again, even the most apparently powerful and successful people in our societies—those to whom many of us, rightly or wrongly, look up—very often need admiration from others and actually suffer psychologically without it. And feelings are often at their best when shared: when we ourselves feel joy, for instance, we automatically look for others to share it with us.[8] Without their attentive presence, our pleasure is diminished. Moreover, when the conditions in which we live, partly set by others, improve, our health can pick up rapidly. With regard to *physical* well-being, for instance, life expectancy across all social classes in the UK rose significantly between the 1970s and the 1990s. Our

7. Sennett, R. (2003; repr. 2004). *Respect: The formation of character in an age of inequality.* Harmondsworth: Penguin.
8. Argyle, M. (1987). *The Psychology of Happiness.* London: Routledge. For a recent review of the literature, see Layard, R. (2004). *Happiness: Lessons from a new science.* London: Penguin/Allen Lane.

health is 'not a fixed property, either of our biological natures or of the society in which we live'.[9] Many or all aspects of life are dynamic. There is every reason to think that this is also true of our psychological health. The outlook is good. People with psychological issues generally really want to get better. In *by far* the majority of cases, they want to come for modern psychological therapy, where it is available; and when they arrive, they want to change if they possibly can. As all good therapists know, when the psychological blockages are removed healthy growth can—and most often does—occur. And sometimes, given the practice of kindness, such healthy growth and recovery occurs most effectively, often with astonishing rapidity.

Yet given the possibilities if we treat each other well, a question might be asked. Have we not, as very successful, evolved beings, actually developed mostly to act mindfully and respectfully—to show kindness towards, and cooperate with one another, rather than causing each other to suffer? Aren't we already doing our best? At present the Darwinian jury members are out, still scratching their often highly evolved beards. To begin with, it is well known that humans, like many organisms, tend to favour their own kind—offspring particularly—over other organisms. In its most basic form, this post-Darwinian idea, kin selection theory,[10] suggests that at least some cooperation, or altruism, between organisms could be explained by the closeness of the genetic relationships between organisms. This accords with common sense. Most psychologically healthy parents, for example, give more money to their children than, say, to charity. Many obvious exceptions come to mind, however: the often excellent care of step-parents towards their children, for instance, to whom they are not genetically related. So from at least one viewpoint, we seem geared to be more kind to those who are (or seem to us to be) close to us.

And in some ways, we may also have evolved to be kind towards, or at least cooperate reasonably with, yet other people. Capacity for altruism towards *non-relatives*, or reciprocal altruism,[11] may have evolved among humans because we may benefit from different types of exchange with *non-related* others; but if need be, equipped with our powerful intelligence and cognitive capacities including memory and face-recognition, we can also identify, and choose to withdraw cooperation from, those who exploit us.[12] This possibility of our continuing with, or withdrawal from, cooperative, kind exchanges also highlights the complex nature of the interactions involved. In any such person-to-person interaction, a single interwoven thread of appraisal, emotion and action is most probably involved—often all within a split second.[13] Above all, however, a *conscious decision* about what to do next is taken—an essential point for my case in

---

9. Marmot, M. (2004). *Status Syndrome: How your social standing directly affects your health and life expectancy.* London: Bloomsbury: 26.
10. Hamilton, W.D. (1964). The genetical evolution of social behaviour, I and II. *Journal of Theoretical Biology, 7,* 1–52.
11. Trivers, R. (1971). The evolution of reciprocal altruism. *Quarterly Review of Biology, 46,* 35–57.
12. e.g. Ridley, M. (1997). *The Origins of Virtue.* Harmondsworth: Penguin.
13. Ryle, A. & Kerr, I.B. (2002). *Introducing Cognitive Analytic Therapy: Principles and practice.* Chichester: Wiley.

this book about treating others well. We can often choose, if we wish, to override our impulses. We don't have to do what we always did.

From one perspective, then, post-Darwinian models of cooperation offer some encouragement, since certain types of kindness appear to have evolutionary advantages, and so seem to be common both among animals and humans—with human family relationships, and trade, as obvious examples.[14] But from another viewpoint—and as certain aspects of day-to-day life indicate—some psychological theory and evidence suggest real limitations to human kindness. For one thing, while human beings often cooperate with and are kind towards those to whom they feel kinship, broadly defined, in proportion to the perceived level of that kinship, it might also be expected that where a person perceives *a high degree of difference* (in social status, say) in another individual or group, the level of kindness will be reduced—and can even tip into a different mode of human activity, like aggression or cruelty. As we shall see in Chapter 2, research in social psychology strongly supports this idea. And for another thing, our physical and psychological closeness to or distance from others can be important. I am frequently and powerfully moved—and to the point of helping—by the stories of courage and survival that are recounted to me by near-strangers whom I meet in my work as a clinical psychologist. Yet hearing about the general distress—no matter how terrible—of anonymous others thousands of miles away can, if I listen inactively and unreflectively, leave me feeling all but emotionally neutral, barely willing to lift a helping finger for anyone or anything. Today, we can *know* everything and *do* nothing.

Whatever the scientific truth about kindness should it ever emerge, though, we may all require others to show it towards us at different times. For instance, all of us—simply by virtue of our being human—have our flaws. Despite what we might often feel, none of us is perfect. We have weaknesses. When times are hard we may lose courage, faith and hope, and feel the drag of despair upon us. We—even the most sensible and reputable among us—make mistakes: sometimes minor ones, sometimes major ones. I have known experienced bus drivers absent-mindedly take the wrong turning; and I have known grown adults, mature professors at Oxford University—of whom more might have been expected (wrongly, since we are all human)—squabble bitterly like babies over the most trivial of points. No one is immune. To act like a jerk, sometimes at least, is human. Everyone does it. Just watch out for the people who deny it.

As flawed, imperfect human beings, we face a dilemma. We need the attention of others at different times throughout life—from first breath to last, we depend on them; but our needs compete with theirs, leading to potential conflict. So human life is partly a balancing act between the needs of self and other. I suggest, though, that in the Western world at least, we as individuals have got the balance wrong. Privileging the modern self, we frequently tend to neglect others. In doing this, because of our essential human interdependence, we can also end up impoverishing ourselves. In this way whole tracts of a person's self can lie fallow, undiscovered for a lifetime, before reaching oblivion at death. Such a wasted life—and I have witnessed a number

---

14. Pinker, S. (2002). *The Blank Slate: The modern denial of human nature.* London: Allen Lane.

of such lives—is a real cause for sadness. This can happen when a person—so often for the most understandable of psychological reasons—is too firmly tied to attitudes, beliefs and patterns of relating that are rigid rather than flexible, life-reducing rather than life-enhancing. This seems to be true of multinational companies.[15] Perhaps the same is true of nations.

Possible solutions to this self–other dilemma exist. Increasing individual and collective psychological self-awareness may ultimately be life-promoting since, more conscious and mindful of our own needs, we may be more likely to pause more, and fully acknowledge and act on the needs of others as well as our own needs. But at every step this journey is difficult. We are easily distracted from our better, altruistic impulses by apparently more pressing concerns—our own. However, if we are prepared to recognise difficulty and press on, it may be that there are hidden treasures to be discovered within each and every one of us—within others, and within ourselves. What's more, one key to unlocking these treasures, as both Christ and the Buddha suggested, may be human kindness.

Why Kindness?

Let's be clear. By 'kindness', I do *not* advocate (as some people will automatically think) an indulgent attitude towards self and other since, taken too far and as I know from my own personal and clinical experience, indulgence often has negative psychological effects—preventing a person from developing their sense of autonomy, for example. In any case, overindulgence of this kind is often based on underlying psychological difficulty in a family: a sense of unexpressed disappointment or sadness, perhaps, which might go back years or decades in someone's life. Nor do I mean an overly-cautious approach to the psychology of self and other, which would be inappropriate since in many ways a high proportion of human beings are psychologically robust. Coupled with intelligence, this robust human nature has allowed us to accomplish extraordinary feats, like the exploration of space. So, too great a sense of caution with regard to the minds of self and other is *not* called for.

Rather, by 'human kindness' I mean two things. First, I mean the basic similarity between people. We are all, essentially, of one kind. As human beings we all share vital needs for life, without which our minds and bodies suffer, then die. From a genetic perspective, the similarities between all of us are huge. We share almost 95 per cent of our genome with chimpanzees. What's more, every human being shares an enormous *99.9 per cent* of their DNA with everybody else, and genetic differences *within* ethnic groups are bigger than genetic differences *between* ethnic groups.[16]

Second, and on the basis of this similarity, I mean a greater sense of awareness;

---

15. Bakan, J. (2004). *The Corporation: The pathological pursuit of profit and power.* New York: Free Press.
16. Tettelin, H. & Parkhill, J. (2004). The use of genome annotation data and its impact on biological conclusions. *Nature Genetics, 36(10),* 1028–1029.

a fuller understanding of the psychological and physical needs of self and other; the delicate shift in consciousness that this entails; and a willingness—maybe once each day, or maybe *even only once in a lifetime*—to put this consciousness into action. Christ said: 'Do unto others as you would have them do unto you.'[17] For Christ this meant, in part, showing care, compassion and love for others, including—or perhaps especially—people who are poor, sick or weak. Or, quite likely these days, all three.

> For I was hungry and you gave me food, I was thirsty and you gave me drink, I was a stranger and you welcomed me, I was naked and you clothed me, I was sick and you visited me, I was in prison and you came to me.[18]

Moving stuff. Or, similarly, take the words of the Buddha:

> To speak no ill, to do no harm, to practise restraint, [...] to devote oneself to higher consciousness, this is the Teaching of the Buddhas. [19]

And that's Teaching with a capital 'T'. This idea, of treating others as one might wish oneself to be treated by them and sometimes called the Golden Rule, exists in some form in all major world religions.[20] In practical terms today this might mean, where possible, giving the self and other the benefit of the doubt. Or having, perhaps, a sense of psychological respect for the self and other, acknowledging possible strengths but being mindful of possible weaknesses. 'Morality', as the writer Iris Murdoch said with only a touch of exaggeration, 'is loss of egoism'.[21]

Take one example. If I want my family relationships to run smoothly, as far as can reasonably be expected, I guess that I would be well advised to try at least a little to respect others' needs, and to negotiate with them about how we live our lives together. But if, on the other hand, I am happy to ruin my family relationships, I am free to act mindlessly, meeting my own needs entirely, according to my own standards and paying no heed to anyone else. But this mindless path would have drawbacks: others might be less delighted than I with our new diet of beer and burgers, nightly football on TV, stained carpets, grubby house, and a change of sheets every six months or so—and only then if they seemed to need it. As another example: while many people encounter, and are easily able to dismiss from their minds, experiences of humiliation and shame during early life and adolescence (a delicate period of human development), some people are marked by such experiences for years or decades and their quality of life is significantly reduced—often as they unconsciously attempt to avoid situations in which it seems that the experience, or something like it, might be repeated. This is one

17. Matthew 7:12.
18. Matthew 25:35–36.
19. The Dhammapada, no. 185. In: W. Rahula (1959; repr. 1997). *What the Buddha Said.* Oxford: Oneworld Publications: 131.
20. Murdoch, I. (1992; repr. 1993). *Metaphysics as a Guide to Morals.* Harmondsworth: Penguin: 468.
21. See e.g. Cooper, M.J., Wells, A. & Todd, G. (2004). A cognitive model of bulimia nervosa. *British Journal of Clinical Psychology, 43(1),* 1–17.

way in which, in those who are vulnerable, psychological issues like eating disorders sometimes develop. By mindfully respecting self and other psychologically, the more resilient and robust among us may be encouraged to develop themselves and others like them further, if they wish; while the less fortunate and the less robust—perhaps people like those above—may be enabled to explore life in their own way and at their own speed. Some people are so psychologically damaged by others and by their experiences that a *very high degree* of caution is required in being around them, so as to help them feel safe, or at least safer, in therapy as in life—at least to begin with. Sometimes and with some people, compassion and gentleness, often spread over time in their treatment, is all. In sum, a balanced, fair-minded sense of kindness towards self and other can increase freedom for all to develop as they will. Liberty for the other can bring liberty for the self. On the matter of love, I'm with the Bee Gees: it belongs to you and me.

Fortunately, it has sometimes been the case in history that powerful groups have taken this psychologically tolerant position, and have taken pains to treat the less powerful in a particularly civilized, compassionate way. It was felt that the privilege of power and finance also bestowed a need to help the less fortunate; this was the concept of *noblesse oblige.* I am suggesting a modern, realistic, psychological version of this caring, mindful attitude towards others. Some people have already begun to call for something similar. One man, who worked in the 1980s for the right-wing government in the UK, has openly acknowledged, for instance, the 'damage' done by socially dominant classes to socially subordinate classes; and also that the least we can do is to try to understand what we have done and help to undo it where we can.[22] Sometimes the ruthless actually do acknowledge their weakness. And men, for so long arrogant and dominant in so many ways in Western societies, have begun to show signs of a healthy self-consciousness. Often, self-awareness—becoming mindful of ourselves, what we think, feel and do—is necessary for behavioural change to occur. But change often *does* occur.

Self-awareness, though, is tricky. In my clinical and personal experience many of our apparently fixed assumptions about ourselves, and each other, are misguided or—still more common—barely even recognized. These assumptions can be very strong. For instance, as a man I have sometimes found it very difficult indeed to admit, either to myself or to anyone else, that things aren't OK in my life, or that I don't feel good. It took me years to see how my beliefs about what being a man meant prevented me from getting in touch with my feelings, and getting help if I needed it. I cannot know myself alone. Whether I acknowledge it or not, someone else needs to help me in knowing who I really am, what I am really about. And getting to know oneself well can take years, decades: perhaps even our whole lives. Engaging *more* with each other and ourselves helps here, as misunderstandings are reduced, and the space between us is reduced or even closed. This might be important in the West, currently the most powerful economic region on Earth but a place where, despite rising living standards, many of us increasingly really look after *ourselves only* and where many of us, increasingly, are unhappy and even depressed. And such self-

22. Mount, F. (2004). *Mind the Gap: The new class divide in Britain.* London: Short Books: 12.

awareness might even encourage us also to look further afield. There may be much suffering in other parts of the world that we, with some kindness, could help to reduce. Or, when other groups, nations or organizations attack us collectively we could—instead of just fighting back, prolonging the cycles of abuse and violence—seek to psychologically engage with them. We could begin to experiment with treating these others in new and different ways. We could begin to try to understand them and help them change—and perhaps even *permit them to change us*—rather than just accusingly pointing the finger at them or at others.

From what I know of psychological life, I believe that when we, acting mindfully, show kindness to ourselves or to others, something special and life-giving happens. The possibilities of abandonment, failure, fear, humiliation, imperfection and loss—or the other ghosts that haunt our daily lives—can be admitted. Feelings of relief may consequently be acknowledged and perhaps shared. The painful and stress-inducing illusion of having always to get things right, to reach perfection, and of having to keep up appearances to others—who are, tragically, often doing the selfsame thing—is replaced by something more compassionate, more humane and more hopeful. This is often the thought that, despite our perceived failings and weaknesses, we still have value and worth nevertheless; and above all, the feeling that we are not alone. The history and culture of even just the twentieth century signposts the many barren places to which the path of attempted perfection can lead. Acknowledgement of imperfection, on the other hand, can illuminate and replenish our present if allowed to do so. Life is here for us *now* to accept and explore, if we can choose to begin to let go of some of our fixed ideas about ourselves and each other. And, linked to this, life is there for us if we can choose to begin to accept and explore ourselves and each other.

In a situation where perhaps something has gone wrong and we might normally rush to judge another, crowing inwardly or outwardly about our own sense of rightness and superiority, we could dare to look beyond our own psychological horizon and ask ourselves a simple question. In the same circumstances, given the same psychological background and outlook as the person concerned, would *we* have behaved any differently? *Really*? Are they really so different from us? In the light of our current psychological knowledge—and especially the notion that our feelings drive how we think—*I don't believe that they are*; but I do believe I understand why we think like that: privileging the self. It's easier for you, me, us to do. I freely admit it; I do it myself. As I'll explain in Chapter 2, so long as we're psychologically healthy, our thoughts and feelings mostly suit ourselves. And that can sometimes cause problems—especially for the welfare of others.

* * *

It may be wondered why, if it is really so beneficial and mindful, human kindness is not more often valued. One reason could be that consciously being kind and mindful of ourselves and others is actually quite a sophisticated psychological position to adopt, and has taken time to evolve, both in developing individuals as people and in species. It may also be that a certain level of material security and wealth is required before our attention can turn to such matters. Now, though, the case can be made with some confidence. As individuals, as groups, and as societies, we can and do have *clear and drastic effects* on others' welfare. We depend on those others and their kindness, just as they depend on us, and it is the *nature of the interactions* between us all that this book argues, is of the essence. From a psychological perspective the idea of the solitary self, standing alone and independent of others, is an illusion; and when we deny the importance of others we deceive and deny ourselves. Whether we admit it to ourselves or not we have the power, when we ourselves act mindlessly, to steal away the psychological lives of others, so that their suffering may last a generation or longer. Yet we also have the ability, with the mindful practice of care and kindness, to give life back to others. Psychological ruins can be carefully restored, a new beginning made.

There are three main psychological reasons why we, as humans, might quite naturally find the practice of kindness and mindfulness fairly difficult. These are connected first with our basic need to survive, our feelings and our neuropsychology; second, with aspects of our social psychology; and third, with human developmental theory (which suggests that adverse upbringings can negatively affect later self-to-other and self-to-self behaviour). I will discuss these in turn. I will then suggest, by referring to the practice of, and scientific evidence for, mindfulness and psychotherapy, that there is good reason to think that the practice of kindness to others and to the self is beneficial. We help to set the psychological climate of feeling in which others live. And we could, if we thought about it, treat each other and ourselves better. We could all feel the benefit.

In what follows I will be appealing, therefore, to the rather old-fashioned, universal ethic found in the teaching of both the Buddha and Christ: of loving one's neighbour—even if they are, as so often now in our short-term society, 'here today, gone tomorrow', and are maybe due to move on again before long. But I shall do so in a modern way, using up-to-date psychological theory and evidence. Of this ancient idea of showing compassion for others, historian Felipe Fernandez-Armesto comments, rather pessimistically, that while 'almost everybody can see its value', 'almost nobody practises it'.[23] I wonder if this might be about to change—not least because, as the economist Richard Layard recently said, 'People are happier if they are compassionate.'[24]

Like the person who, after a rather shaky beginning, is a few sessions into his or her psychotherapy, we are as a species now well aware of the issue of our treatment of others and the chain of delight and difficulty it can cause. I think it would be fair to say that we do have a problem: a rather large one, in fact, which can be made to go away quickly—and then just temporarily—only by a number of strong drinks. And that wouldn't do. Instead, such a recognition as this is doubtless the best place for psychological change to begin. As in all real psychotherapy, we can start only from where we are.

---

23. Fernandez-Armesto, F. (2003). *Ideas that Changed the World.* London: Dorling Kindersley: 167.
24. Layard, R. (2004). *Happiness: Lessons from a new science.* London: Penguin/Allen Lane: 8.

2

Explaining Mindlessness

Those who do not feel pain seldom think that it is felt.
Dr Johnson

Self–Other

We are closer to one another than we think. A clue exists in the related processes of impregnation, gestation and birth. Physically—and psychologically—we emerge from each other. But in the knockabout world in which we live, where harsh judgements come quickly, and where getting and spending so often get in the way, it's all too easy to forget this. In this chapter I'll explain some of the psychological reasons why we need each other in many ways, but are often not so good at looking after each other.

Current neuroscientific and social psychological research indicates that from birth onwards, rather than simply existing as *individuals*, separate from others, we have from the first moments of our existence an acute sense of them, and their interactions with us, as we depend on them for our welfare. As many religious teachings suggested, including those of Christ and the Buddha, we have at any time the power to nurture or to negate well-being in others. Those others have the same power over us; but we could ask some key questions here. What are we doing with that power? What shall we choose to do with that power?

Up to a point, this interactionality is common sense. Most of us—the more fortunate—consider ourselves part of a family, an organization, a nation, a world. But it is the recently revealed level of interactionality—the delicate, shifting, psychological interface between ourselves and our fellows—that is the key. We can test this easily. Next time you pass a stranger, try smiling at them. Chances are, even without thinking or knowing why, they'll smile back. This is because we, like animals, are naturally designed to interact with, and respond to, each other. Just looking into someone else's eyes automatically produces an easily noticeable reaction—physiological arousal, including higher heart rate.[1] Or think of major life events: the stark desolation after the death of someone beloved; the fantastic hope and joy of someone's birth.

Interactionality begins early. The beginnings of interpersonal bonds, prepared for before birth during gestation, have been noted in newborn infants as young as 18 hours. Such infants reproduce mouth and facial movements displayed by the adult they are looking at—and with parts of their body (the mouth and face) to which the children have no visual access. Here, visual information about observed behaviour is translated into motor commands for reproducing behaviour. So by the time an infant is 18 hours old, a self–other space[2] between the child and adult begins to emerge, with one person naturally aware of and reciprocally influencing the other, and in turn being influenced by that other—a process that continues, in more sophisticated ways, throughout life. In its most basic form, and from birth, our human self constantly interacts with other people and objects in its environment. Information, verbal and non-verbal, goes back and forth quicker than the blink of an eye, and the infant sends signals—often with very strong feelings—to try to get his or her needs met. All this is quite natural, of course. Despite certain limitations in their social skills—their inability to speak comes to mind—babies want to be big friends with you: with good reason. They need your help.

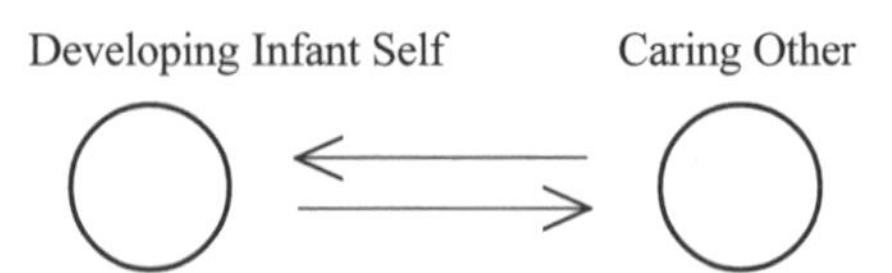

Figure 2.1 Interpersonal communication from birth

Then, from the second month of age at the latest, the infant and his or her caregiver show signs of emotional connection—'affective attunement'. Here, in a process of imitation, an aspect of the behaviour that reflects the person's feeling state is matched. These expressions that are produced by the infant may differ slightly in form and intensity, but they are *emotionally resonant* with what they see in their caregiver. This resonance between caregiver and child is essential for a good bond to develop between them and, in the longer term, for the healthy psychological development of the child.[3] In this way a stable psychological foundation begins to be laid for later, adult life. Children can then learn to work out, safely, who they are and what they are. As part of these processes, they can also establish a meaningful relationship with the world of others. And since we are social animals, learning to work out correctly how people

1. Argyle, M. (1994). *The Psychology of Interpersonal Behaviour: 5th edn.* Harmondsworth: Penguin: 31, 47.
2. Gallese, V. (2003). The manifold nature of interpersonal relations: the quest for a common mechanism. In C. Frith & D. Wolpert (eds.) (2003). *The Neuroscience of Social Interaction: Decoding, imitating, and influencing the actions of others.* Oxford: Oxford University Press: 159–182.
3. Schore, A. (2003). *Affect Regulation and the Repair of the Self.* New York: Norton.

feel, why they might feel like that way, and *our ability to imagine all that for ourselves*, does matter.

Once it develops more as we grow, our ability to imagine what others might be thinking and feeling is called 'Theory of Mind' (ToM). ToM generally becomes obvious in toddlers—partly visible because of their growing dishonesty, or rather their comic attempts to be dishonest—from around age 2. You accuse your toddler of eating something it's been agreed he shouldn't. He may reply: 'I never ate it. Scrumpy put chocolate on my face with his paws. He is a naughty doggy.' Further investigation may be required into Scrumpy's face-painting skills: but this ability to 'mind read' others' thoughts, and be aware that others—even dogs—might have thoughts and intentions, is called second-order intentionality. Over time, our ToM abilities become more sophisticated. As adults we are yet more able to guess quite accurately what others are thinking and how they might be feeling; we manage complex interpersonal reflections on the state of self and other. While these abilities are also seen in many other animals in more simple forms, they are best-developed in us. It is for this reason that we might, as adults, be expected to be able to reflect on and act on our own and others' behaviour, particularly if that behaviour is clearly destructive. And while there is good scientific evidence that women's ability to empathise with others is more finely tuned, on average, than men's,[4] most members of both sexes are likely to possess at least *basic* empathic skills.

The issue I will address, though, is that while the psychological evidence mounts to suggest that we are designed to be aware of, interact with and depend on others from birth, our ability to be empathic towards them, to imagine how they might be feeling and vice versa, often breaks down—or at least *seems* to break down—later on. We very easily, and especially when under threat, switch from consideration and thought for others (whether others quite close to us in our families, or others further away from us in the wider human community) back to self-preservation.[5] We may 'want to be kinder, but what is driving us cares all too little about this particular want'.[6] Reflection on this point might, I think, help prompt us as thinking, feeling adults to begin to recapture our lost sense of the other.

Such reflection, and a deliberate extension of our empathic, Theory of Mind abilities of which human beings, infinitely creative, are easily capable, might also lead us to begin to treat others and ourselves more thoughtfully and more mindfully—with more kindness. As a practising clinical psychologist I'd hypothesise that this could make us all feel better; many people already do. I met one this afternoon, in fact. I showed a bit of focused kindness and she perked up considerably. Human beings *love* that stuff. Like a bee drawn to flowers when it has the choice of all the air, we know, instinctively, that kindness lifts our spirits. It is honey for the soul.

---

4. Baron-Cohen, S. (2003). *The Essential Difference: Men, women, and the extreme male brain.* London: Penguin.
5. Wang, S. (2005). A conceptual framework for integrating research related to the physiology of compassion and the wisdom of Buddhist teachings. In P. Gilbert (ed.). *Compassion: Conceptualization, research and use in psychotherapy.* London: Routledge: 75–120.
6. Phillips, A. (2005). *Going Sane.* London: Faber: 239.

Blind to Ourselves

So perfectly smooth is the habitual functioning of our minds that we have little or no idea of the complexity and power of the neurological and psychological processes that allow us to be aware, self-aware, and to choose what we do, both to ourselves and to others. Despite what we might like to believe, we can be partly or even completely wrong in our ideas about ourselves, others and the world we live in.[7] The economist Paul Ormerod recently pointed out that, as enormously complex creatures living in an enormously complex world, while we very often behave with purpose, and

> take decisions with the aim of achieving specific, desired outcomes, it is very difficult or impossible to predict the consequences of decisions in any meaningful sense.[8]

So from the viewpoint of our psychological health, if we have less power to affect future outcomes than we might often think, is it really worth the worry to fret as much as we do? These ideas might also give us further pause for thought. Actually, the very smoothness of our brain's functioning can cause problems that might require us to stand back from ourselves just a little.

The brain consists of about one billion brain cells, or neurons, which together produce our waking and sleeping life. Clarity is emerging in certain fields of study here. It is also well established by research that a significant amount, perhaps most, of the mind's processing—taken for granted each day by most of us—is *unconscious*. In this, Freud was right. There is much experimental evidence for the processes of unconscious emotion, learning, memory, perception, and skill acquisition, to take some examples. Given this large body of research, 'it is now abundantly clear that extensive perceptual processing does indeed occur without conscious awareness, and can exert an influence on experience and behaviour.'[9]

Furthermore, it may be that fundamentally different rules govern conscious and nonconscious psychological operations. For instance, while our conscious, cognitive abilities decline gradually as we grow older, age differences seem to have less impact, or even none, on nonconscious learning ability. Many older individuals show no impairment relative to young adults on tasks involving learning sequences.[10]

Some of the most striking studies in this field show that in a given situation in which information is presented to us, our bodies can begin to act before the psyche has given the order to do so. This kind of evidence has led certain psychologists to question whether human will, which we take for granted each day in the sense of our

---

7. Fine, C. (2006). *A Mind of its Own: How your brain distorts and deceives.* Cambridge: Icon.
8. Ormerod, P. (2005). *Why Most Things Fail: Evolution, extinction, and economics.* London: Faber: 99.
9. Williams, J.M.G., Watts, F.N., MacLeod, C. & Mathews, A. (1997). *Cognitive Psychology and Emotional Disorders: 2nd edn.* Chichester: Wiley: 258.
10. Howard, D.V. & Howard, J.H. (1992). Adult age differences in the rate of learning serial patterns: evidence from direct and indirect tests. *Psychological Ageing, 7,* 232–241.

being able to make conscious decisions and take actions—is viable at all. Our reliance on consciousness may be, in part at least, reliance on an illusion.[11] This research has generated the notion that while our conscious thoughts may have key, unconscious connections to our actions, our general experience of conscious will emerges from a process of *interpreting* these connections, but not from the connections themselves,[12] as our personal world is created in a moment-by-moment process in a dynamic interaction between our minds, bodies and environments. In other words, despite our strong instinctive feelings about the matter we may not—in the strictest sense—consciously 'know' what we are doing, such is the nature of the hidden machinery informing and guiding our choices, and the speed and effectiveness with which it operates. This hidden machinery becomes clearer at certain times. In some types of psychotherapy, notably eye movement desensitization and reprocessing (EMDR) (discussed more in later chapters), swift associations between previously apparently unconnected, and often forgotten, memories are made. Often this helps to explain and eventually reduce current psychological symptoms.

From the viewpoint of cognitive science, then, there should be good reason to question the very process of 'rational' decision making, and how we habitually go about our business, including our conduct towards other people. There are also other, equally good reasons.

I'm Feeling Selfish

Another reason for the breakdown in our sense of other people and our mindlessness towards them is our feelings, and the survival function of our feelings. Under stress or threat our feelings, like those of any organism, rise up, tell us to pull away from others and to put our own needs first. Generally, the turkey is not the greatest advocate of Christmas. Quite so. Feelings, though shared by everyone, are experienced *personally*. Unchecked, this can make us transparently and sometimes ridiculously self-interested.

Above all, we want to live. Except in unusual circumstances, the human psyche focuses on survival, and some of our chief means of navigation through life are our emotional states: our feelings. In all situations they provide us with vital, often partly unconscious feedback about our physical and psychological environment. Combining this information with conscious thought, we make decisions about what we need to do and what we can do—all in an attempt to perpetuate our well-being. Neuroscientist Antonio Damasio puts it like this:

> The entire collection of homeostatic processes governs life, moment by moment, in every cell of our bodies. This governance is achieved by means of a simple

11. Wilson, T.D. (2002). *Strangers to Ourselves: Discovering the adaptive unconscious.* Cambridge, MA: Harvard University Press.
12. Wegner, D. (2002). *The Illusion of Conscious Will.* Cambridge, MA: MIT Press.

> arrangement. First, something changes in the environment of an individual organism, internally or externally. Second, the changes have the potential to alter the course of life of the organism (they can constitute a threat to its integrity, or an opportunity for its improvement). Third, the organism detects the change and acts [...] to create the most beneficial situation for its own self-preservation and efficient functioning. All reactions operate under this arrangement and are thus a means to appraise the internal and external circumstances of an organism and act accordingly.[13]

If life is easy, we never need give these processes a moment's thought. Few are so lucky over the whole span of their existence. If life is difficult we may become, and really need to become, more self-aware—particularly if, as is sometimes the case, our basic assumptions about our lives are in the process of being shattered, whether by accident, change or chance.

Take the process of anxiety. It begins with the awareness of some kind of threat.[14] That could be an external object, person or situation actually perceived or, indeed, a memory, thought or other internal stimulus. An image or images of the stimulus are then represented in the visual or auditory parts of the brain. Signals relating to the image are then made available to emotion-triggering sites in other brain areas. The amygdala, in the temporal lobe; the ventromedial prefrontal cortex, part of the frontal lobe; and the supplementary motor area and cingulate, another frontal region of the brain, are examples. These and other sites then activate other, emotion-executing sites of the brain: the hypothalamus and the basal forebrain, for example, which detect certain neural signals. This process then sets off a cascade of events that can become an emotional state that may, depending on circumstance, become stronger or weaker. The hypothalamus executes many of the chemical responses required. Directly, or via the pituitary gland, chemical molecules are released into the bloodstream that affect the internal climate of the body, our organs, our central nervous system—and our behaviour.

Our conscious thoughts can then modify, and be modified by, the ongoing dynamic processes, as an initial stimulus recalls other emotionally significant material. In this way our thoughts can be seen as being thrown up by the brain, together with the body, as an *interpretation of and reaction to the organism's environment* at any given time during our lives. This may, say if the material is anxiety-provoking, maintain the earlier emotion; or, if the thoughts are of a different, perhaps more reassuring type, the earlier emotion may change. We may relax. Whatever the outcome, feelings arise from an ongoing, silent symphony of psychological and physical processes, culminating in body-sensing regions of the brain. Feelings translate our ongoing life-state—our awareness of bodily processes—into language. In other words—words; and images.[15] If our organism finds itself in a satisfactory internal and external

---

13. Damasio, A. (2003). *Looking for Spinoza: Joy, sorrow, and the feeling brain.* London: Vintage: 35.
14. In this section, I have drawn on *ibid.* 57–65.
15. *ibid.* 85.

condition, and the regulation of life processes is straightforward—if the living is easy—we feel good. Or, as William James put it in 1892: 'Our judgments concerning the worth of things, big or little, depend on the feelings the things arouse in us.'[16]

Every experience in our lives brings an emotion, or emotions.[17] They affect how we feel from day to day. Over time our range of responses to situations, including social situations, develops. Different situations and the feelings that characterize them are connected with our way of seeing ourselves, others, and the world. Our personal narrative—the story we tell ourselves about all the different parts of our lives, from our career histories to how we chose our car—is formed, layered in different areas of our memory. We learn, if we are fortunate to have the kindness of others when we need it, to put feelings into words. I did this because Dad thought it wouldn't be a good idea. Then that happened, so I decided to do this, which led me there; and so on, in detail. Connections are made between the conceptual categories we form of situations, also at brain-cell levels, with emotion-triggering apparatus in the brain. Options for action, and different outcomes, become associated with different emotions and feelings. As Damasio says, when we find ourselves in a familiar situation, we 'rapidly and automatically deploy the appropriate emotions'.[18]

Given previous experience, and whether fully recognised or not, our emotions and feelings are sentinels for our *personal* future survival. And their operation is, as the above account suggests, at least partly beyond our conscious control. If we are fortunate and our lives—our upbringings in particular—have gone well, we move towards positive affect regulation, and a quiet and stable internal psychological world.[19] We develop a positive sense of self, and can experience the world from quite a stable emotional position.

Emotional signals, in this body-based process, may actually enhance decision making as part of these processes.[20] Any decision we make occurs at least partly on the basis of our previous experience in similar circumstances, draws more or less on emotion and leads us to what we consciously and unconsciously feel will be overall the *best available outcome for us and our interests*. So from the perspective of our feelings, we are wired to put ourselves first. And the world we experience is personal to us, created and changed by the constant interplay of mind, body and the environment that, in the light of our learned experience, calls forth an appropriate reaction and response from us. In any given situation, our mind and body produce the feelings and responses that, given our collective experiences during evolution, are most likely to help us to survive. Take a stick, poke a dog sitting in his basket. He bites, reacting to us. And if the poor dog has been hurt, he will react when we go near him with a stick

---

16. James, W. (1899). On a certain blindness in human beings. In: W. James. *Talks to Teachers on Psychology: And to students on some of life's ideals*. London: Longman, Green: 228.
17. Damasio, A. (2003). *Looking for Spinoza: Joy, sorrow, and the thinking brain*. London: Vintage: 146–150.
18. *ibid.*: 147.
19. Cozolino, L. (2002). *The Neuroscience of Psychotherapy: Building and rebuilding the human brain*. New York: Norton: 26–27.
20. Which now has empirical support. See: Damasio, A. *ibid.* 148, 315–316.

in future. He learns to associate it, and us, with pain. We do that too, but in rather more complex ways. Our feelings, thoughts and behaviours represent our reactions to the environment we encounter. If you are kind to me, I will most likely relax; yet if you are unkind to me, or frighten me, the state of my body and mind will change in reaction. Over time our patterns of thinking, feeling and behaving develop. We may learn a pattern of responding that involves our welcoming guests into our house; or, if we are fearful or suspicious of others, we may learn never to invite guests in at all. But make no mistake—our feelings exert powerful effects on our thoughts, in ways that can seem irrational. To take a positive example, consider my cat. Having brought her up from when she was a stray kitten, when *I* look at my smallest cat I see a furry princess: Mittens, the most wonderful cat the world has ever seen—an amusing and mischievous mini-munchkin with little white paws of snow. When *you* look at my smallest cat, you see an untidy animal, badly behaved and of no particular pedigree—a scruffy ragamuffin of the street. What's the big deal—it's just a cat, isn't it? Not to me. I'm *crazy* about my cat. Feelings-wise, I'm hooked in completely and would never, could never, get out. My feelings have warped my thoughts, in a good way.

Fig. 2.2 The power of personal feelings. To you, this cat may seem to be a scruffy ragamuffin of the street. To me, she is a furry princess.

This cycle of events also appears in various connected forms in all common psychological issues. An event produces a particular feeling, and the responses in thought and behaviour that almost automatically come with it. Think of self-harm—a way of behaving that many people, who are not sufferers or psychological health workers, find hard to understand. Here, often after negative earlier experiences, people learn that one way to gain relief from apparently unbearable feelings is to hurt themselves physically and psychologically. So when the person becomes aware of something stressful (an external event like a relationship break-up, or an internal event like a painful memory or thought), and they feel blocked from other courses of action, they may cut themselves rather than adopt an active coping strategy. The self-harming behaviour releases, among other things, pain-killing chemicals, opiates, that are naturally produced by the body and give a strong, temporary sense of release or relief. But over time—often until the meaning of the behaviour, and possible alternatives, are considered—the self-harming and the underlying sense of badness or negativity felt by the person may remain.[21]Until then, self-harming is often considered to be a useful tool of mood-control by the person. Very often it is: since it helps them to cope with very difficult, negative, underlying feelings that need ideally to be talked about with someone else—most likely in a way they haven't done before. This brings us to an important catch.

People's thinking and feeling about themselves and their behaviour very often depend on how they feel about themselves because of what has already happened in their lives, and so which patterns of feeling, thinking and behaving have been set up. If people have experienced difficulties, perhaps in being cared for during a sensitive period of their development, there may be a lack of connection between their psychological systems for feeling, behaviour and thinking. Children who have been seriously abused, for example, are more likely than others to show abnormalities in regions of the brain that are important for the connections between behaving, feeling and thinking.[22]

In other words, what people have *learned* while being around others, and the feelings they have had at these times, both early in their lives and later on, are important. If these early, difficult, underlying feelings are not talked about, made clear and linked with other parts of their experience, people's responses in similar situations remain the same—which means that their reactions almost always lead them back to the same emotional place where they were put by the original negative experiences. So, while we are born psychologically healthy, if we experience poor or mindless treatment from others, these traumas help to form the principles according to which our feelings and behaviours are organized. We carry the imprint of others' actions, and we ourselves leave our own imprint on them.

These processes are very clear in self-harm, when inner feelings of badness, under stress, produce behavioural responses—burning or cutting of one's own skin, perhaps—that eventually return the person back to the negative feelings, which in turn often come from an early life of poor-quality care from others. Until, that is, the original negative feelings themselves, and their meanings for the person, are talked about, reflected on and eventually integrated. And strange as it may seem self-harm, like all other human behaviour, makes complete sense to the person at the time. All of us, in any given situation, tend to cope in the best way we know how. No one actually *wants* to feel messed up like this. It's a really unpleasant way to live, before you get any psychological help, with chaotic and unstable emotions leading to chaotic and unstable relationships.

---

21. See e.g. Huband, N. & Tantam, D. (2004). Repeated self-wounding: women's recollections of pathways to cutting and of the value of different interventions. *Psychology and Psychotherapy: Theory, research, and practice, 77(4),* 413–428.
22. Cozolino, L. (2002). *The Neuroscience of Psychotherapy: Building and rebuilding the human brain.* New York: Norton.

Yet, as I mentioned, we are *all* capable of similar patterns of relating to others and to ourselves, regardless of our social background. I myself am a past master at harshly criticizing myself and others. Having—like many people—a slightly shaky psychological set-up myself (as I'll explain in Chapter 4) when feeling stressed or under threat, my mind can produce strong feelings and thoughts about people and circumstances around me, and I sometimes quickly revert to criticizing and dismissing others, if only silently to myself. This criticizing of them reduces my anxiety and makes me feel safer—at least temporarily. Such critical habits of mind are common and often evident in the general population in the UK and the US. This is a pity, since it is also damaging to both self and other—pushing others away rather than drawing them closer to us. Consequently, it becomes more difficult for us to understand each other, and so helps to maintain any problems between us. This is one reason, incidentally, why psychotherapy consists of people listening and talking to one another.

Such psychological patterns are not always easy or pleasant to recognize in ourselves. Clinical psychologists, despite their abilities to understand and help others, and perhaps because of something to do with their middle-class origins and quite hard scientific training, can sometimes be harsh critics of themselves and other people. Until I had my own personal therapy and began, around the same time, to practise mindfulness meditation, I had little idea—in fact, *no idea at all*—of my own earlier self-critical habits. Looking back now, it frightens me to see how I lived. Week after week, to begin with, I produced a torrent of self-criticism. This now seems to me like a non-stop tide of psychological sewerage that polluted my innocent mind. Not good enough at this. Not good enough at that. Failed at the other. Shouldn't have done it like that. Shoulda, woulda, coulda. All the time; all my fault. What a joke I am! Facing a difficult period in my life I was, in effect, hurting and hammering myself still more, rather than giving myself the care and time I needed.

Our judging of ourselves and others, though, is as psychologically understandable as it is globally widespread. We need to survive around others, and sometimes this means defending ourselves against them, whether physically or verbally. But when these behaviours become too strong or habitual, they can become psychologically and physically damaging. These critical, judgmental habits of mind are also a key reason—perhaps *the* key reason—why we often do not treat others as well as we might.

Christ recognized these patterns of mind, and warned against them:

> Judge not, that you be not judged. [...] Why do you see the speck that is in your brother's eye, but do not notice the log that is in your own eye? [...] First take the log out of your own eye, and then you will see clearly to take the speck out of your brother's eye.[23]

Or in the Buddha's words: 'The fault of others is easily seen; but one's own is hard to see.'[24]

---

23. Matthew, 7:1–5.
24. *The Dhammapada*, no. 250. In W. Rahula (1957; repr. 1997). *What the Buddha Taught*. Oxford: Oneworld Publications: 252.

Fortunately, we now have a good psychological explanation for this behaviour and, indeed, the beginnings of a modern solution that Christ and the Buddha touched on, which we'll come to later.

In sum, the human organism, like its animal cousins, is ultimately geared for survival. We interpret our environment and act accordingly at any given time. It is for this reason that, among all human feelings, thoughts and behaviours throughout our historical past, the theme of self-concern is prominent. This point was made in 1954 by Albert Einstein, who noted that while

> … a human being is part of the whole, he experiences himself, his thoughts and feelings as something separated from the rest—a kind of *optical illusion of consciousness*. This delusion is a kind of prison for us, restricting us to our personal desires and to affection for a few persons nearest us. Our task must be to free ourselves from this prison by widening our circle of compassion to embrace all living creatures, and the whole of nature in its beauty. Nobody is able to achieve this completely, but the striving for such achievement is, in itself, a part of the liberation and a foundation for inner security [my italics]. [25]

As Einstein says, it is only by a deliberate, conscious, mindful effort that we can escape this imprisoned state that, like all matters of the psyche, is invisible to the naked eye. Our feelings, as Darwin and Freud knew, keep pulling us back.

I Can't Think Straight: Cognitive or thought biases

Another reason why we suffer from Einstein's 'optical illusion of consciousness' is the working of strong personal biases in our thinking. These automatic 'cognitive' biases, like the feelings with which they are interdependent, are also superlatively designed for survival. They help keep us safe, and they help us to think well of ourselves—even when our circumstances seem to suggest otherwise. At the same time, though, they can make us vulnerable to neglecting the needs and rights of others. Recognizing these thinking errors in ourselves might have benefits though: the operation of such biases shows that, in a very real sense, *we ourselves* create—or at the very least partly create—the world that we experience. Our feelings, thoughts and actions depend not only on what we find in the world, but also on our own psychological and physiological condition when we find it.[26] For this reason, the same place, at the same time, may seem to be a land of milk and honey to one person, but a vale of tears to another.

---

25. Einstein, A. (1954). *Ideas and Opinions.* Trans. by S. Bargmann. New York: Crown Publishers: 126.

26. Harvey, A., Watkins, E., Mansell, W. & Shafran, R. (2004). *Cognitive Behavioural Processes Across Psychological Disorders: A transdiagnostic approach to research and treatment.* Oxford: Oxford University Press.

The psychological evidence firmly supports the conclusion that, far from their being a simply 'rational' truth, our 'rational' thoughts rely on our bodies, minds and feelings being *in balance*. A judge with, say, damage to the emotional and memory circuits in his or her brain is likely to make very questionable judgments. A person whose only alleged crime was to buy more than one Jean Michel Jarre album might be sent to prison for life. Whatever we might think of such a sentence being handed down by a judge, without the neurological and psychological systems of feeling being intact in a person there *can be no* 'rational' thought. From a distance, our legal and government structures all seem to make rational—if rather stuffy—sense. Zoom in close up, though, and it becomes evident that, like all rational decision making, they depend on a healthy basis of feeling in the people who create such structures. Or, to put it another way, the worst regimes in human history are run by people who are deeply emotionally disturbed, whatever their gifts of leadership.[27]

Understandably, though, from the perspective of surviving day-to-day life, it is very beneficial to us to be, or more accurately to *feel,* sure about what we perceive, and to be able to act on that information. It's nice to feel you know where you are. The creation of apparent certainty is a basic tendency of the human psyche; but this apparent certainty about the world and its inhabitants can be hugely misleading. Our minds play tricks on us every day—most often without our being aware of the fact. For example, as numerous psychological experiments have shown, they can tempt us to make poor judgements about risk—overestimating the dangers facing us, say, on little or no firm evidence.[28] In the case of many, or perhaps all of us, the illusion of certainty can falsely govern how we live our lives from moment to moment. Sometimes, indeed, this can occur over generations in a family, when a particular distorted belief, founded on false or questionable principles, is passed on and affects behaviour. Scotland is a bad place to go on holiday, because Aunt Mabel was hit by a flying haggis there in 1876. Cats make bad pets, since a big one ate little Stevie's ice-cream, making him cry, in 1922. The bicycle is a bad form of transport, because Uncle Albert, bumped by a milk-float, drove his bike down a manhole in 1940. To be fair to him, though, it was blackout at the time. In such cases, it is the internal machinery of our minds, complex and effective in so many ways, that is in error, naturally operating in biased ways. Yet the creation of seeming certainty is not the only issue here.

Remarkably, one of the most potentially destructive human cognitive biases is—from our own, personal point of view—*positive*. If we are fortunate, our learning in the care of significant others through our early development teaches us that we are physically and psychologically safe, and that we are capable of interacting well with our environment. On the basis of such positive early learning experiences, happy and fulfilling lives are built, and the possibility of happiness may—if we are blessed with good luck—be passed to the next generation. And if we are psychologically healthy,

---

27. See e.g. Bullock, A. (1991). *Hitler and Stalin: Parallel lives.* London: HarperCollins.
28. Gigerenzer, G. (2002). *Reckoning with Risk: Learning to live with uncertainty.* Harmondsworth: Penguin.

we 'big ourselves up'. We all, if we are well, possess an internal, mini-Anthony Robbins of the mind. Even though this little guy, or his neuropsychological equivalent, doesn't actually try to make us stand up and clap like the real thing, he does make us think better of ourselves than we actually are—more confident, effective, successful; getting the maximum from the minimum. In other words, people without psychological problems, and who feel good about themselves, tend to privilege themselves when interpreting what happens to them. In attributing causes to events, if we are feeling good we tend to take more credit when things go well compared with when things go badly. This tendency, experimentally confirmed many times, seems to protect or enhance self-evaluation, and is known as the hedonic or self-serving bias. Psychologically healthy people also attribute positive events to causes that are more stable and global, or comprehensive, over time compared with negative events.[29] If I win the game, it's because I've always been a good player; but if I lose, it was because the weather today was lousy.

Similarly, when isolated events in our lives go badly, there is also evidence of an anticipatory self-serving bias. Here, psychologically healthy people anticipate failure intentionally, and publicly make 'external attributions' about such an event. 'I'll never make it,' we might say, cushioning a potential fall. This process, known in psychological circles as a self-handicapping strategy, can help us to explain away failure and protect our positive feelings about ourselves. Together, these ideas suggest that one aspect of being psychologically healthy involves making unrealistically optimistic appraisals about the chances of good things happening in future, and our ability to make them happen.[30]

Such healthy optimism has advantages and disadvantages. On the positive side, it means we keep feeling good. We can live quite happily, imagining that others feel similarly. On the negative side, it is easy to imagine how, content with our own lives and feeling optimistic overall, we could overlook the suffering of others—particularly if they are physically distant from us and we know little about them. In other words, part of being psychologically healthy may—rather curiously—entail feeling more optimistic about, and being *less aware* of, others' experiences. This human psychological characteristic explains our ability to overlook suffering elsewhere for as long as possible—so long as we ourselves are unaffected or at least not directly involved. Most of us do not dwell too much on what we do not want to know: how a cow in a field becomes a burger in a bun. My guess is that, even as you read the previous sentence, your feelings began to tell you to recoil, and to avoid an unpleasant idea. This perceptual bias in itself might serve as a good reason for our further self-reflection. Even though I am feeling pretty good today, I wonder how those others over there might be feeling? And why might that be? It's actually quite difficult for us to know how others feel. We may need to ask.

---

29. Abramson, L.Y., Seligman, M.E.P. & Teasdale, J.D. (1978). Learned helplessness in humans: critique and reformulation. *Journal of Abnormal Psychology, 78,* 40–74.
30. Bentall, R. (2003). *Madness Explained: Psychosis and human nature.* Harmondsworth: Penguin: 244.

The operation of these self-serving biases explains many interesting aspects of human behaviour, including the habitual neglect of those people with psychological issues by the rest of the population. Statistically, most people feel psychologically fine, most of the time. And since feeling psychologically fine means we are either unaware of or untroubled by *others'* troubles, or both, people with psychological issues are a minority who are, most of the time, basically ignored.

* * *

When we are anxious, depressed or stressed, though, our minds work differently. Another kind of bias kicks in. With little science to support him, the English philosopher Francis Bacon noted in 1625 that:

> If there were taken out of [our] minds vain opinions, flattering hopes, false valuations, imaginations as one would, and the like, it would leave [our] minds poor shrunken things, full of melancholy and indisposition, and unpleasing to themselves.[31]

Bacon was right about our shift, in psychological ill-health, from 'false valuations' towards being 'poor shrunken things'. But with the benefit of modern psychology, we now have a much more precise idea of how and why this happens.

If we are less lucky in our early psychological development, we may learn through various early experiences that, in one way or another, we are *unsafe*. This is where problems can arise. Simply, if consciously or unconsciously we sense or feel that our needs may not be met, the chain of physical and psychological events described above may start, beginning with the awareness of a negative or threatening stimulus. Again, the aim of this is—consciously, unconsciously or both—to protect ourselves and promote our survival.

At such periods, other negative, cognitive or thought biases operate, according to our sense of self at a given time.[32] These biases arise from learned patterns of thinking that guide our perceptions and judgements. Evidence suggests that such a mindset develops early in life, depending on what happens to us and how we perceive what happens to us. It may be nurtured by many factors, including poor parenting,[33] poor social skills in childhood, maltreatment and stressful life events. To take another example, children who are sexually maltreated at the hands of others who behave mindlessly may become despondent as they grow up. They may experience strong feelings of helplessness and hopelessness, connected to their lack of control over the abuse. They may then be

---

31. Bacon, F. 'Of truth'. In: J. Pitcher (ed.). *Essays* (1991). Harmondsworth: Penguin. 61–62.
32. I have drawn here on: Lyubomirsky, S. & Tkach, C. (2004) The consequences of dysphoric rumination. In: C. Papageorgiou & A. Wells (2004) (eds.).*Depressive Rumination: Nature, theory, and treatment.* 21–41.
33. Blatt, S.H.J. & Homann, E. (1992). Parent–child interaction in the etiology of dependent and self-critical depression. *Clinical Psychology Review, 12,* 47–91.

forced to attempt to understand and control the negative feelings they experience; but compared with *active* ways of solving the problem, this may be ineffective. They may be led, rather, into self-reinforcing cycles of rumination and depression as they mature.[34] So compared with that of the more carefree, happy-go-lucky person, a different internal world begins to develop.

If our psychological development is like this—and it is, despite what we often believe as we drift along every day secure in our own minds, a far from unusual pattern—we may be more prone to organize our memories automatically in particular ways later on, making it harder for us to 'think straight' and be mindfully aware of what we are doing, and how we are doing it. Low, stressed moods are associated with the tendency to focus especially on negative information. And generally, people with psychological issues 'typically attend to information that is specifically related to their problematic concerns, and ignore information that is unrelated to them.'[35]

Various experiments have shown that people who are depressed, when presented with cue words or statements, tend to be able to recall negative events more quickly than positive events.[36] Similarly, if we are depressed we often tend to ruminate (women more than men, on average), thinking endlessly about how we feel—as part of trying to feel better. But not managing this improvement, we tend to choose more negatively biased and negatively distorted interpretations of life events ('My success was due to the help I had'). We may minimize successes or overgeneralise from failures ('I didn't make it this time, so I'll never make it'). We may also make more negative self-evaluations ('I'm unlovable'; 'My problems can't be solved'); make more pessimistic predictions about our future ('It'll never change'); feel less optimistic about our ability to solve problems; and, importantly, have low expectations of engaging in enjoyable activities ('It won't make any difference anyway'). This is one reason why, when we are feeling low, it is easy to remain trapped, doing depressing things over and over again, so our mood becomes self-perpetuating. This self-reinforcing cycle confirms Einstein's idea that madness consists of 'doing the same thing over and over again, expecting different results'. I wonder if this might also be true of our treatment of each other?

When psychological difficulties of this kind emerge, one way out of such self-maintaining craziness is simply to make contact with others. Indeed, we human beings maybe have evolved to show, in clear ways like symptoms of distress, easily recognizable from our body language, that *we cannot go on as we are*. Sometimes this is obvious; sometimes not. As a stressed, unhappy teenager I felt for about a year—a whole year—that I could not feel my legs. They felt numb; the muscles, as I tensed them, no longer

---

34. Spasojevic, J., Alloy, L.B., Abramson, L.Y., Maccoon, D. & Robinson, M. S. (2004). Reactive rumination: outcomes, mechanisms, and developmental antecedents. In: C. Papageorgiou & A. Wells (2004). *Depressive Rumination: Nature, theory & treatment.*. Chichester: Wiley: 43–58.
35. Harvey, A., Watkins, E., Mansell, W. & Shafran, R. (2004). *Cognitive Behavioural Processes Across Psychological Disorders: A transdiagnostic approach to research and treatment.* Oxford: Oxford University Press.
36. For this section I have drawn on Lyubomirsky & Tkach, *ibid*, 21–41.

felt as though they were responding. Looking back, this was a bodily sign to myself and others that I couldn't go on, or didn't want to keep soldiering on—at least in the way I was. One way of understanding what was happening for me at this time was that my legs didn't want to take me where I was trying to go. I was running a poor psychological economy and was working too hard—for reasons I'll explain in Chapter 4—and this behaviour was giving me no space for myself, my own personality, to develop. At such times, if we are fortunate, beneficial contact with others occurs and new possibilities emerge. In one form or another, this is called help, of course.

When we are in such low mood states we are likely to *feel* less in control of our lives overall and perhaps completely trapped—unhappy in our jobs and relationships yet feeling powerless to change them, even though this is not actually so. Our perceptions and thoughts can become very distorted.

So whereas psychological health—which develops partly from good care from others—is associated with a self-focused, optimistically distorted thinking style, psychological ill-health—which develops partly from poor care from others—is associated with a similarly distorted, self-focused but pessimistic thinking style. Either way our perceptions may be quite inaccurate, and a different inner world appears, on the basis of which we act. And whether we're psychologically healthy or unhealthy, it may be helpful for us sometimes to become a little more mindful of ourselves—of what we're doing and of how we're feeling; to take a step back from our own misleading perceptions and emotionally based patterns and wonder what's *really* going on, both in the worlds of ourselves and of others. Reason alone is no longer enough. Greater psychological self-awareness and a little mindfulness, in the general sense, may be required.

Living in a Mindless Bubble

As I have mentioned, modern psychological views of human behaviour say that our need to survive is so powerful that often all other considerations—actually, in most circumstances, the consideration of others—come second. Driven by the need for survival the human psyche, and the feelings felt within, very often pays a *disproportionate amount of attention* to its own welfare. Trapped in a loop of scanning the environment for physical and psychological threats, monitoring its own state and that of the body as part of the processes of self-regulation, and reacting cautiously to any threats sensed, it is little wonder that the human psyche—like that of its animal cousins—is habitually, though understandably, self-absorbed. Whether we are psychologically healthy or unhealthy, we mindlessly spend much or all of our lives in the bubble of our own individual consciousness. And most importantly, there is good scientific evidence that our perceptions of ourselves, each other and the world are significantly distorted—and that these distortions can and do change according to how we feel. Now, key conclusions emerge.

If our feelings, for survival purposes, are *the* default guide for our thoughts, actions and behaviours, this helps to explain why generally (though with some exceptions) people act in, and are focused on, *only their own interests*—and why stepping back from ourselves mindfully to recognize this may be vital if we are to treat others fairly and compassionately. To underline the point: how many times today have you done deliberately something *against* your own interests in every way? If we are psychologically healthy, this does not happen.[37] It is no coincidence that human newspapers are full of news about socially important and/or sexually attractive humans—rather than, say, dogs. If dogs had a newspaper, *The Daily Bone* might be edited by a Rottweiler. *The Bone* would be full of doggie stories, of interest mostly to dogs: assertive, bright dogs—perhaps labradors—might be on the front pages, while scantily clad, fluffy poodles would fill the gossip columns with their funster animal antics. Like dogs we act in our own interests, to suit ourselves. And our allegiance, arguments, feelings and thoughts change as our interests shift, depending on the circumstances in which we find ourselves.

We can put this to an imaginary test. On meeting you, say, if you are friendly I'll like you, particularly if we discover that we have things in common. If we carry on talking, chances are I'll like you even more … until you start disagreeing with me. And the more strongly you disagree with me, and the ruder you are, the more my feelings will change—and rise up to deal with the situation. Then a familiar relational pattern begins to emerge. I have a bone to pick with you. You against me. Us against them. Young against old. Men against women. Black against white. Capitalism against communism. Conservative against Labour. Democrat against Republican. Rich against poor. West against East. Al-Qaeda against the West. Developing world versus Developed world. Me against you. X against Y. My, oh my: you name it, and I'll probably be against it! I've occupied many of these positions in quite mindless ways myself, at different times. Put together, they all seem rather ridiculous. They—and we—can't all be right about the same thing, at the same time. We fear each other, and fight each other, so often. Must we?

We act in this mindless way partly because, as a species, we are self-justifying and self-seeking organisms. Human beings are the incorrigible rogues of the animal kingdom—and still deny it. Bright enough to do so, we cheated our way to the top of the food chain, without meaning to. We are talking about deep-seated conscious and unconscious mechanisms—and so long as we are psychologically healthy, we habitually overlook others' needs and put our own individual or collective case before others, at almost every turn and in a scientifically predictable way. Often, this is fine: except that sometimes others need us to be mindful, to see their distress, and require us to show help and kindness.

---

37. Indeed, even the psychologically unhealthy person's often self-damaging behaviour fits with their basic, negative feelings about themselves and/or others.

They Would Say That, Wouldn't They?

The modern psychological explanation of feelings also begins to explain why we literally self-centred human beings, and some of our animal cousins, are such frequent and effective deceivers of self and other.[38] In pursuit of our own ends, guided by our feelings, we sometimes feel as though we need to be dishonest. Most human beings are dishonest, in some way, every day. Intellectuals, happily advising humanity on how to conduct its affairs while often in flight from reality to a more comforting, problem-free world of ideas, can be notoriously dishonest. Freud, the great, hugely and obviously ambitious early archaeologist of the psyche, for instance, was a self-deceiver *extraordinaire*, denying any ambition at all.[39] And Karl Marx, champion of the underdog, valued his residence in the exclusive area of Hampstead, London, to an unseemly degree, given his stated aim of equality. Put another way, driven by the underlying need for survival our human belief and behaviour systems, both individual and collective are, in part at least huge, complex, and often ridiculous rationalizations. They are *post hoc* reasons, dreamed up after the event, for thinking and behaving in the way we do. Indeed, it is a scientifically established habit of human beings to create narratives, stories, after an event to fit what we *think* happened rather than what *actually* occurred.[40]

This human tendency of quietly tailoring what we believe to our feelings within ourselves, rather than to facts in the world we share with others, is clear when the characteristic belief systems of depressed poor people are compared with the belief systems of depressed, wealthier, middle- or upper-class people. Often—and understandably—depressed poor people develop, and when asked supply, a narrative or story about the world being a dog-eat-dog place, run by greedy, harsh capitalists who conspire with one another and care nothing for the exploited masses lower down the human food chain, as they live off the fat of the land. Such people frequently say that the situation is hopeless and that, since they see themselves as powerless, there is nothing they can do to help themselves. On the other hand, the wealthier person who is depressed suffers from similar psychological symptoms (tiredness, say) and is likely to feel similarly negative about their own person; but, given their affluence, sees no such problems with the *status quo* which—because they themselves benefit from it in the form of a materially comfortable life—they either ignore or consider to be benevolent, where most people's needs (as far as they know or want to know) are taken care of. And where people are noted to be poor, wealthier people often tend to blame the poor themselves for their own poverty. It's hardly surprising that the rich and poor, individually and collectively, struggle to understand each other—and indeed blame each other for perceived shortcomings. Their world-views, for good, scientifically explicable, psychological reasons, differ greatly from each other.

---

38. For a recent summary, see Livingstone Smith, D. (2005). Natural born liars. *Scientific American, 16(2),* 16–23.
39. Storr, A. (1996). *Gurus: Feet of Clay.* Oxford: Oxford University Press.
40. Loftus, E.F. (1979). *Eyewitness Testimony.* Cambridge, MA: Harvard University Press.

Of course, the rich and poor people are *both* right in their own way. That's right: both right at once, and about the same thing. Guided by their own feelings and experiences, they just see issues—as we all must—from *their own* viewpoint. To some extent, when it suits us we *all* distort the truth, or even lie in our own interests, both to ourselves and others. Yet we are largely blind to this, and continue to act mindlessly. There are few things so vast as our indifference.

These highly dishonest, though understandable human tendencies affect our everyday lives in innumerable ways. I myself admit to being sometimes dishonest, both to myself and to others. At the milder end of the dishonesty spectrum, I might deceive myself that it's OK to tell my friend that I'm feeling too busy to meet—when in fact I really can't be bothered and would far rather please *myself*, sit in Starbucks, and greedily read the newspapers. At the extreme end of the spectrum sexual offenders, guided by powerful feelings but hampered by poor emotion-regulation skills, routinely deceive themselves (and try to deceive others) that their victims somehow 'provoked' or even 'enjoyed' the crime they suffered.[41] Thinking distortions of this sort require treatment. Part of this involves helping the person concerned to be more aware of others' feelings and rights. But the central point remains: human beings can, if circumstances are right and they are happy to act mindlessly, persuade themselves of anything. We sometimes choose to believe nonsense, if that nonsense suits us and our needs at the time.

Take a war waged by a dominant nation or nations against another oppressed, subordinate nation. Such a war can be catastrophic, with human rights being blindly swept away as the interests of the dominant group are privileged, unquestioningly, by themselves. And too few questions get asked. Mindlessness, in other words, affects groups as well as individuals; and the consequences for individual, ordinary people can, if they are unfortunate, be very powerful.

The Mindless Group

Self-serving processes of the kind noted in human individuals also operate in human groups. Again, our evolutionary development is most probably involved, going back to the time of *The Flintstones* and beyond. If Jellostone Park was threatened by outsiders, Fred, Barney and friends needed to club together—and in more than one way—so that they and their families survived.

The results of these processes can be seen in groups of all kinds, from small groups, like the people in *The Office,* to much larger groups, like the people who make up nations. Research in cognitive and social psychology suggests that these proven psychological biases help to define group boundaries, to stereotype outgroup members and, very often, to discriminate against the 'Other'. These biases may lead us to exaggerate the differences between social categories, favour ingroups over

---

41. Salter, A. (2003). *Predators: Pedophiles, rapists, and other sexual offenders: who they are, how they operate, and how we can protect ourselves and our children.* New York: Basic Books.

outgroups,[42] attempt to reduce uncertainty,[43] and be (over-)responsive to potential threats rather than gains. Together, the scientific evidence confirms what many have suspected. Individually, we human beings are often no angels. Collectively, we are often the pits.

To take maybe the most important example above, we know that people are 'ethnocentric', tending to value people they perceive to be of their own kind—their ingroup—more than people they perceive to be different—their outgroup. Together with others we often put ourselves, the ingroup, first; the others, the outgroup, second, in various ways. For one thing, Western people tend to make what are called in the jargon 'dispositional attributions'—blaming the person—for others' behaviour, even when there are clear external or environmental explanations for what happens.

Here, desirable or positive behaviour by ingroup members, and undesirable or negative behaviour by outgroup members, are internally attributed to dispositions. But negative ingroup behaviours and positive outgroup behaviours are externally attributed to situational factors. We also tend to believe other groups' behaviour is more stable and predictable than our own.[44]

In other words, if we did the right thing, we always tend to do that—we're just those kinda guys. If those guys over there did the right thing, circumstances must have helped. And if we did the wrong thing, something must've made us do it, Sir. If those guys did the wrong thing ... well, they would, wouldn't they? This tendency, an ingroup-serving bias, to attribute observed behaviour internally to the person playing a role, is known as the 'fundamental attribution error' or FAE. One explanation for such strong, ethnocentric, intergroup attributional bias involves stereotypes—pre-existing, fixed ideas about others. That guy likes football, drinking and fighting because he's English, doesn't he?

From such psychological roots, prejudice grows. As two respected professors of social psychology recently put it, 'Human beings are remarkably versatile in being able to make almost any social group a target of prejudice.'[45] Not the finest character reference you could wish for. Our own daily experience tells us that certain groups are most frequently the victims of prejudice. These target groups occupy low-power, low-status positions in society, and include sex, race, ethnicity, age, sexuality, and physical and psychological health. Sex, race and age, research shows, are the most frequent basis for stereotyping. Of course, the effects of stereotyping can be drastic. One researcher suggests that sex-selective abortion and infanticide—most often when baby girls are killed—have led to over seventy-six million 'missing women globally'.[46]

---

42. Brewer, M.B. & Miller, N. (1996). *Intergroup Relations.* Pacific Grove, CA: Brooks Cole.
43. Wilson, G.D. (1973). *The Psychology of Conservatism.* San Diego, CA: Academic Press. 207–232.
44. Baxter, T.L. & Goldberg, L.R. (1988). Perceived behavioural consistency underlying trait attributions to oneself and another: an extension of the actor–observer effect. *Personality and Social Psychology Bulletin, 13*, 437–447.
45. Hogg, M.A. & Vaughan, G.M. (2000). *Social Psychology: 3rd edn.* Edinburgh: Pearson / Prentice-Hall: 345.
46. Klasen, S. (1994). 'Missing women' reconsidered. *World Development, 22,* 1061–1071.

What makes it more difficult is that relatively automatic thinking processes may be involved. And against our expectations—I'm a liberal kinda guy myself, aren't I?—such automaticity, to some degree at the very least, seems to affect *all* of us.

Even just *seeing* a member of a certain social group can trigger a chain of non-conscious processes. Stereotypes can be automatically generated by categorization—by putting people into boxes when we see them, in effect. You know the kind of thing: young man; older woman; black man; Chinese woman. And categorization, in turn, can automatically arise from certain triggers (an accent, perhaps, or a face). If the stereotypes are outside consciousness, as they often are, we have little control over the stereotype that is operating. In US research, African American primes (e.g. slavery, blacks, athletic) that were presented too quickly for people to be aware of them caused people to interpret a later, neutral act by a person in stereotypically negative ways. This suggested deep-seated negative stereotypes of African Americans—despite the overwhelming genetic similarities between all races. While such automatic effects may be more marked for people who score highly on measures of prejudice, we may *all* be prone to preconscious priming of this kind.[47]

One means of noticing these processes may be linguistic. When talking about positive outgroup (and negative ingroup) characteristics, we tend to use very concrete language that describes events in simple terms; but we use far more general and abstract terms, relating to enduring characteristics, when talking about negative outgroup and positive ingroup characteristics.[48] We become abstract and general when talking about our prejudices. There is a football hooligan in all of us. You know them human beings? Oh, they're a shocking bunch …

* * *

Let's be clear: we're not *all* bad, but we do have a more negative side. One reason for this is that as human beings we generally view and treat the 'Other' so mindlessly—both in each other and in ourselves. Rather than allowing ourselves to approach and eventually get close to other people of different kinds and, as often as not, begin to like them, we all too easily remain at a distance. Wired to be naturally fearful and suspicious of them, our prejudices, because of the processes above, are easily reinforced. To take one obvious example: elderly people in the West—despite their many valuable abilities, and not least their experience and allied skills—are often treated as worthless and powerless members of the community. Older people are denied many basic human rights, and their basic needs are often untended.[49] Since

---

47. Devine, P.G. (1989). Stereotypes and prejudice: their automatic and controlled components. *Journal of Personality and Social Psychology, 56,* 5–18.
48. Maass, A. (1999). Linguistic intergroup bias: stereotype-perpetuation through language. In: M.P. Zanna (ed.). *Advances in Experimental Social Psychology* (Vol. 31). San Diego, CA: Academic Press: 79–121.
49. Kitwood, T. (1997). *Dementia Reconsidered: The person comes first.* Milton Keynes: Open University Press.

the younger generations generally have little to do with older people, intergenerational encounters activate group, rather than individual perceptions. This leads to avoidance of older people, and minimization of intergenerational contact; so older people tend to remain socially isolated and marginalized in Western society.

Looking at our Western cultures, even the most charitable observer would be forced to conclude that human beings' perception and treatment of groups other than those they themselves belong to is rather less than ideal—and that's putting it very diplomatically. But more surprising still, our poor treatment of other human groups—though partly non-intentional and unconscious—may actually be *systematic*. And this could be important since, at least in the UK, a black male remains twice as likely to go to prison as to university, and social class divisions 'not only persist but actually appear in some important ways to be deepening'.[50]

Above all, recent medical research here has firmly established that human physical and psychological health is strongly affected by a person's relative place in the social system, since 'where you stand in the social hierarchy is intimately related to your chances of getting ill, and to your length of life.'[51] Basic human needs like autonomy and social engagement are systematically thwarted 'for people lower in the hierarchy'.[52] Furthermore, it may well be that in groups we do these things to each other. But why?

A possible psychological answer comes from the US. Social dominance theory (SDT)[53] is one of the most comprehensive and empirically supported attempts to explain negative aspects of intergroup relations. While the theory is not perfect—no scientific theory is—given the amount of research evidence on which it is based, reaching back to the 1970s, it builds a persuasive argument. SDT helps to explain from a psychological standpoint how and why members of certain groups in society—subordinate people—suffer more than others—dominant people—because of key, evolved patterns of human behaviour. Here the self-serving psychological processes of the person, discussed in Chapter 2 above, are writ large—in jumbo form, and with jumbo results for us all. For example, while there is no time to look in detail here, there is good evidence that poorer people are more likely to be discriminated against by the more wealthy in terms of employment, education and health, and to neglect their own well-being and that of their families. Also, men who are low in social status are particularly vulnerable to discrimination from the socially dominant.

From the SDT perspective, the operation of human mindlessness—which is *not*, for the most part, conscious or intentional in any of us—comes to seem systematic and to follow specific patterns. In brief: dominant individual people and groups look

---

50. Mount, F. (2004). *Mind the Gap: The new class divide in Britain.* London: Short Books: 13. Information also from the Commission for Racial Equality, 2004.

51. Marmot, M. (2004). *Status Syndrome: How your social standing directly affects your health and life expectancy.* London: Bloomsbury: 1.

52. *ibid.*: 266.

53. To which I am indebted in the following section. Sidanius, J. & Pratto, F. (1999). *Social dominance.* Cambridge University Press.

after their own interests,[54] while subordinate individual people and groups in effect turn on themselves self-destructively. In this way our social systems, with their dominant and subordinate groups, emerge and remain relatively stable in their structure. This wouldn't matter—particularly if you're relatively wealthy: enjoy the sunshine in Monaco if you get the chance—except that subordinate individuals and groups can suffer hugely, both physically and psychologically. Indeed, while they occupy the same or similar physical space, dominant and subordinate people inhabit very different physical and physiological inner worlds. And whether or not you buy the whole theory, it's hard to ignore the evidence.

Overall, just as the behaviour of the human individual has evolved, as neuroscientist Antonio Damasio says, to 'create the most beneficial situation for its self-preservation and efficient functioning',[55] so human groups, operating collectively, seem very likely to work in a similar way. It may be that we like to think that equality is most often practised between us, but:

> The widespread assumption of equality of treatment fails to be consistent with the best evidence available in every democratic nation in which serious research on these questions can be found.[56]

Not much doubt about that, then. SDT and the evidence that backs the theory suggest that systems of group-based social hierarchy are produced and maintained by the activities of *both* dominant *and* subordinate people.[57] We do it to ourselves. And, of course, to each other. It all depends on how we're feeling: about ourselves, about each other and about the world outside.

Social Climbers of the World Unite

It may be, then, that the structure of our societies and the patterns of human well-being observed within them can be quite directly connected to our individual and collective common psychology.

This is because, given our basic make-up and experiences, we are most often guided in our choices and actions by our feelings—for purposes of survival. But though our feelings and sense of well-being depend greatly on others, and their well-being on us, conflict emerges. This is due in part to the sheer number of other individuals and groups in our many societies. It can often feel to us, and with good reason, as though our needs compete with those of others—and that our own needs *must* come first, most or even all of the time. I might well want to be top dog myself. It'd make me feel good. But you might also want top spot, and the psychological

---

54. See also Connif, R. (2003). *The Natural History of the Rich.* London: Arrow Books.
55. Damasio, A. (2003). *Looking for Spinoza: Joy, sorrow, and the thinking brain.* London: Vintage: 35.
56. Sidanius, J. & Pratto, F. (1999). *Social Dominance.* Cambridge University Press: 43.
57. *ibid.*: 45.

rewards that go with it. You wouldn't care too much about me then; you'd probably be enjoying yourself too much. Because of the often overwhelming concern with our own personal feelings, the other—person, group, organization or nation—very easily and not always noticeably (for example in the case of lower social class groups) gets pushed aside, away or down. If my needs feel so important, it may feel to me that there's no room for you in my personal world.

There is, as I have suggested above, much evidence suggesting that if these processes of self-assertion and entitlement are left unchecked, and all are pitched against all, not only can human life become brutish, but great and unnecessary suffering occurs for specific, unfortunate groups of people—those people who are in one way or another socially subordinate. Historically, and for good psychological reasons that are rooted in our feelings and in our own internal interpretations of them, we as a species have tended not to be mindful of this suffering. This need not be so.

One solution to this conflict—simple in theory, tricky in practice—was offered by Christ, and by the Buddha. It was to consciously treat each other as we would wish to be treated ourselves. But there may seem to us little point in this, since it does not instinctively *feel*—from our default, evolved guide as to what we might do—as though it is in our interests. Deeper exploration of how human psychological development can be affected by poor treatment may shed more light here. It may encourage us to step back and become still more mindful of the needs of others, as well as ourselves. Since they are at the beginning of life, might it make sense to start with children?

3

The Mindless Treatment of Children

Our patients suffer from reminiscences.
Sigmund Freud

Children of Circumstance

Where psychological damage is inflicted between an adult and a child, one thing is almost always certain: the kid comes off worse. His or her mind may be temporarily or permanently scrambled to a greater or lesser degree—and there are likely to be knock-on effects for others later on. As a child, he or she is simply psychologically sensitive and needs to be cared for. And cared for pretty well.

Psychological practice and research suggest that when people are poorly cared for as children they may be prone, consciously and unconsciously, to treat others and themselves less well, or even badly, as they mature into adulthood and later life. Having had little opportunity to learn skills of care—both for the self and for others—the range of caring behaviours of such people, and their ability to be kind, can be reduced. So even bearing in mind other matters like the impact of biology[2] and genetics, personality and temperament, these people in turn tend to treat others, their children and themselves in ways that reflect their own early experience. While numerous factors form a complex developmental picture in which many issues combine with one another, the nature of the parenting we receive affects us. It is vital for children's later health that they are treated well.[1]

As we saw in Chapter 2, parent–child interaction starts at birth—or even before the child has been born.[2] The mother's expressive face, very attractive to the infant, is

1. Carr, A. (1999). *The Handbook of Child and Adolescent Clinical Psychology: A contextual approach.* London: Routledge.
2. For a recent summary of the available evidence, see J. Nadel & D. Muir (eds.). (2005). *Emotional Development.* Oxford: Oxford University Press.

the key visual stimulus in his or her world. And conscious and unconscious communication between the caregiver and child is essential to good psychological and physical development. In healthy mothers and children, 'mirroring' between partners—a minute, split-second process of affective attunement—allows emotions to be quickly shared and managed. Pleasant emotions can be enjoyed by mother and child; unpleasant emotions can be jointly handled. This enables 'interactive repair' of difficult feelings. During psychological development, experience of such healthy parenting allows children to understand that at certain times of stress, negative feelings may emerge, but can eventually be coped with and lead back to more positive states. In this way children come to feel attached to, and feel safe with, their parents or caregivers. Such children, equipped with skills of emotional self-management learned from their parents, are then well prepared for future stresses, which they can face and swiftly recover from. Psychological 'resilience' develops; psychological health can be reached and then maintained with the challenges of normal life that everyone experiences.

Our interactions with children, then, strongly affect their later development across their lifespan. It is the frequency and quality of these parent–child interactions that are vital, because they help set the direction for later psychological and physical development. Detailed studies of interaction between parents and children, and adolescents and their peers, have provided precise accounts of the kinds of interpersonal interaction that produce, and maintain, positive and negative behaviours in children and young people.

The traumatised child's mind

Where people are less able to parent effectively, so that children receive less-than-adequate care, psychological issues may result. There is evidence, for example, that where there are 'attachment' or bonding difficulties between children and parents, children are more likely to develop dysfunctional attitudes that, as they innocently mature, can leave them more prone to depression.[3] And where children are actually abused or maltreated, later psychological problems become more likely. Such problems include anxiety and depression, behavioural problems and delinquency, and (in severe cases) post-traumatic stress disorder (PTSD).[4] A look at the effects of abuse on a child's mind shows clearly how we human beings can affect one another through our contact with each other, sometimes in quite drastic ways. Neuroscience helps to explain why. But get ready for this: the Bad News Bears are really on their way. They won't be here long—that wouldn't feel good and we know that we wouldn't like it—but here they come, just for a short while.

---

3. For a summary of the evidence, see Scher, C.D., Segal, Z.V. & Ingram, R.E. (2004). Beck's theory of depression: origins, empirical status, and future directions for cognitive vulnerability. In. R. Leahey (ed.). *Contemporary Cognitive Therapy: Theory, research, and practice.* New York: Guilford: 27–44.

4. In this section I have drawn on Cicchetti, D. (2003). Neuroendocrine functioning in maltreated children. In: D. Cicchetti & E. Walker (eds.). *Neurodevelopmental Mechanisms in Psychopathology.* Cambridge: Cambridge University Press: 345–365.

Brain development is partly genetically determined, but is also critically affected by the environment and what happens in it. Child abuse, whether emotional, physical or sexual, can itself be a massive stressor. In animal research, threats of physical injury and pain have been shown, not surprisingly, to produce intense activation of physiological systems associated with fear and stress. Early stress can affect young brains, by reducing the child's ability to adapt to challenges flexibly. Later in life, the physiological and psychological results of these processes may pave the way for more severe psychological problems. Early trauma is linked with long-term changes in coping, emotional and behavioural control, responsiveness of the neuroendocrine system to stress and brain structure, neurochemistry and gene expression. Put simply, the traumatised young mind finds it more difficult to cope with stress. All of this means the child may be more vulnerable to later psychological problems; but these issues can, in turn, be strongly affected by the social environment in which the child matures, and how life is lived there.

One thing leads to another: social context and child development

The social context in which children develop can greatly affect the feelings they have about themselves. Children's social context can increase or reduce the level of stress or other negative feelings they and their families experience, the risk of the children's being abused or maltreated, and of their having psychological problems later on. Many such factors can, separately or together, affect the developing child.

Here, the kinds of individual and group processes noted in Chapters 2 become relevant. Above all, the psychological health and feelings of children depend, at least partly, on the psychological health and feelings of their parents or caregivers. And the psychological health of parents *and* children is in turn strongly linked to the social environment in which they live, influential factors associated with that environment, and the quality of life there. If, as a parent, I feel bad in myself and in my life, it's going to be harder for me to make you, as a child, feel good. Look, I'm stressed out—OK? Give me a break, kid! In view of the group psychological processes we looked at in Chapter 2, and our evolved, default tendency to look after ourselves first while overlooking the well-being of poorer groups in Western societies, locally as well as globally, the effect of local social conditions on child welfare may *actually* be a concern for all. We all affect each other's well-being, however indirect our impact on each other may seem to be. We are all in this together. But which social factors are important as causes of stress, ill-feeling and psychological difficulty, so that they affect how parents and their children feel and behave towards each other?

Factors like parental stress levels, low social status, parental depression, exposure to parental smoking or drug intake before or after a child's birth may negatively affect a child's brain and emotional development, and so can make it more difficult for the child to lead a balanced psychological life as they mature. Similarly, the type of discipline received by a child from their parents or caregivers is likely to influence their psychological health and future. Importantly here, children with persistent behavioural problems receive harsher punishment, yet in a less consistent way than other children. The emotional tone of their family may be hostile and pessimistic, partly because any negative behaviour from the child often leads to coercive and conflictual parent–child interchanges. In such family situations, it often eventually happens that children's positive behaviours (like trying hard at school) are ignored or overlooked by their caregivers, while their negative behaviours (like hitting their brothers and sisters) are rewarded with inconsistent negative attention (like being shouted at). 'You little so-and-so! You're always picking on your sister! Right, that's it, you're not having your dinner!' One psychological solution here is to help parents and caregivers put consistent boundaries or limits down about what is, or what isn't, acceptable behaviour from children; but also to begin first to *notice* (not easy), and then *reward* (also not easy, particularly to begin with), more positive behaviour. So then a new 'story' or 'narrative' about a 'problem' child is encouraged to develop. Here the child's behaviour, rather than the child him or herself, comes to be seen as the issue. But from the earliest point of development—well before birth—at-risk children may be exposed to more social stresses and fewer protective factors than is usual. Such circumstances increase the chance of later behavioural and emotional problems—until psychological help arrives.

The presence of even *one* risk factor like those above—say, the mother and father both parenting their child harshly—may affect how the child feels about themselves, and raises the chance of later psychological problems in the child. But there is also good evidence from long-term research to show that *many* environmental risk factors of this kind are linked to producing later psychological problems in children.[5] These risk factors are found in people at all levels of society, but are concentrated in financially poorer areas. They may affect children's academic performance most strongly, followed by their psychological health. The researchers of one recent study said that:

> Gender, race, ethnicity and income level alone may have statistically significant effects on adolescent behaviour, but *these differences pale in comparison with the accumulation of multiple negative influences in high-risk groups* [my italics].[6]

So the sheer number of psychological risk factors to which a child is exposed may negatively affect their psychological development; and the number of risks tends to rise significantly in poorer populations. As everyone with children knows, it is harder to feel that we are doing a good job—or even a 'good enough' job, which will help our children mature as normally as possible—as a parent when we face real stress ourselves.

---

5. Here I have drawn on Sameroff, A.J., Seiffer, R. & Barko, W.T. (1997). Environmental perspectives on adaptation during childhood and adolesence. In: S.S. Luthar, J.A. Burack, D. Cicchetti & J.R. Weisz (eds.). (1997). *Developmental Psychopathology: Perspectives on adjustment, risk, and disorder*: Cambridge: Cambridge University Press.507–526.
6. *ibid.*: 520.

Developing Mindlessness: Psychological effects of child abuse

Mindless behaviour

Regardless of where children are living or who they are living with, though, once abuse has occurred the child's relationships with, and feelings about, themselves and others can be strongly affected—both in the short and long term. Research shows that abused children *learn* to be more aggressive towards others later on; also that the abusive treatment from others affects their style of thinking and feeling, as well as their behaviour. Their way of being can change. These issues can impact on the child's development and threaten to knock them off a psychologically healthy course. Other people in the child's community can then also be affected in a negative way because of the earlier abuse. While abuse is an extreme example of child maltreatment, it shows clearly how our interactions with them can affect their development. These changes have been explored over recent decades by researchers including John Coie and Kenneth Dodge and their colleagues.[7]

First, Coie and Dodge note that abused children's *behaviour* often changes, clearly reflecting through their actions and words what they have experienced. Having been hurt and threatened themselves, they often—and logically, when you think about it—come to hurt and threaten others. The children's minds are, in effect and in the light of their experience, defending themselves in case of attack. Faced with what is to them a recognizable threat, their feelings automatically rise up internally and produce an appropriately (from the child's viewpoint) aggressive response. Long-term studies conducted with the same groups of children in the US show the possible links between physical abuse and later aggressive behaviour towards others. With a sample of preschool children, parents were interviewed about the children's developmental history from 12 months of age onwards. The following question was included: 'Do you remember any times when your child was hit severely enough by any adult to be hurt, or to require medical attention?' Children who had been physically abused were significantly more likely than non-abused children to show aggressive behaviours later in playgroup.

Centrally and linked to this, abused children may find it more difficult to be empathic towards others, and to treat others mindfully and with kindness. Early treatment of the self often affects later treatment of the other. Damaged, hurt children become *significantly less* mindful of the needs of others. Such children often have little sense of what it means to take care of something or someone—to be kind, in other words. To anyone. They struggle to see anyone else's point of view at all.

Careful research observations of very young children aged from just 1 to 3 show, for instance, that abused children were much less likely to respond in a concerned way to other, distressed children than non-abused toddlers were. Instead, abused

---

7. In the following section I have drawn on Coie, J.D. & Dodge, K.A. (1998). Aggression and antisocial behaviour. In: N. Eisenberg (ed.). *Handbook of Child Psychology: 5th edn.* New York & Chichester: Wiley. Volume 3: *Social, Emotional and Personality Development:* 779–862.

children, reflecting their own less-than-ideal treatment at the hands of their caregivers and feeling more easily threatened because of this treatment, responded with either fear or aggression to try and cope with the sense of threat.[8] Furthermore slightly older, 3- to 6-year-old physically abused children in day-care settings were observed to have fewer interactions with peers, but also proportionately *more negative interactions*, than a carefully matched comparison group.[9] These studies show greater aggressive responding to conflict and distress by physically abused children, and a higher level of emotional reactivity to perceived stress. So where children who have been abused see—or even just *sense*—conflict between others, because of the strong feelings that are produced in them they are more likely than other children to respond with either personal distress—which can lead to escape or avoidance behaviours (like just running away from the situation)—or with aggressive acts (like just hitting the other child involved). The children's feelings of distress in the present were learned straight from their experiences of threat in the past.

In other words, there are clear signs from the research done by Coie, Dodge and their colleagues that people can be directly psychologically affected by the early treatment they receive. The connection can be simple. If children are abused by other people in their past, it often becomes more difficult for them to get close to others, and enjoy being with them, in future. Children's relationships with others are affected. Because of their early experiences of maltreatment, kind, sociable behaviour goes against their feelings; they are more likely, as they begin life, to behave antisocially towards those around them. This pattern is not always present: but it often is. Antisocial, negative behaviour in adulthood is seldom, perhaps never, psychologically inexplicable. It makes sense when we decide to take enough trouble to find out what that person has been through.

For this reason alone, we might pause to think about the psychological consequences of allowing children in more deprived communities to continue to suffer, where early experiences of abuse, and other stresses, are significantly more common than in other places. Allowing such deprivation and abuse to continue is to encourage the cycles of negative, damaging behaviour to persist. Because of the long-term results of such experiences, helping to prevent such abuse in future would very probably go some way to helping *all of us,* directly or indirectly. The sum of abuse would be reduced, the sum of human kindness increased. Where people, as children, have been victims of abuse from others, whether emotional, physical or sexual, simply expecting them to be good, caring, polite citizens may be too much too ask. Their inner lives may have been drastically changed; and they may need help of some kind, personal or professional, from other people to return to a healthy course of development.

---

8. Main, M. & George, C. (1985). Responses of abused and disadvantaged toddlers to distress in agemates: a study in the daycare setting. *Developmental Psychology, 21,* 407–412.
9. Howes, C. & Eldredge, R. (1985). Responses of abused, neglected, and non-maltreated children to the behaviours of their peers. *Journal of Applied Developmental Psychology, 6,* 261–270.

Seeing threat where none exists: biased thoughts and feelings

Second in their sketch of the abused child's mind, Coie and Dodge show how children's *thinking style* may be affected.[10] As we saw in Chapter 2, thinking or cognitive biases can occur, affecting children's daily lives at home and at school. The precise ways in which such children see themselves, others and the world may change sharply—yet be invisible to the observer. Understandably, when compared with other, non-abused children they show much greater sensitivity to threat, and learn to look out for many kinds of danger in life as they mature. Sometimes they perceive dangers, particularly personal dangers from other people, that do not even exist when the situation is seen through the eyes of others.[11] And the resulting social information-processing patterns in the child, assessed yearly in research during the child's development, can account for aggressive behaviour later in childhood.[12] These processes are not conscious, however. They are mostly learned at an unconscious level—then acted out with others later on.

After early experiences of abuse in which children themselves felt a great sense of threat, aggressive children show gaps in attention to relevant social cues, as well as hypervigilant, over-anxious thought biases. They are, to put it simply, overoccupied with potential dangers. And aggressive children also pay more attention to aggressive social cues from others compared with non-aggressive children, as well as finding it more difficult than other children to *divert their attention* from aggressive stimuli of which they are aware.[13] This makes perfect psychological sense. It is only natural, if a child feels or has felt desperately threatened at an early point or points in their life, for their mind and body to prepare for future attacks.

One young man, who grew up seeing his parents physically fighting from the age of seven, felt that as the eldest child he should be stopping the fights. Because of this he would try to get between his battling parents, with the result that he would often be hit hard on the body and directly in his face by his own father. Understandably, he learned that the world was a dangerous place, and that people were not to be trusted and could not be trusted in future. Consequently he kept at a very safe distance from others as he grew up, fighting his way through life for himself. He learned to be 'the boss' or 'the man' in any social situation, including at home and at work, so as to keep out of danger. But this surface strength cost him much personally, because it affected his relationships. It meant that his 'female' (or human, we might say) feelings were always hidden. Until he felt he had no choice but to give up emotionally, and learned that sometimes being 'weak' was acceptable after all, no one else was allowed

---

10. See Coie & Dodge, *ibid.* 824–828.
11. Dodge, K.A., Bates, J.E. & Pettit, G.S. (1990). Mechanisms in the cycle of violence. *Science, 250,* 1678–1683.
12. Dodge, K.A., Pettit, G.S., Bates, J.E. & Valente, E. (1995). Social information processing patterns partially mediate the effect of the relation between socioeconomic status and child conduct problems. *Journal of Abnormal Psychology, 104,* 632–643.
13. Gouze, K.R. (1987). Attention and social problem-solving as correlates of aggression in preschool males. *Journal of Abnormal Child Psychology, 15,* 181–197.

to get close to him. He could not share his intimate feelings with anyone, even his own wife. Obviously, until that changed, marriage was not much fun for the couple. For many years, and though they cared deeply about each other, neither really knew much about what the other was feeling. Though they lived together physically, emotionally they were far apart.

Supporting the idea that early experiences of threat and abuse affect the way children see the world, many reliable studies have found that, in social circumstances that are unclear, and where it's hard to tell what's going on, aggressive children are more likely than other children to make hostile interpretations of others' intentions. Such children think ill of people, with little evidence for the conclusions they draw. In such studies, experimental participants are asked to imagine being provoked—maybe by having water spilt on them—and to interpret the other person's intent.[14] Aggressive children interpret even *neutrally meant* acts as *intentionally damaging*—seeing negative intent where it does not actually exist in another person.[15] As one might expect, there is evidence that children's hostile biases predict aggressive behaviour many years into the future. Children's thoughts about others also predict acceptance by potential friends of the same age. The more aggressively the child interacts with others, the less he or she is likely to be accepted by them.[16]

There is good evidence to suggest, then, that young children reared in a home of abuse, conflict and threat develop a heightened awareness of conflict that reduces their ability to properly and fairly process others' intentions in social situations. This cognitive and emotional difficulty leads them, when compared with other children, to react more aggressively to others, and to be less able to control their own angry responses. The kinds of psychological process examined in Chapter 2 come, after experience of early abuse, to lead to strong behavioural and emotional biases in children. Very young children who have been victimized and have felt threatened come naturally—and through no fault of their own—to expect hostility in or attack from others, and learn to be hypervigilant to these cues. Since they are more than usually oriented to defending themselves and attacking others, they may sense limited social possibilities. Consequently they may be less able to respond positively to others, to act with kindness in response to others' distress or even to neutral situations, as though they themselves are in danger.

Overall, then, aggressive children who have themselves often been ill-treated find it more difficult to make good social decisions based on full and accurate information. This occurs because of the understandably and, after abuse, naturally biased way these children's minds process information presented to them in everyday life.

---

14. Graham, S. & Hudley, C. (1994). Attributions of aggressive and non-aggressive African-American male early adolescents: a study of construct accessibility. *Developmental Psychology, 30,* 365–373.

15. Dodge, K.A., Pettit, G.S. McClaskey, C.L. & Brown, M.M. (1986). Social competence in children. *Monographs of the Society for Research in Child Development, 51 (2, Serial no. 13).*

16. Rabiner, D.L. & Coie, J.D. (1989). The effect of expectancy inductions on rejected children's acceptance by unfamiliar peers. *Developmental Psychology, 25,* 450–457.

Rejection and anti-social behaviour in adolescence and adulthood

Finally, as Coie and Dodge have shown, early abuse often re-emerges in different, destructive forms after childhood.[17]

Over time, after children have frequently shown aggression towards others, the effects of early abuse can lead to their being socially rejected. Unconsciously, children who themselves have been abused push other people away, leaving them isolated in a vicious circle that brings them back to the original bad feelings; and perhaps because of the effects of their behaviour, aggressive children experience more feelings of loneliness than others. If unchecked, such feelings can lead to further anti-social behaviour since, feeling abandoned or rejected, the children may be more inclined to be aggressive around others, alienating those others even further.[18]

The effects of early abuse can also last into adulthood in the form of actual antisocial behaviour. Early self-control problems are predictive of, and lead to, a broad range of adjustment problems in grown men. Such problems typically include spouse abuse, drunk driving and severe punishment of children.[19] In one study of 182 men that used interviews with them, their spouses and their children about their education, work, marriage and parenthood, those who as children had temper tantrums (biting, kicking and screaming, for example) at age 8, 9 and 10 were compared, in their later years, with those who had had no such tantrums. The boys with bad tempers achieved less in educational terms than others. Similarly, the marriages of men who had self-control problems were less stable. Divorce among such people has been noted to be twice the usual level.[20]

Abusive early relationships in life can, then, negatively affect later key personal relationships like marriage. This is perhaps because, internally, the abused person's feelings are often similar to how they always were, following the initial experience of abuse. Until these feelings are thought about and reflected on, they are hard to change. Even where genuine love and kindness is offered by another person, they may find it very hard to see, and hard to feel. Instead, marked by the early feelings of threat from the experiences of abuse, they may sense—incorrectly—that the other person may be trying to abandon them, or even hurt them intentionally. Even the smallest signs of this—such as wanting, quite innocently, to go out for a drink with friends—may be taken by the abused person as a sign of threat. In turn, the abused person may become more hostile and rejecting. And so on until the end of the relationship, which confirms what the abused person always thought—that there's something wrong with them; that living life alone, and lonely suffering, was all they deserved. It's bad and it's sad,

---

17. See Coie and Dodge, *ibid.* 830–835.
18. Asher, S.R., Hymel, S. & Renshaw, P.D. (1984). Loneliness in children. *Child Development, 55,* 1457–1464.
19. Huesman, L.R., Eron, L.D., Leifowitz, M.M. & Walder, L.O. (1984). Stability of aggression over time and generations. *Developmental Psychology, 20,* 1120–1134.
20. Caspi, A., Elder, G.H. & Bem, D.J. (1987). Moving against the world: life-course patterns of explosive children. *Developmental Psychology, 23,* 308–313.

but this is how things can often work when psychological damage has been done. Unless the cycle is broken, hurt can easily become self-reinforcing.

* * *

What happens to us as children powerfully affects our later psychological development. This includes, crucially, the relationships we have with others and above all the quality of those relationships. All children bear the imprint of those who have cared, or not cared for them. But at the extreme end of the parenting spectrum, where experiences of abuse are involved and children are treated mindlessly, the psychological results can be drastic, as our beliefs about ourselves and others, our perceptions, our feelings and so our behaviour can change. The production in children of early, lasting, negative feelings in themselves can take them—and us, as adults—to behave in ways that if they are unchecked can lead them, and others with whom they share their lives, back to the original bad feelings. In some cases, as the work of Coie and Dodge so clearly shows, where conditions are wrong it can lead children off from a healthy developmental course towards feelings of rejection from others and antisocial behaviour towards them. Often these psychological habits persist in adult life.

On the positive side, though, not all children and young people who have suffered and been abused at the hands of others, and have gone on to develop psychological issues like behavioural problems, continue to suffer themselves or cause others to suffer in later life. Good marital experiences—where people *treat each other well, over time*—and job commitment and stability can act as protective factors. They can significantly reduce the chances of antisocial or deviant behaviour in early adult years.[21] This may be because a sense of being valued and cared for by others, after childhood—either at home or at work or, ideally, both—can help to make good the problems caused partly by early abuse or maltreatment. In such cases, more positive cycles of interaction are set up. Often, people come to feel less threatened in themselves, and more positive about themselves, even though they frequently have very clear memories of the difficult times of their early lives and how hard things were when they started out. Feeling a little better about themselves, while being able to reflect on how things have changed for them over time, makes it easier for such fortunate people to relate well to other people, to come closer to them and allow them to be close, rather than pushing them away. In time they come psychologically and physically closer again to the rest of the community. Everyone benefits.

Sometimes these recovery processes occur with psychological help. Talking the problems through with another person leads the affected individual to begin to develop different views on themselves, and on their lives. But such is the inspiration, resilience

21. Rutter, M., Quinton, D. & Hill, J. (1990). Adult outcomes of institution-reared children: males & females compared. In: L. Robins & M. Rutter (eds.). *Straight and Devious Pathways from Childhood to Adulthood.* Cambridge: Cambridge University Press: 135–157. Sampson, R.J. & Laub, J.H. (1990). Crime and deviance across the life course: the saliences of adult social bonds. *American Sociological Review, 55,* 609–627.

and strength of the human spirit that people often make such changes themselves. By awareness and insight, as well as learning from others, they begin to see how early deprivation of one or more kinds has led them to treat themselves and others less well than they might. Frequently, they begin to make important changes in their lives; maybe beginning to look after their own needs and feelings for the first time. Perhaps just pausing to think before they reach for 'one more' drink—or in my case, currently, another tub of tasty ice cream. Or stepping back internally, and remaining mindful and quiet, before they feel their anger growing with their children where it is not really justified. In these common cases—in millions of them—people's self-awareness changes their lives, and the lives of their families, for the better.

4

Me and My Shaky Psyche

If I knew myself, I'd run away.
Goethe

Explaining my Shaky Psyche

There is good reason to think that the mind—especially the young mind—is sensitive, and that what might appear to be relatively mild stresses in childhood and adolescence can mark us, and affect us and those around us, later on as we develop. Many people know this for themselves in different ways, and experience it in their own lives.

My own personal experience of psychological issues reflects these matters. I've had quite a shaky psyche myself. While I am a clinical psychologist, exploring with psychotherapy and mindfulness the inner landscape of others so as to discover, with them, grounds for hope, as part of my previous private bids for the dubious title of The Unhappiest Man in the World I have experienced, at various times earlier in my life and by turns, significant levels of anxiety, depression and panic, as well as bulimia. These, as I shall explain, had clear psychological foundations deeper down, in a feeling of low self-esteem (or, if you like, just a negative, unflattering view of myself). For decades these issues had many effects on the quite rigid and restricted way I lived my life. I strove for imagined glory, to hide my psychological pain. There I go again: that sounds too grand, considering what happened. What follows is an everyday story of psychologically painful experiences that affected someone—me—and my feelings and behaviour through the years. I was really quite a screwed-up kid, and a troubled young man. Because of this, I had to look inward to find and begin to resolve the issues before I could look outward in a more healthy way. I didn't want to be Woody Allen for ever. What were the symptoms of these problems? Well, certain patterns of my previous feeling, thinking and behaving provide some clues.

In the following account of my personal issues, it might be worth remembering that my issues—just like anyone else's, are just human 'stuff' of one kind or another.

They're pretty normal hang-ups with pretty normal causes—definitely not too important in the cosmos—but they did affect my life and how I felt about myself. We all have such psychological stuff that affects us and, since I've regularly sat in both the therapist's *and* the client's chair in psychotherapy, it makes sense to draw on my own life to show you how we develop, and change, psychologically. I also feel that it's time for some honesty. While plenty of books discuss psychological problems, few writers can be clear, or perhaps can dare to be clear, about the psychological origins of, and solutions to, their own problems.[1] I will do things slightly differently. In the light of much self-reflection I can be clear, and I will be clear. Almost without fail my clients respond very well to such honesty and transparency—not that I'd go on about my own issues inappropriately in their time, as that's not my job. In that way, I think, everyone's best interests are served. We are all fallible humanity: even psychologists. Or sometimes, perhaps, *especially* psychologists. In any case, forgive me if you will, for I have sometimes been a muppet.

Fear and self-loathing: how my problems showed themselves

Until the last few years I've always avoided—and been secretly terrified of—authority and authority figures. This fear showed itself in various forms. Faced with school or university exams, for instance, I'd work like *crazy*. It felt as though if I didn't work very hard to protect myself, I'd somehow get hurt, or something would go badly wrong. Feeling threatened like this, I'd begin working hard preparing for the exams months or even years before other people. At its most extreme, in my attempt to defend myself against the threat I perceived during my exams in my first year at university, I basically hid in my room there. My little room became, looked—and felt like—a kind of battle HQ, as I covered the walls with revision papers. I felt in a way as though I was under attack; I sat there working for 14 hours a day, 7 days a week, starting at 8 am and finishing at midnight, with breaks for exercise, meals: and then giant mega-meals—bulimic-style binges on food when the feelings became apparently unbearable.

Frankly, I often felt scared during these times: really worried that things wouldn't turn out all right, that something serious was going to go wrong—and that I'd be paying a heavy price for this. At night, lying in bed and trying to sleep, I'd imagine that I was sleeping, protected perfectly under an angel's wing. There, in this imagined place away from the worrying present, I felt I could be safe. There I would be untroubled by anyone who (so I felt) would try to hurt me. But all the time I felt as though, working away like mad, I was saving up ammunition for battle in the looming examinations. And when the exams came, after a nervous start most often, I felt myself giving them a massive and sustained hammering. I often imagined myself, strange as

1. See, for example, Solomon, A. (2001) *The Noonday Demon: An anatomy of depression*. London: Chatto & Windus; Wolpert, L. (1999). *Malignant Sadness: The anatomy of depression*. London: Faber. A trend towards greater transparency may be evident, though. See Dworkin, M. (2005). *EMDR and the Relational Imperative: The therapeutic relationship in EMDR treatment*. New York & Abingdon: Routledge.

it sounds, bombing them to destruction below me, after which I would sweep off—in my threatened mind only—victorious again; a winner, happier, now much safer than I had felt, with the enemy for the time being at least successfully destroyed.

I can well imagine how curious that must seem to you, if you're reading: what on earth is the guy talking about? How disproportionate, how over-the-top, those feelings seem and sound now. But that's how scared I felt at the time: terrified. Terrified that things would go wrong, terrified that I would not be safe and that things would not be OK at all, and terrified that, somehow, even my basic needs in the future would not be met.

Feeling desperately threatened at this time of my life, it seemed only 'rational' to me that I took desperate measures to survive. At these times, the tension would build during the days (though I was barely aware of this at the time) as stresses mounted up and up. I would dimly feel, for example, that it was impossible for me to pass the exams that I was facing, since the philosophy books—particularly the logic—that I had to study were too difficult for me to understand. Once the tension had hit its peak by late evening, around 10pm—I was often alone in my room by this point, all possible company departed—I'd tidy my desk, pack up my papers, and walk at speed to a place that sold junk food: a supermarket, a fish-and-chip shop, a kebab van. Once I'd reached one of these, I'd buy something—say fish and chips. Then, walking around, I'd eat that very quickly, taking massive bites and gulping it down. Then I'd go somewhere else to buy something more, and eat that. And so on, and so on until after two, three or four food-stops I'd feel so full that it felt badly uncomfortable and I couldn't eat any more. At that point I'd stagger home to college, hurting physically because I was so full—sometimes being uncomfortable when walking, my stomach aching because of what I myself had done; and hurting emotionally too, because I was so unhappy. Because I felt I didn't have the guts, I didn't make myself sick, like many people who binge-eat but, as well as the feelings of unhappiness and self-disgust that my mega-meal produced, I also felt a child-like sense of fullness with all the food. So the binges, which happened around two to three times a week, gave me a curious mix of feelings; they seemed to confirm my feelings of misery, keeping me there, but they also provided a temporary feeling of comfort. I felt that even if I couldn't rely on anyone or anything else, I could rely on the words that I was reading in poems, and I could rely on food. In a time of great personal uncertainty, both felt as though they offered certain good. Looking back now, though, this sounds like such a lonely period. I wish now that I, as an older man, could by some trick of time return and cherish, encourage and father the boy I was. I also wonder whether Oxford itself could have done more to look after me and others like me—though I was good, I guess, at hiding the problems.

Given my early experiences of threat, which I'll explain shortly, the situation I was in as a young man at university produced an appropriate reaction in me, curious as it may sound above. Because of parts of my early life, I felt that the staff would treat me badly there at university. Since they seemed to have power over me, and seemed to be in control, they could hurt me. It felt to me as though they would be cold, hard, and unfeelingly harsh with me. Who was I, after all? Just an unattractive, socially unwanted lad from nowhere, I felt, with nothing going for me. Who, in the wider world, would care about *me*? It felt, very strongly, as though I had to *do* something about it, and defend myself against this threat. *Do something!* I did—I worked brutally hard. And when the exams finished, I felt safe. Temporarily invulnerable, I felt that no one could touch me or harm me then. Of course, in the busy world we inhabit this feeling of safety didn't last long. The cycle started again, and I began to feel psychologically and physically vulnerable once more, as I came to face new challenges.

This fear of authority figures, and what they might do to me, also affected me strongly when I came to think about getting a job in the real world a few years later. I felt sure that the world was full of strong, powerful, good-looking people who were ready to criticize me, hurt me or punish me for little or no reason. Above all, I felt, *no one should be allowed to have power over me, because they could not be trusted.* And I felt that on no account whatsoever should they be allowed to get any more power over me than they already had. I instinctively felt and knew—or thought I knew—that they might abuse their power, which would leave me feeling vulnerable and at their mercy. I tried to escape reality, but life caught up with me, as it always does. Eventually, I simply had to face my problems.

So when it came to leaving the quite protected academic environment at age twenty-two and getting a job with other people, I wasn't just scared of London—the place where most of my college friends were heading—I was scared of life. Also, since women at that time hardly seemed to be interested in me, there was little sense in leaving the 'life of the mind' at university. So I hid myself away behind books again for yet another five years, still basically too frightened to come out into the world as an independent adult, responsible for myself.

Seeing the world and the people in it as dangerous and threatening also left me, sometimes, feeling trapped and stuck. Part of me wanted to be free, yet part of me was also too scared to do anything and leave the prison that circumstances had created for me, and that I myself had helped create. Not surprisingly, I also sometimes felt low. Mostly during this time I propped myself up psychologically by the use of study (giving me a feeling of increased status), and physical exercise (running) most days. Both of these generally kept my mood at a reasonable level, but sometimes the feelings went further into low moods and depression. I would then feel very tired, confused, slow to react in my mind, and inwardly feeling out of control and frightened. All these are some of the well-recognized symptoms of low mood and depression. And in situations with others at such times, I'd feel like being especially submissive, with them feeling to me (if not to themselves) much more capable and powerful than I was. I'd wake up in the morning, and the feelings hadn't shifted. Often I had the sense that there seemed to be no prospect of change, or of my life improving.

When I finally began work as an assistant clinical psychologist, at the age of thirty in 1999, some of these problems—particularly those regarding authority figures—remained in their basic form. Although my food-binges had stopped almost a decade before, when I was twenty-one, my perceptions still became distorted at certain times, especially under stress, when the feelings were stronger; and still more so in the presence of authority figures, who instinctively seemed to me to have some or all of the power over my life and career. At times I felt physically smaller than I was, and authority figures, like my boss at the time—even when we were there together in the flesh—came to seem much bigger than they actually were: certainly bigger than me, which was absolutely not the case in reality. And more curious still, very kind and well-meaning professional people—in one case a lady of 5ft 1in and around 7 stone—came to seem angry, critical and threatening to me (5ft 10in and around 12½ stone), when there was no outward evidence *whatsoever* for this. As you might have guessed, these fears changed the course of my existence in various ways. And where did all this come from? In fact I can tell you quite accurately where it came from, using what we know of human clinical psychology, including what we know about the working of feelings when we feel under some kind of threat as described in Chapter 2.

Through self-reflection and psychotherapy, I came to see that at least two connecting issues from my early life were involved in my problems—my fear of others, and my sense of being unattractive. In anyone's psychological development, it's quite normal for two or more key issues to be involved in the origins of their problems. As you might expect, these issues led me to behave in certain ways, all of which were humanly understandable when the psychological details are known. Let me explain what I mean. To begin with, though, I need to say a little about the psychological background of my own family when I was growing up, since that affected me, just as our psychological family background affects most, if not all of us.

Starting out: me as a loved but fatherless child

Born in London in 1969, I was an only child brought up by my mother, a middle-class, professional woman who had middle-class English values such as tolerance and the importance of being conscientious and hard-working—with not too much emphasis on how one was feeling. Although I may not have been an entirely planned pregnancy, I know that I was very wanted and loved by her, who worked hard to keep us—and she never once mentioned a feeling of being tired, or of having had enough. My mother gave an enormous amount of love to me, and I am very fortunate in that. Sigmund Freud suggested that the boy who is his mother's favourite may draw, to his great benefit, on a lifetime's store of love, which can sustain one during challenging times. So far, so good.

But while I know my mother very well, and benefited from her caring presence, I had, and still have, no idea who my father was, never having met him. So I had *no* idea of how it felt to be safe and protected by a father, or stepfather, which can be important for a child; or, indeed, how a father, or a man in general, might be or act, or what such a person might be expected to do. Often (though it depends on the father), children learn valuable psychological skills from good fathers (though not from bad ones), like how to successfully control their emotions, to accept boundaries and limits regarding what is reasonable behaviour, and to pick themselves up when things get difficult or times are hard. There was no such father-figure around as I developed. This, in itself, left me somewhat psychologically vulnerable in certain ways. For one thing I've often felt rather unprotected. I think I can understand why a disproportionate number of British Prime Ministers have either been fatherless or have lost fathers. If you're on top it could feel as though no one wields power over you. I've sometimes also had difficulties managing my emotions—dwelling too long on low or sad feelings in destructive cycles of rumination, for example, instead of taking my attention away to more encouraging matters and then actually doing something about the issues.[2] I have also often struggled to be clear about, and to accept, my own limitations and the boundaries set by ordinary reality.[3] So sometimes this has led me to think I can do more than I am capable of, leading me, in the past especially, to overstretch myself, try too hard and land myself in trouble. Or I felt really strong feelings of frustration at quite normal things, such as having to do things I didn't want to do.

It is also likely that my lacking a father or father-figure may have had other, indirect effects on my psychological development. It may also have encouraged my mother to indulge me in certain ways more than was healthy. At the very least, when two relatively healthy parents are present they most often feel OK about saying 'no'. I think my mother, alone, sometimes found that hard to do, which led to my getting my own way too much of the time and to having false, over-inflated expectations about later, adult life.

Try not to laugh: but I basically expected, for instance, not to have to do any work after a certain age. I know; it's difficult to believe. Having finished university at age 22 with a good degree, I actually thought to myself that I had achieved all I needed to. I'd felt very vulnerable and threatened; I'd won the battle I felt that I'd been in—and I thought that the work of my life was over! Of course, this youthful, foolish idea —and boy, does it seem silly now—was almost completely mistaken. I had worked very hard at exams from the age of 15, true; but I had not yet even approached the challenging, interesting reality of the world beyond the walls of university. This would take me still another seven years. In view of this, it's maybe no surprise that I was thirty before I got my first job. Partly because of the unpleasant, threatening feelings that came up when I thought about being in the outside world, I managed to avoid it—and all the pleasures (like money) and pains (like responsibility) that went with it—by staying in college. There was no limit-setting father-figure around to help me separate from my (over)generous mother, and specifically to listen to my plans for avoidance of the world and then to say, firmly but fairly: 'Get on with it!' So, not to put too fine a point on it—I didn't. I wish, in vain of course, that I could have done what I needed to do in recognizing these problems for myself, and taking better, more adaptive decisions. But I'm afraid I couldn't at the time.

Having explained some of my own psychological background, we can move on to my specific psychological problems, beginning with the fear of others and authority figures especially.

---

2. Nolen-Hoeksema, S. (2003). *Women Who Think too Much.* London: Robinson.
3. On the negative effects of fatherlessness, see Pilgrim, V. E. (1993). *Muttersohne.* Frankfurt: Rororo.

Feeling unprotected: me as a frightened child

Regarding my fear of others: actually I'd felt very scared and threatened as a small child of around 4 or 5. Although it was nothing out of the ordinary, I was treated pretty mindlessly. No one stopped to think about the possible psychological effects of what they were doing or saying.

These events occurred in around 1973 and 1974. The processes of care—or the lack of it—that I talked about above became relevant. I wasn't abused, but I had some difficult and unpleasant emotional experiences that stayed with me. At that time, when I was young, my mother was working full-time, all day, five days a week. I was also 'cared for' after school, and in some of the school holidays, by a woman who had children, and stresses, of her own. That would have been fine, except I felt strong feelings of being abandoned, isolated and unsafe when I was with her. Unlike my own loving mother, she shouted at her children. She often looked angry. I was frightened of her anger; I was also scared of her husband, who talked about the belt he used on children who misbehaved, and it felt as though there was no one there to protect me from all this. Only now do I see how much I *hated* being with her, as well as having the threat from him lurking in the shadows when he came home from work. I *really* hated it. I was simply too scared to say so to anyone, for a long time. I was a little kid. In the early 1950s, a psychological experimenter found that he could easily create experimental neurosis with unpredictable mild shocks to lambs, but only if the mother was not present. If the mother was present: no neurosis, no freaking out.[4] I was the lamb without the mother present—without my mother, but sometimes being shouted at and frightened by another adult. It freaked me out.

One of this woman's worst interactions with me—and I remember it vividly over 30 years later—was being out alone with her on a street close to her hated house. I wanted to use the toilet, but was too afraid to say so to her since I felt she might shout at me. So instead, something inevitable and natural for a child happened. Unable to hold myself any longer, I urinated and defecated where I was standing. I can still see the delicate streams of urine running downhill between the cracks of the pavement. I can still feel my trousers full and warm with my own faeces. The very situation I had wanted to avoid—provoking the woman's anger—then occurred. She began to shout at me, so to try and stop this I tried to beat her to it by saying, 'I'm sorry. I'm bad. I know I'm bad. I'm bad.' So, like a lot of people in similar situations, I got my pre-emptive attack on myself in first, before she could do it. It felt better at the time to feel as if it was under my control. I'm sorry to say it, but I wonder if many children nowadays, often cared for by people who aren't related to them, have similar frightening experiences.

Certainly, my experiences of childhood difficulties and ill-treatment are little—although not nothing—when compared to the horror and terror experienced by some

---

4. Wang, S. (2005). A conceptual framework for integrating research related to the physiology of compassion and the wisdom of Buddhist teachings. In P. Gilbert (ed.). *Compassion: Conceptualization, research and use in psychotherapy.* London: Routledge: 75–120.

people whom I meet in my work as a clinical psychologist. There's no doubt about that. My traumas noted above were not great. Yet even those experiences, as an effectively defenceless, frightened, vulnerable child cut off from my caregiver and protection, marked me powerfully, just as experiences of threat or abuse mark other people powerfully. And, as I write those words above about myself, I feel real sadness, also real anger. Sad that I was exposed to such poor care as this, and a situation like this. Where was the protection I needed? Where was my mum? Where, come to that, was my dad? And who *was* my dad? I may never know. Angry, too. It sickens me to think of this now: to think that I felt as though I had to criticise myself to keep myself safe from that woman. It makes me feel that if anyone were to treat a child of mine like that—not that I have any, yet—they should be in fear of their lives. I'd feel like wanting to hunt them down, personally. It'd make me feel like ram-raiding my car into their living room. These are crazy feelings, obviously: and I look like a mild-mannered, reasonable clinical psychologist! That's the level of threat and insecurity I felt at the time—leading to the predictable departure of my empathy for others when I think about what happened. So this episode, and a few others like it, left me with a strong sense of feeling threatened, of vulnerability, of not feeling protected. The powerful memories and their associations stuck, as did the sense that other people, particularly people in authority who had, or seemed to have, power over me could be very dangerous to me. That's one of the feelings that has stayed with me from that time.

Feeling unlovable: me as a rejected adolescent

Second, the other main theme from a slightly later part of my development—around the ages of 13 to 16, between 1983 and 1986—was a sense that I was unattractive. While I had quite a high level of belief in myself academically and physically, as a boy—thanks in many ways to the encouragement from my mother—one of the things I *couldn't* control (much as I wanted to) was how attractive I was to the people I was interested in: girls. To begin with, I remember feeling as though not being successful with them really didn't matter. This was around the age of 10 or 11. But the picture changed over the next few years. Although I made my first hesitant attempts at being with girls, I unfortunately got rejection after rejection from them. It's still a bit difficult to look back on, even over two decades later. I feel sad for the boy and young man I was then. But I clearly remember feeling a sense of attraction to certain girls in my class at school; say. then—probably in a clumsy way, given my inexperience—making an approach to them; 'asking them out'. After that, I remember numerous times when I was rejected. I'd just be standing there, feeling ashamed of myself. In one of the most painful of these memories (which, of course, many of us have from adolescence), I had gone specially to see a girl whom I liked in the shop in which she worked part-time. It was 1984 and I was about fifteen. I had put on my best clothes and trainers to go and see her, and even brushed my (1980s) hair to create the best possible impression. But my request for a date was rejected and, as I stood there going red, the plastic bag I was carrying burst, and out of it dropped my hairbrush onto the floor. This just made things worse, as my feelings of shame increased. Hesitantly, I picked up my hairbrush and stumbled out of the shop, feeling like the world's biggest fool. I never spoke to her again. I never dared to, for feelings of shame; I felt so stupid. Another occasion from about the same time had a similar result. When I was fifteen, I remember approaching a girl at a party after she had been calling out loudly, 'Bring me a boy.' She was lying on a bed, looking fairly drunk but happy. In my doubtless clumsy, adolescent way, but doing the best I could at the time, I approached her but, as soon as I got near she just said, 'I didn't mean you. Send up one of the handsome ones.' I turned away and left the room. Obviously, this shaming statement hurt a very great deal—cut me to the core. I was only a kid then. Maybe the mullet put them off. Maybe I should have just 'got over it'; but I did try. I really did try. Sometimes, though, it's not that easy. Many of us in adolescence have similarly difficult experiences.

Striving to compensate: trying to be a 'successful' man

Having had a number of such negative psychological experiences around this sensitive, adolescent time of my life, I learned the memorable, painful lesson that girls (all of them, as I wrongly deduced from my limited experience of the time) didn't find me attractive. Indeed, it felt to me back then that I was *unattractive*, that I was *ugly*—that there was really something wrong with me, which is a really unpleasant feeling to have about yourself. In some people these feelings can eventually lead to a sense of despair and hopelessness. In such cases, the person may simply give up trying to achieve what they had desired. But for me back then, it felt as though I could make myself attractive by achieving things in life. If I were to do well academically, and make something of myself that way, I felt girls then might find me lovable, or worth loving. So, perhaps by absorbing some of the lessons around me—on television, in the media—about how to be a 'successful man' (but having no obvious positive or even neutral in-house model to learn from as a Dad), I consciously set about becoming a man: an attractive, successful man. This must be possible, surely, I felt. Sylvester Stallone did it: surely we could all do it?

But there were problems with this plan, simplistic as it may now seem. One of these was that it put me under great pressure to try to succeed. If I wasn't an academic success at school and university, say, it really felt as though I would *have* nothing, and *be* nothing. It felt as though I would be nothing to anybody—that I would be left all alone and that nobody would care. And another by-product of these experiences was that I thought in order to be attractive to any girls, I'd need to lose weight and build muscle. Definitely. I really thought that would change things. This then set me on a six-month course of anorexic-style dieting, when I'd eat no more than 800 calories a day (as a male adolescent who needed at least 2500 calories a day to grow healthily). Pumping iron at home in the evening, I became very proud of my muscles, not least when, since I was losing weight at the same time, the veins in my biceps began to stand out like those of the guys in the weightlifting magazines. Sometimes, even though I didn't feel good inside, I felt strong on the outside. Little did I know at the time, however, that I was planting both feet squarely on yet another psychological banana skin. Oops … I did it again.

This period, after facing exam stresses, was followed by a crash into bulimia, at the point when my body became so desperately hungry that I felt I had to binge. That then led to my feeling disgusted and disappointed with myself, leading on to further strict dieting—and then another binge. So much unhappiness by the age of eighteen: what a fun time that was! I wish, naturally, that it could have been different; but looking back, I wouldn't want to return to the 1980s, at least in the way I experienced them. I'm so glad it's over, that my life has changed since; and that I feel differently now.

* * *

How did these experiences add up for me psychologically, and do the damage they did? It was partly or mostly for these reasons, based in my early experiences of fear and feelings of powerlessness, coupled with an early feeling of unattractiveness, that I've often felt so terrified of authority figures. That was one reason why I felt so insecure at the age of 19 at university. After my time at the hands of the carer-woman above, having had little sense of being protected from her at key times by a mother or father when I felt I really needed it, I felt deep down that I really was bad or unacceptable in some way—that the apparently threatening university would discover this, and that if I did not work extremely hard and effectively punish myself before anyone else could, I would be treated very harshly and thrown out like the bad, worthless idiot I was. And worse: given my sense of unattractiveness and ugliness, I felt that this would mean that I would *never* find a girlfriend or female partner. It might sound silly now, but back then it felt as though the stakes were very high indeed—and the feelings were certainly powerful. I felt strongly that I had to perform in order to be lovable enough to find a partner; but powerful and threatening authority figures stood in my way. Every day felt like a very pressurized fight for psychological survival. And it's not surprising, when I look back now.

Given what we said in Chapter 2 about the origins of feelings in body and mind, we can begin to understand what was happening at those times. Having been primed to perceive threats as a child, so as to react for my own protection, I tended to over-react later on whenever a potential threat (like having to write an essay at university) seemed to show itself. Then the whole self-maintaining bodily process of defence and reaction would be regularly deployed. Uneasy feelings would lead to anxiety, negative thoughts ('If I don't work to the point of exhaustion, I'll fail'), and negative behaviour (like extra hard work and extra worry), designed to avoid the threat by one route or another. A similar psychological process would occur regarding the other issue to which I had been sensitized: women of around my age. But taking these things together, my mind would all too often send me signals that in some important-seeming way my needs, whether for safety or for close relationships, were not going to be met. All these issues can be usefully shown diagrammatically. This, in the clinical psychological trade, is what we call a 'formulation'. It explains what is happening psychologically for a person. Here, on the next page, is a simple version of mine. These early experiences of fear and threat at the hands of another person also marked

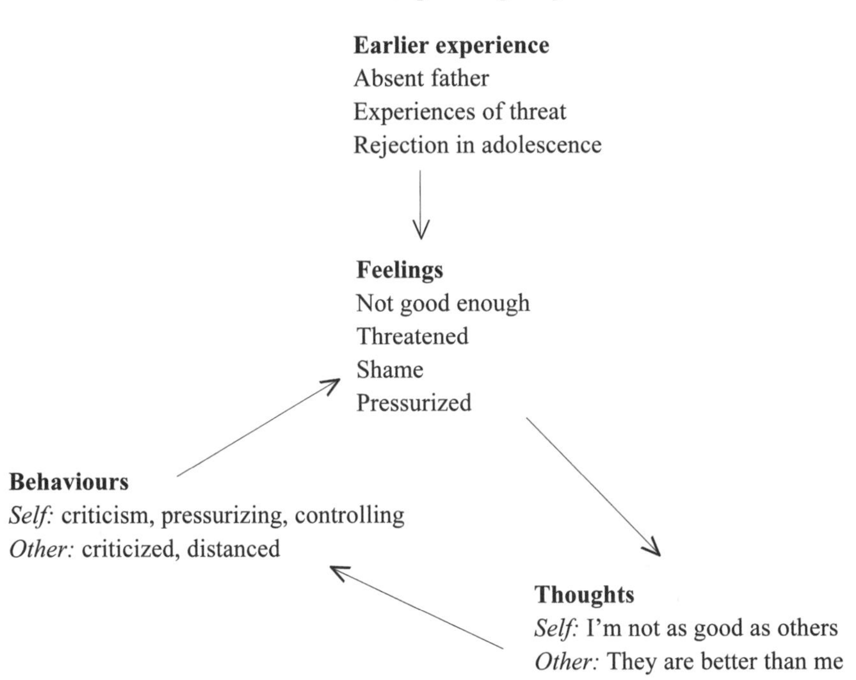

Figure 4.1 My formulation

me in more subtle ways. I've come to understand this as my psychological grasp of my past has increased over the years. Like some of the people described in the research in Chapter 3, having felt under threat myself when I was small I became more aggressive and critical towards myself *internally*, submissive to others *externally*, and only secretly aggressive towards them or critical behind their backs. As part of this psychological set-up, I became more submissive than usual in my behaviour when facing, say, shop assistants in uniform, who have a kind of authority no matter what they do. In shops, my voice used to go up in tone—suggesting fear and submission—and I would say 'please' and 'thank you' more than I needed to—sometimes three or four times in one interaction. 'Thanks.' 'That's great.' 'Lovely.' 'Thanks very much.' But what am I doing? Boy, *I'm* the customer here. They need me at least as much as I need them, and maybe more.

Also, and perhaps most curiously, I came to see that a large part of my deeper motivation for doing things came from wanting to show the woman above—and any one else who cared to see—that I wasn't so bad or unattractive after all. This is where the secret aggression comes in. It would take me away from the bad experience of feeling not good enough, inferior. I wanted to show that I was superior, better than others; better than anyone else. I often enjoyed imagining myself in superior positions compared to that carer woman (this, of course, could not happen in reality now: I have no idea where she is and haven't seen her for over thirty years). In my imagination, in this way, I'd feel victorious. Look what I've achieved. Look at me now. I've shown you, haven't I? *Look at who is the man*! I imagined myself standing over the person, with them conquered, with my foot on them, like a soldier who has won the war, who has annihilated the opposition, and is now safe, can no longer be got at. Nonsense, of course, but that's how it felt to me at the time. I'd felt really bad about myself, and really threatened—and there was a natural drive in me to try and change this situation so that it felt better, at least temporarily.

And when confronted with everyday stress, say pressure at work, I can still sometimes come to feel a bit freaked out and overwhelmed more quickly, perhaps, than I otherwise would have. At these times I notice I can quickly go into feeling crushed and trapped—the kinds of feeling that arguably go back to my childhood experiences of being 'cared for' by that woman. What might feel like day-to-day challenges to some people can sometimes feel like life-or-death battles to me, until I take a psychological step back. Similarly, I sometimes feel a bit frightened of colleagues at work, particularly if I don't know them very well: a little as though they are the powerful—and possibly threatening—adults and I am the child. Me in a submissive position, them in a dominant position. I now consciously know this not to be true—we're all adults with equal rights; but that's sometimes how it feels. This feeling sometimes leads me to push others away, to seem a bit aloof and to keep my distance from folks. I may not mean to, but I sometimes do. However, I recognize it now, and that helps me to step back and calm myself.

Furthermore my early experiences of rejection, coupled with the lack of a father or close, older role model from whom I could learn how to interact well with women, and particularly how to flirt, affected my early approaches to women. Having had negatively memorable experiences of rejection, and relatively few early experiences to counterbalance them and help me feel any different, I consciously and unconsciously expected this to be repeated. One result of this was that, when in the company of eligible women in adolescence and as a very young man, I showed typical shamed, submissive behaviours such as anxiousness and averted eye-gaze, reinforced with self-criticism—all of which gave a clear message that I felt bad about myself.[5] I came across to women as though I had no confidence at all in my own worth or attractiveness—which of course was true at that time. Predictably, my lack of success recurred, and my underlying feelings about myself and the sense of myself as unacceptable were reinforced. For a number of years in early manhood I got precisely nowhere, and remained psychologically stuck with this negative feeling about myself—all as part of the predictable, simple, self-maintaining psychological cycle above.

I remember that I was lying once on my psychotherapist's couch (you only do this in certain types of therapy,[6] and then only if you want to)—an odd-sounding place to be, I admit, with a therapist sitting behind me as I talked on my back—when I became aware of some of the deeper motivations for doing what I did. Suddenly my desire for achievement came to seem ridiculous to me and, I guess, to my psychotherapist. I'd never, ever see again the relevant people whom I wanted particularly to impress. They could easily even be dead. What did I have to gain by

---

5. Beattie, G. (2003). *Visible Thought: The new psychology of body language.* Hove & New York: Routledge.

6. This is sometimes done in types of psychoanalytic psychotherapy; and it does feel a bit funny, especially at first.

trying to get to a position of such apparent strength? It was, like many of the things that we think in our daily lives, an illusion. I'd got it wrong, and wrong for many years. Not everyone was out to get me. Looked at in the light of the present day, this old idea of mine was pretty much bonkers; actually, perhaps *no one at all* was out to hurt me, or shame me, any more. My early experiences of feeling very threatened by that woman, who was supposed to be caring for me, had marked me to such a degree that, like some of the children mentioned in Chapter 3, I became aggressive in myself in part of my deepest motivation. Some of my actions, even some of those concerning care for others, were driven not by kindness but by sheer desire for dominance and revenge and, beyond that, by my need for feelings of being safe from others and the hurt they could cause. That is, dominance over people I had not seen for virtually a generation, and would almost certainly never see again. Did my fight and struggle against them have to go on? No, I could stop the internal fight—by recognizing what was going on, and not fighting any more. Luckily, after the help of psychotherapy and self-reflection on these matters, these issues are much less painful and less pressing for me now than they once were.

On Reflection …

Looking back from a distance now to these difficult times in my earlier life, it is easier for me as a clinical psychologist to see what I needed back then. I really needed someone independent to talk to openly, to help me work out what in my life was making me distressed (feeling under pressure workwise, and my really strong sense that I would be thrown out of the university very quickly and always be unattractive to others if I didn't perform to very high standards). I needed a little help, kindness, and time to work out why my past meant that the present was so distressing (my experiences of insecurity and threat in childhood, as well as the perception of being so unattractive). And I needed someone (a good psychotherapist) to be there for me for a short time while I tried out my new understanding that I could be safer—*much safer*—than I felt after my early life and the psychological marks I was left with; that I no longer had to hide at some times and aggressively fight for dominance over others, all for the feeling of wanting to be safe.

And on occasion, at difficult or stressful times, I still need to remind myself that I'm very likely to be safer than I feel. It's usual for people to re-experience difficult feelings—emotional flashbacks, you might say—especially at times of stress. When this happens to many people for the first time, they may feel that all is lost, that things will be as bad now as they ever were. In fact, that is rarely so. What often helps is to briefly 'check out': to take a little more care of oneself—a little mindfulness meditation, maybe; take a little time and perhaps try to see what the trigger of the problem was. Very often a little self-care like this is all that's needed to help us get back on our psychological feet, like a toddler learning to walk. Sometimes it takes only a few minutes; then, when we are ready, we can carry on walking in the direction we wish to go—or change direction a bit, if the original direction doesn't suit us any more. Or we can simply take a rest; or have someone listen. Maybe that was what we needed all along.

I *did* go to see a clinical psychologist when I was 20 and a student at university, between essays and food binges; but, unfortunate though this seems now, I attended only one session. I went, but I didn't go back. I wish now that I had stayed for more, even though it mightn't have been easy—these are difficult feelings we're talking about, as you yourself may know. I tried to ask questions about *her, the female therapist*. Who was she? Where did she train? My mother was a clinical psychologist—perhaps she knew her. All this was a giveaway to the therapist; she quickly spotted that I was trying *not* to talk about my own feelings—anything so as not to have to talk about how *I* was feeling inside. I felt so insecure that I simply didn't trust her to care for my interests in any way. I felt if I said what was wrong, and then changed and stopped working so hard, I would definitely be 'found out' and thrown out of the university. Like many other of my understandable but overdone fear- and threat-driven perceptions at the time, this was not quite right, not quite accurate. My mind, feeling threatened, was filtering out the positive information that was in my favour. In fact it was *far from accurate*—I could have relaxed much more than I did, and even if things had gone wrong, I would have got a second and possibly even a third chance from the university if I had needed it (this happened to some of my friends, but I didn't notice at the time). So I left therapy, at this early point in my life, before it had really even begun. As sometimes happens with people I now meet, I wasn't ready to hear what was going to be said, and even less ready to begin to do anything about it—because I instinctively but inaccurately felt that it would mean my leaving university, and with it the chance of a career of any kind. And without a career, I felt, I'd never get a girlfriend; and, without a girlfriend—never mind a fiancée or a wife—I could never, would never, be happy. That's the way I thought; but like many other things in my life, I wasn't quite right about this either. My feelings and perceptions had been distorted by my past negative and threatening experiences. I was wrong; I see that now—but it felt completely right and true at the time. It wasn't.

* * *

How *did* things change psychologically for me? Well, I have been helped enormously myself by different aspects of psychology. Reading psychology, including different self-help books, over the years, and having some therapy myself, have both helped greatly. At first, when I was at my most troubled in my late teens and early twenties, at a time of my life when I felt most miserable and pressured, I came across the idea that we ourselves partly construct our own world that we live in—and are free, to at least some degree, to change it if we wish.[7] That gave me hope, and I also came to see that I could *feel* better if *I myself* treated myself well. Later, as I studied psychology

---

7. See e.g. Rowe, D. (1987). *Beyond Fear*. London: HarperCollins. At a stressful time in my life, in 1991, this book made living a whole lot easier. I remember reading it, and a great deal of psychological weight lifting off me.

more formally, I came to realize that while I was fortunate in many ways, some parts of my early life may have directly or indirectly set me up, potentially, to be unhappy—for instance, by certain aspects of being in a single-parent family and lacking a father, and by having had early feelings of insecurity, as I have described above. Also I came to begin to use psychological theory to check out and change some of my beliefs, thoughts and feelings about myself, others and my place in the world. In a word, over time I came to be more mindful of myself, my life, and how I did things.

Stepping back a little from my life, mindfully—and this process included my own ongoing work with mindfulness meditation—I came to see that after my early experiences of rejection, I had often acted around others as though I was second-class or somehow inferior to them. This sometimes invited an appropriate response—so my needs, or I as a person, wouldn't get taken quite so seriously. These feelings about myself, I also realized, had affected my behaviour when things were difficult regarding my eating habits. In my late teens I really did feel as though I wasn't *worth* looking after, or worth being with: that there was no point to it—and that's partly why I binged, knowing that eating lots of food would, as well as helping me to feel full and comforted, make me put on weight and be still more (as I saw it back then) unattractive. Yet stepping back from my own behaviour and being more aware of what I was doing, I also came to see that sometimes when I felt that things were going well, and I felt a bit superior to the people I was with, I could—I am sorry to have to admit—be rather a bully. Sometimes I'd ignore people who deserved attention, even among the friends I had then. Although I often didn't show this contempt for others, I felt it quite strongly within.

Looking back on my own behaviour, though, this last example suggests something else that I have since learned psychologically about myself. Underneath all this contempt for others was a man who had been hurt during his development, who felt really ashamed of *himself*, and who actually wanted to be accepted and cared for by other people, not spurned by them. I came to see mindfully that much of my behaviour was unconsciously intended to isolate myself, and push others away or down in status, because I was frightened of them and how they might make me feel. Now, happily, I've mindfully come to see how I was acting, what I was doing to myself and others, and what negative effect this was having. For one thing, it was affecting my health. It feels physically and psychologically better—and happier, too—for me to be closer to others, and to experiment with letting go of some of my previous critical, silly and snobbish ideas about them, the latter largely a product of my family background.[8] I no longer act like Lord Snooty, always in the right about certain matters—academic ones, for instance. Whatever else happens, we are all people of value in different ways. Few people actually deserve our contempt and withering criticism—despite what we might sometimes feel when under stress.

So over time, with the benefit of better relationships with others and with the benefit of psychological knowledge, as well as having had some therapy, I've been

8. On English class-consciousness and its effects on our behaviour, see Fox, K. (2004). *Watching the English: The hidden rules of English behaviour.* London: Hodder & Stoughton.

able to step back a great deal from myself and my own life in quite a mindful way, and change much as a result. I now feel much more content in myself. I can be fine as I am; I don't have to prove anything to anyone any more. These are big psychological changes. There has been a shift from feeling as though I was basically not good enough as a person—a feeling that was driving the psychological symptoms I experienced—to feeling that I am at least OK. I can be me, just like you can be you. And I can tell you, that feels much, much better.

This more positive feeling has emerged and has been expressed in various ways. I haven't binged on food for fifteen years—I just haven't felt the need. I no longer push a supermarket trolley at speed round Sainsbury's or Tesco collecting crisps, chocolate and pies which I then gorge on miserably alone, all in one sitting. I no longer have anxiety and panic attacks, so that I have to get off my bike before I fall off from worry. I not only believe in a thing called love, but I believe that I am at least quite attractive and lovable now: that I can be loved by someone else, that I can love them. I do this. I can even believe that the person who loves me won't—as I used to feel—simply abandon me, running off to leave me for someone better as soon as they come along. I also believe, as I never used to, that things can work out for me. When I was young I used to believe that I was destined to have a lonely, unhappy life; also that I simply didn't deserve any better. Lots of people I meet in my work feel like that. And you know what? There has been a big psychological turnaround. I just don't believe that bad stuff any more—and I'm really glad I don't. Looking back now, that was just a thought, a feeling or set of feelings from the past. It wasn't necessarily true. All things change. And we ourselves can change, if we will allow it. We can, with help, learn new psychological skills that we didn't have before. We can move on.

Above all now, departing from the issues that led me to have such a shaky psyche in the first place—feelings of fear, and being rejected—I have begun to treat myself with the mindful care and respect I deserve as a human being with human rights. It feels so much better to treat myself with kindness: good for the body, and good for the mind. And a final word here about the possible personal benefits of mindfulness. As part of helping me to treat myself and others better, it also helps to curb some of my natural excesses. Mindfulness—and sometimes even *only the thought* of mindfulness, a brief check on *what I'm actually doing or not doing*—just helps me not to act so 'bananas'. I drink less alcohol, eat less junk food and spend less money on things I don't need. I do more of what I really need to do. I want to live. I want stuff. I want a dog, a husky dog. In all these ways, positive changes have taken place in my own personal psychology and those changes can be expressed in the updated, more positive formulation as follows. As we can see in Figure 4.2, after periods of psychological reflection and psychotherapy the negative maintaining cycles have been replaced by more optimistic, life-giving ones. I feel different things now, do different things, and so get different, more positive psychological results. Phew!

OK. Maybe that's not much of a story, but that's some of my inner life, and some of the ups and downs I've had after some specific early difficulties. I had more issues than *The Beano*, but I eventually got through them. It shows how psychological factors can affect our sense of ourselves, how the path of our lives can be changed by our

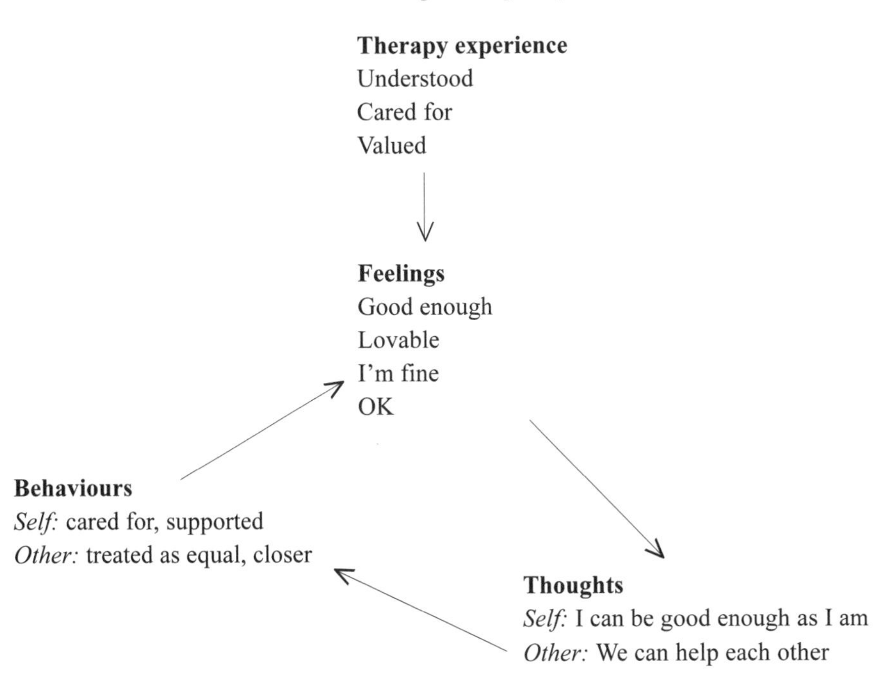

Figure 4.2 My formulation after therapy

early experiences, and how psychological tools only—no medication required on this occasion, at least—can contribute to helping us change how we feel about ourselves.

Research, clinical, and indeed personal experience show, then, that what we ourselves go through, how we are treated, and in particular, the nature of our interactions with others when we are young, can powerfully affect our development. Negative experiences can stay with us in our minds, affecting how we feel, what we do and who we can become: not just for weeks or months, but for years, or even decades, of our lives. It happened to me, and maybe it has happened to you. Since this is so, it is the point of this book that we and others might benefit, over time, from attending just a little more carefully to, and being a little more mindful of, how we treat one another. Not just how we treat children and young people; *everyone*, including ourselves. But how?

5

Kindness and Mindful Psychotherapy

The curative effect can, in the final analysis, only occur between people.
Jung

Are You Experienced?

If we *are*, as I have said, psychologically and physically interdependent on one another, sharing self–other space throughout life but also vulnerable to mindless treatment and psychological damage from others, we might arrive at certain ideas. For one thing, if we wanted to improve all our lives rather than the lives of just a few, a particular approach to living might be adopted. This, the 'Golden Rule' of world religions I mentioned in Chapter 1—preached by many, but practised by few— is the deliberate, mindful, reflective practice of kindness by one person towards another. You might wonder what good the deliberate, mindful, reflective practice of kindness might do; and indeed, why it has been emphasized by almost all major religions throughout history.

One possible answer comes from psychotherapy. Originating in religious practices like confession[1]—where again, people *talked* to and engaged with one another: funny, that—and using Freud's brilliant idea that our psychological past with others affects our present, at its best psychotherapy begins to undo early damage. Where suffering has been caused in one way or another by others, the deliberate practice of kindness in psychotherapy—and elsewhere in everyday life—offers something very different from what has happened before. At best, psychotherapy offers hope and possibility. Where early suffering at the hands of others has had a long-lasting, even shattering effect on a person's self and their relationships with both themselves and others, psychotherapy helps to make good the losses—or at least helps the person to accept

---

1. See Ellenberger, H.F. (1970). *The Discovery of the Unconscious: The history and evolution of dynamic psychiatry*. London and New York: HarperCollins.

the reality of the losses. It is for this reason that whether they work with children, adults or older people, many therapists act as a kind of parent, offering a similar kind of interactive repair of difficult feelings and emotional states, helping us to cope better with the reality that confronts us.[2] After someone has been psychologically hurt in some way, or feels that they have become 'stuck', a good psychotherapist wishes to help them grow again, to become more free in themselves, and to mature in the best way that circumstances internal and external to the person will allow. Gradually, the therapist helps the person to develop the emotional skills to eventually help themselves and become more autonomous and independent. And where difficult early experiences have in some way left the person with a lack of love—either for themselves, for others, or very often for both—the careful use of compassion and kindness in psychotherapy helps to restore it. By kindly offering help, the therapist gives, and models, a new way of being that can be much more life-giving, and kinder to the self. One of the most remarkable things about psychotherapy—and a matter that never ceases to amaze me, however often I see it for myself—is that what we feel, do and say with others can help to change their lives for the better. Suffering can be expressed and given by one person; accepted and held by another; worked on together; and then reduced. With the help of others, our feelings—about ourselves, our lives, our people and our world—can be changed. Let us be clear: psychotherapy does not *always* help.[3] In a small proportion of cases it can even make things worse. But most often, with a suitably qualified and skilled therapist, benefits occur.

It is the possibility of kindness that makes mindfulness meditation an obvious companion to, and part of, psychotherapy. While there are differences between the two, there are also clear similarities. Above all, mindfulness, like psychotherapy, involves increasing our awareness of what is happening in our lives; and in particular it involves increasing our awareness of the contents of our minds, including our perceptions, and what we do. Once this awareness has increased, making us more conscious of patterns of feeling, thought or behaviour that are self- or other-damaging, we may be more able to do something different. Above all, mindfulness and psychotherapy have kindness and compassion in common. Both suggest that treating ourselves and others with care and kindness is most often life-giving and creative, and is likely to lead to harmony, growth and health.

Often, though, people's initial experience of being cared for by psychotherapy and mindfulness, as in other parts of life, can make them feel uncomfortable; and then they turn away, not wanting to look, not wanting to see what is there. They avoid the caring contact when it is offered because it feels somehow wrong, painful or aversive to them—very unlike what they are used to from childhood, adolescence or adulthood. Some people leave therapy before it has properly started because of this, not ready to hear what is being said, and unable or unwilling to listen at this point in their lives. Indeed, some people who might well benefit from psychotherapy feel so

---

2. See Schore, A.N. (2003). *Affect Regulation and the Repair of the Self.* New York: Norton.
3. See e.g. Bates, Y. (ed.). (2006). *Shouldn't I be Feeling Better by Now? Client views of therapy.* Basingstoke: Palgrave Macmillan.

uncomfortable about it that they never even start it, or get to that point. This is very often understandable, given their earlier experiences at the hands of other people.

I did so myself when I was younger. As a confused and troubled boy in the final years of school, struggling with feelings driven by the earlier negative experiences in my childhood that I talked about in Chapter 4, it felt far too threatening to allow someone else to know how I was really feeling. I couldn't ask, and didn't ask, for the help that I needed. At age 17, feeling myself to be *completely* unattractive to women, bad and shameful, and that I *had to succeed* academically to stand any chance in life, I put myself under huge pressure to work at school and at home. I unthinkingly pushed myself on and on, working for hours each evening, holiday and weekend. I left myself almost no time or space for my own feelings, thoughts and development. Hundreds of lines of poetry were learned off by heart for exams. And when I wasn't working, I was pushing myself on my home gym. I was doing, as part of my over-hard exercise routine, two hundred sit-ups before breakfast. I did so many sit-ups, as part of my quest to be an acceptable man, that I still have the scars on my back from the original carpet burn, where I made myself bleed—but in the process of doing this, my needs as a young man were temporarily lost along the way.

Not surprisingly, feeling under pressure, gravely (and disproportionately) worried about my future and with emotional management skills that were not so good, I then also somehow became falsely convinced that I was suffering from, and about to die from, a brain tumour. Fantastico! Just what I needed. I'm not even twenty, yet think I have only *months* to live! I'm sure that something terrible's going to happen! And how about this?—even better: I feel too ashamed to tell anyone! A worry about death and dying, then—again a common concern. My worries about the exams, together with overwork and not enough space for my own needs, produced anxiety symptoms like feelings of breathlessness and dizziness that I then hypochondriacally misinterpreted, in strong obsessive thoughts that lasted for around nine months, as indicating a brain tumour, part of a fatal illness.[4] Unfortunately at the time, I really didn't feel able to say what my worries were, and my GP didn't pick up the underlying problem, so I wasn't able to connect with anyone then in a psychologically meaningful way. What I really needed was someone to see that, deep down, I really felt as though I was in danger: not safe. Hence the worry about illness, which was a different and to me more acceptable way of my psychological and physical system saying this.

I was feeling really frightened at this time—not only of the exams, but of life. I really had *no idea* what to do, nor explanation, nor even words, for what was happening to me and around me. I didn't know who I should be; or even whom to ask. It took me another *12 years* to feel able to ask for, and get, some therapy. Even then I couldn't openly admit, either to myself or anyone else, that I was really unhappy and possibly not even aware of it—and that I needed someone to help me sort things out. No, 'I just want to explore,' I said to the psychotherapist, feeling too ashamed to say the truth about my deeper feelings, my unhappiness.

---

4. Wells, A. (1997). *Cognitive Therapy of Anxiety Disorders: A practice manual and conceptual guide.* Chichester: Wiley.

In a way, I just needed a little help to be shepherded through the difficult periods. I didn't find at this time what I needed: the feeling and sense that I was acceptable as a person, and that my psychological issues were understandable and could be resolved and let go of, even if this would take time. Fortunately, many more people stay when they first get the chance of therapy because, deeper down, they know a good thing when they feel it.

And let us not forget: in one sense at least, and while they would deny it, many of those who undergo psychotherapy are heroes or heroines. Not the obvious kind, who cope with terror and threat in the outside world; instead, they are often heroes and heroines of their own internal world where, until treatment, they may be stalked by past terrors that are represented in patterns of brain activity and connected bodily reactions, worsened under stress. It takes courage to withstand the repeated onslaught of the experience, and then the memory of the experience. Yet many people who come for psychotherapy have done this alone, in silence and with dignity, for years. And now you may be asking: how does the basic plan of a psychotherapy look?

Beginning Therapy ...

Typically, psychotherapy has a clear overall structure within which—as with any organic thing—there are many variations, depending on the life-stage of the client and the model (or models) or therapy to be used by the therapist. At first, partly because the person coming for psychotherapy usually has sustained some psychological hurt, there is a period of understandable anxiety, doubt and hesitancy when being around someone, the therapist, whom they don't yet know very well. At this stage the person often tends to be rather shy or (as I was) slightly ashamed of themselves, or even *very* ashamed of themselves. Also perhaps, depending on their perception of the situation, they may be a little defensive or even critical. This is often reflected in the verbal language they use and in their body language, which tends to show how they are feeling. Their mannerisms, speech and tone of voice, for example, may be somehow restricted or stifled. Then again, feelings of anxiety may make them talk rather too much—giving too much of themselves away to the other person. The person might do certain things that suggest psychological issues. They might check, as some people do, that the door of the psychotherapy room is not locked (suggesting possible anxiety), or make judgemental comments about the structure of the building (suggesting a possible need for control). Or, as I did when I was at university, they might try to get the therapist to talk about themselves as a way to avoid talking about their own experiences and feelings. That was a giveaway! I was clearly trying to dodge talking about my own stuff! And, rightly, my therapist moved on to different material—mine.

If the person has had a very difficult or traumatic life before reaching psychotherapy, it may be obvious to the psychotherapist that they are frightened. Perhaps they are too fearful to talk because of what they feel might happen to them; or the person may have a sense that the feelings inside them are too painful and too powerful for them, or anyone else, to cope with. Usually, though, talk about psychological issues often tends to be more superficial to begin with, perhaps focusing on everyday problems that are worrying them, or their expectations of what will happen during therapy. Many people are surprised to find that talking—the right kind of talking—can be enough, and that talking about your feelings actually *heals* rather than hurts. Perhaps they expect me, in an ostrich outfit or something similar, to open up their heads and look with a torch directly into their heads, identify the problem and fix it. If that is the case, I explain to them that, for better or worse, this type of drastic action will not be necessary. This kind of talk can be reassuring to people as they come to feel a little more secure in the situation, and most often soon learn to get used to it.

With a little time, then, this initial anxiety drops; people come to see what is likely to happen, sense the possible benefits, and a feeling of trust between the people develops. This early stage might take an hour or two, or sometimes it can be just minutes. But if in their perception the person has for some reason had particularly difficult or frightening experiences earlier in their lives, or they have had poor early care that left them with a low level of emotional skill, it may take months or even years before they feel confident enough to talk openly about their feelings. Taking the step towards talking openly and frankly about the self can take enormous courage for some people. Often, actually *talking* takes more courage for them, and is more of a shock to them, than if I were to hide away and then come out of the cupboard in my ostrich outfit, ready for action. But, when it happens, this is the second stage. Here, *great* progress can occur between the people. Much of psychological interest can be learned by both persons present.

... And beginning to explore with mindfulness

If it seems appropriate (and this is not always the case: it depends on the person, their issues and how stable they feel),[5] this early stage in therapy might be a good time for the person to begin to explore a little mindfulness meditation. Until they reach therapy or other forms of healthcare, relatively few people have experimented with mindfulness. They may be a little surprised to hear about its possible uses, but they are often pleased to hear how simple it is to practise—though the benefits can be psychologically complex. I simply explain that, in its essence, all mindfulness requires is to be aware or 'mindful' of our thoughts and feelings. Normally we aren't—except when things go wrong in our lives and we become anxious, stressed or depressed. Unlike many other parts of our lives, mindfulness isn't a pass-or-fail situation; it's non-doing—just being aware. This can feel strange to us when we do it for the first time, but I demonstrate a simple method. There are many useful books and other

---

5. Mindfulness should always be used with caution. Situations in which I would be very unlikely to recommend its use, even with supervision, are when people are experiencing psychosis, severe depression, a manic episode as part of bipolar disorder, or severe anxiety. If I'm aware that a person has highly traumatic memories that remain problematic, I'm very careful here, too. If in doubt about beginning to use mindfulness for yourself, please consult a qualified practitioner.

materials on mindfulness practice[6] that can be helpful for people if they are interested, but beginning mindfulness work can be straightforward. I tend to say something like this when I'm working with people. 'Probably with your eyes shut, focus your attention gently on your breath, being aware of your chest and stomach rising and falling with the breath. And when you become aware of different thoughts or feelings as they enter your awareness, allow your attention to go to perceive those things. Then, having been aware of the shift in your attention, just let them go, and gently escort your attention back to your breath.'

This process will then repeat and, as it does so, we can simply follow it, all the time being aware of the movements of our attention. We might do this for around 15 minutes per day if the person feels able to, or for less time if for any reason they find it especially difficult. If people are anxious, they can sometimes work with their eyes open.

Most often, people find it fairly straightforward to explore mindfulness for the first time. But some people may find it disturbing, upsetting or weird; perhaps they are very anxious, and may feel very jumpy indeed when we try to slow their psychological clock down; or they may be clearly troubled by frightening or painful thoughts, feelings or memories. For these people the answer—if they are to continue their exploration of mindfulness—is to go very carefully indeed, best accompanied by someone experienced with mindfulness. Sometimes such people find it just *impossible* to be mindful; but often even very anxious people can learn, second by second, to be just aware of what their attention is doing, where and how their mind is wandering. And if that is so, that's a good basis for our further work. Luckily for us, our mind is like the sky: just as the sky is often cloudy—dark storm clouds may be present, and it may be pouring with rain—our minds may fill with dark thoughts. But just as the clouds and rain pass, even our most desperate feelings also move on, often leaving space for sunlight behind them. And by beginning to be mindful, we can start to be aware of these changes that, by their very nature *as* changes, may give us grounds for hope. By being mindful, we feel the movement in the world and in ourselves.

The Middle of Therapy …

By now the psychological sketch, or formulation, of the issues is beginning to be more complete, and the middle stage of therapy has been reached. Like fearful animals in the wild, understandably quite wary of approaching each other initially, the two people, therapist and client, can now begin to trust each other. Often (but not always), familiarity and friendliness grow between them. The psychological issues can be more openly discussed and, as it were, be held up for inspection between the two people, as two jewellers might examine gemstones together in a bright light. The person's fears, sometimes of the most basic kind can be admitted—of going 'mad', or of dying, of

6. A clear introduction is Kabat-Zinn, J. (2004). *Full Catastrophe Living: How to cope with stress, pain and illness using mindfulness meditation: 15th anniversary edn.* London: Piatkus.

not coping, of not being good enough, or of being humiliated or shamed, to take some of the most common (and some from my own personal extensive collection of groundless fears that, in fact, when I look at the evidence, amounted to precisely nothing). They can be worked on together; then, often, the *real* issues start to emerge.

Even the simple admission of the fear concerned can bring relief, and the feeling that help from another kind, mindful person may be at hand. This can be a great form of consolation and encouragement. Sometimes such people—whether or not they are psychotherapists—have an extraordinary, kind presence that in itself seems to have a kind of healing force. To such precious people we may, thankfully, feel that we can say anything and they will accept us, or even show us a strange kind of love: not the sexual kind, clearly, but love nonetheless. This can be very important, since we often have a sense that our underlying feelings and fears are shameful and that people will definitely reject us for having them, leaving us feeling terrible, worthless—even abandoned. It can be a powerful experience to find instead that whatever we say, kindly and mindfully, others can accept us. The other person may not like what we say. They may not agree with it. We might have ridiculous political views, or spend our free time in unusual ways, but they show that they can accept our talk, and accept us—even the parts of ourselves that we have felt to be completely bad and unacceptable, surely (we think) worthy of rejection by other people and by us ourselves. Or we may feel the angry part of ourselves to be worthy of rejection; or the needy part; or the frightened part of us, that seems too shameful to own up to. Not everyone will accept us and our feelings: that is clear. But some people *can* accept us for what we are, and who we are, and whatever we feel— just as ourselves: nothing more, nothing less. And that, you may agree, is a marvellous thing.

Once acknowledgement is actually made of worrying feelings and thoughts and—no matter how terrible they *feel*—they are admitted, their origins can gradually be explored. Often, indeed perhaps almost always, the origins of psychological issues are found to greater or lesser degrees in people's earlier experiences. The worried little girl turns out to have heard her parents shouting at each other, maybe hurting each other, in the middle of the night. The depressed man's career, it turns out, didn't live up to the expectations of his hard-driving father or, now, given his memories of and learning from his father, of himself. The lonely older lady was teased at school and developed a lifelong fear of people, so never really feeling able to trust them enough to get close. In my personal and professional experience, once the facts of the case are known, there are *almost always* obvious reasons for the psychological symptoms that present themselves. In fact I have *never* met a person whose feelings were inexplicable, given what I came to know about their previous lives.

... And making molehills out of mountains with mindfulness

In the middle phase of therapy, too, if a person is finding that mindfulness suits them, the practice of mindfulness is likely to bring benefits. They are likely to be feeling a little more relaxed by now—although this is a by-product, rather than an aim, of being mindful. Often people have not only begun to get used to being mindful, however they are doing it—perhaps when lying down, sitting or walking—but they also may become more aware, with kindness and compassion as they gently assume control and awareness of their attention, of what is actually happening in their minds and of their internal psychological contents. This can frequently come as a shock. As may be discussed in psychotherapy, the person may find, by stepping back a little from what is on their minds and simply observing where and how their attention is moving, that their minds contain many powerful negative thoughts and feelings. These can be depressing, frightening, sad or otherwise unsettling; but whatever the person experiences, if they are practising mindfulness daily they will be more conscious of what is happening inside their minds. And with this simple awareness, something else important emerges: the person comes, in a kindly way, to know themselves a little better and to begin to recognize what is happening to them. As part of that process, the issues that concerned them may begin to reduce in force. Standing very close to the problem, it may appear to us like a mountain; but standing back with the help of mindfulness, it can appear more like a molehill— perhaps one of a number, but nevertheless something that we can cope with and see more in proportion.

Around this time also, the therapy approaches a particularly interesting phase. Client and therapist can observe what happens within, and between, therapy sessions—noting which patterns of feeling, thinking and behaving emerge, in whichever and whatever ways, an infinite variety of combinations. Early learning, and the sense of self that develops as people mature into adults, affect how people relate to their therapist.

Having sometimes felt very frightened and threatened as a child, as I said in Chapter 4, and being at a difficult time of my life (feeling, inaccurately and over-negatively, that I was getting nowhere at work and was unhappily single when I desperately wanted to be attached) when I began therapy, I felt *sure* —100% certain—that my therapist would be devastatingly critical of me, since that is what I deserved. My character would, basically, be assassinated by him. I've failed at this; I'm a failure at that; I should be doing so much better than I am—or so I felt. That's the kind of negative thing I thought he would say. Actually, and thankfully, he was the opposite, giving me the gentle, life-giving nurturance I needed, odd as this sounds, to question the crushing, life-denying self-criticism that I took for granted within me. The vital message was quietly given to me as I sat there (to begin with) and as I lay there on the couch (later on): 'You do not think it yet, or feel it yet. But *you are OK as you are.'* I am really thankful for that. Together, client and therapist can make links to the possible origins of the patterns in the person's earlier development. Where and how was this way of being learned? With a little help to reflect back on their lives so far, people most often find this quite a simple question to answer. Once important aspects of the pattern of relating, and its origins, have been recognized by the two people together, change can begin.

In the middle of psychotherapy also, regardless of whether eight sessions or eighty are involved, new, more complex, kinder, more positive, self-protecting and self-compassionate stories about ourselves and our lives can begin to develop. This seems to be important, or even essential. Just as parents can help their children to manage their negative feelings by encouraging them to explore them and their psychological origins, so as to arrive at possible solutions or at least compromises,[7] the psychotherapist encourages safe exploration of past and present experiences. The therapist provides and models the emotional regulatory functions of the healthy, or healthier, social brain. Feelings that seemed unbearable to begin with can be discussed, put into meaningful words and begin to be understood. This may include feelings like anxiety, despair, loneliness, sadness and shame—all ones I've known myself.

Most often, with help and perhaps with some mindfulness, these feelings *are* found to be somehow bearable, as the repeated exposure to stress in the supportive environment of psychotherapy allows the person to begin to tolerate increasing levels of arousal. Just as in childhood, the repeated cycle of attunement between the people, the rupture of attunement (including difficult feelings), and then re-attunement slowly creates the expectation of reconnection and of safety in the person who is having psychotherapy. And this learned expectation of future relief allows the person to come to tolerate, and successfully cope with, stronger feelings.[8] That's right: I can feel the bad feeling, think the bad thought—and still, eventually, feel fine. That's the way. Such thoughts and feelings can be approached mindfully. Rather than simply reacting to the negative internal and external experiences that we have, if we have a little experience of mindfulness we can see the difficult thought or feeling coming and encounter it, rather than avoiding it. Although we might not expect it to do so, this can actually reduce our suffering, since we do not react so mindlessly, spinning off into emotionally driven cycles of avoidance and defence. Perhaps also at this time we may become aware of beginning to let things go a little—whether negative thoughts, feelings, or over-high expectations relating to different parts of our lives.

After feeling ashamed of myself for much of my youth and early manhood, I can allow people to be close to me and to really look at me now, seeing all the contours of my face. These days I don't even think about it. That's a change. Once I would never have dared do this, because I thought that people would see how unattractive I was and would then leave me—instantly. And just as for adults as well as for children, we are wired in such a way that some solutions are almost always possible for all psychological problems— particularly when those problems are looked at a little more objectively by two people together, and perhaps divided into smaller, more manageable parts as they so often can be. In these ways new, more accepting and positive stories about ourselves can gradually be created. Though the light may seem almost lost on the horizon of our experiences, the sky is never entirely dark. With human kindness, solace, seen or unseen, is always present.

There is very probably something essential about having the opportunity to reflect in the presence of another, kindly person. Perhaps at some level, deeper than the

---

7. Gottman, J. (2001). Meta-emotion, children's emotional intelligence, and buffering children from marital conflict. In: C.D. Ryff & B.H. Singer (eds.). *Emotion, Social Relationships, and Health*. Oxford: Oxford University Press: 23–39.

8. L. Cozolino (2002). *The Neuroscience of Psychotherapy: Building and rebuilding the human brain.* New York: Norton: 32–33.

conscious, when we are able to talk freely to a kind person we begin to see—really see—that they are actually there for us, and that in the presence of another we can be cared for. Where before we felt as though we were lost and abandoned we can now be safe, or at least have the possibility of being safe. Being more mindful, we may also come to see that we can be there, with great compassion and kindness, for ourselves. Whereas once we might have criticized, attacked or abused ourselves, we may come to treat ourselves more mindfully, as though we have value. A switch can then gradually be made within us—like badgers in their setts gradually sensing that it is safe to go outside—from caution to exploration. We become more ready to explore ourselves, our environment, and our lives. This day-to-day work in clinical psychology suggests that cycles of disadvantage can be interrupted and actually stopped if people, whether young or old, learn to reflect, psychologically, on their experiences. That is great news, not least because reflectiveness is not just the preserve of the rich. Happily, the ability to think and the ability to reflect and change are free. This is an enormous gift that we have, and one that we often forget in the rush of life.

And how such reflection, with another person, can help us feel better and recover ourselves! Like anyone else when my interests are threatened, or appear to be, I can still behave very childishly and mindlessly in my mid-30s, before realizing what I am doing and correcting myself. After failing a psychology assignment, I raged like an angry two-year-old who's had his favourite toy taken away. I cursed the markers, and above them the exam board; they all became—most politely—'idiots', trying to do me down. I swore on the telephone at family and friends and, feeling so angry about what I thought to be a misjudgement, I considered demanding a re-mark, but by 'different idiots'. I felt like throwing my mobile phone against the wall and having it shatter in a thousand pieces, if possible. The idea of its exploding, preferably with coloured lights and noise, seemed very satisfying. Having felt hurt by others, I wanted to feel as though I'd done some real damage of some kind that others would notice.

In time, though, the kindness of other people helped me to see a different picture. A new vista was opened up to me now. The whole course was only an add-on, anyway; I had *volunteered* to do it. It wouldn't have mattered if I'd never even *started it,* let alone finished it. If I'd had to drop out and leave the whole thing, it would actually have made my life easier. Eventually I had to admit that I had rather—not for the first time—vastly overestimated the importance of the event. In the heat of the moment, caught up in myself and with my pride hurt, I had got things wrong. Indeed, thinking about how I reacted above makes me look a bit … well, *silly*: a bit of a monkey. I shouldn't have been surprised at my own aggressive reaction, though, since my interests were threatened, or they seemed to be. But hey!—which of you monkeys took my bananas? I wanna get you, and I'm gonna make you pay! Look, I've gone and done it again …

But reflection and self-reflection are not quite enough in therapy. The focused practice of compassion and empathy, at first by the therapist and then by the client towards themselves, is vital. This is partly because one aspect of psychotherapy, originally noted by Freud, is the process of loss, including the shedding of illusions about ourselves, each other and our world. This is a painful process that can temporarily leave us feeling vulnerable, and again requiring the help and kindness of other people. Freud argued that depressive feelings can emerge when we give up our connection to a valued object: a person or an idea. According to Freud a period of mourning, of depressive feelings, is natural before, if all goes well, new connections to other people, things and meaningful aspects of the world are made. A similar process often occurs in psychotherapy, as illusions or unrealistic ideas that we have valued are shed. It may be very painful to let go of cherished ideas, objects or people. There are many kinds of such ideas: that we must be successful; that we can't show our feelings; that we have to live our lives in a certain way; that we can't live our lives in the way we want; that we have to think certain things; that we have to keep control of ourselves at all times; that the person we carefully chose to be our partner for life isn't the person we thought they were; that we were right. Or that our lives always turn out just as we want. In psychotherapy and in mindfulness such ideas, and the feelings that go with them, can be looked at by the people present, client and therapist, and in time let go. While this happens, we may need to feel comforted by someone else as we go through the painful experience.

Letting go, or 'giving up' in some way, can be very difficult for some of us to do, particularly if we are proud people. As a man, like many of my fellow men—and having watched *Rocky* a little too carefully for my own good—I have often found it hard to stop fighting and struggling in different situations: to simply give in and let go, and perhaps to ask for help. This tendency has caused me much suffering over the years. Foolishly not wanting to admit defeat, I have tried to save and cling on to various situations that made me feel much worse psychologically—sometimes for months or even, sad to say, years. In my early working life, for example, feeling overwhelmed by business, I sometimes wished that the incoming work would just stop. Having got used to getting many things my own way as an only child, I falsely imagined I could often or even always do so. This didn't help me at all. It is better for me to let go of my expectations, and to accept my difficult adult responsibilities and really do something about them. And actually, once I get over the shock of it, this feels a lot better than staying trapped in my 'grumpy child' role. Yes, when I don't get my own way—and get what I want—I can become upset, bitterly resenting the boundaries imposed on me by responsible adult life. But by carrying on like this, and making a song and dance about my situation, I just make things worse. I also sometimes make myself feel much worse than I really need to. I'm sorry to have to admit it, but I have made these mistakes in my life. I'll probably still do the same thing a bit in the future. I'm human, after all. You too?

It took me a long time to learn this, to see the operation of this pattern, and even now I quite often need to remind myself of the choices I have. Sometimes, however, if what we hopelessly wish for is out of reach, then giving up what we are trying to get is good. It can feel so good to give up and let go at the right time in our lives.

When we give up in such a way, positive feelings can soon follow and guide us as we gradually negotiate our path into new ways of life. One of the best things about psychotherapy is that when people *are* finally able to give up some of these ideas about themselves, and the issues that have been causing them problems—and this can take some time—natural feelings of energy and enjoyment often come to take their place. Ah, we say to ourselves at such times: *this* may have happened, *that* may have happened, but life—*my life*—can go on after all! This is why the psychiatrist Jung used to welcome something apparently bad happening in his clients' lives. Something good was bound to follow, and body and mind naturally wish to recover as best they can if they have the chance. There are many wonderful things to do, places to go and wonderful people to meet in the world, but sometimes we stop ourselves from seeing it and then doing something about it. What we initially see as pure misfortune can help us do this, and recover our natural perspective as well as our physical and psychological health.

One man was often told by his abusive parents when he was growing up that he was not a human 'boy, but a monster'. His arm was once broken by his mother who didn't understand how to care for him. He understandably internalized this, hurting himself physically and psychologically for years; feeling so ashamed of himself, he averted his gaze so he would not make eye contact with others—a common signal of shame feelings, and linked to depression. But in psychotherapy all this began to change. After a wary beginning, in which he spoke in barely more than a whisper and made little eye contact, tentative connections were made between his current behaviour and his early experiences of abuse. Before long, sympathetically invited to help the therapist understand how he was feeling and why that might be so, he began, gently at first, to wonder whether, as a human being, he too might have rights like everyone else. At first the idea itself was hard to think of, sending him ricocheting around a learned internal circuit of hurt, damage and misery. But mindfully letting go of the painful, shaming ideas of the past, he became more free to be himself and to live his own life. A sense of humour developed for the first time. He wanted to depend on others less. The focused light of kindness, sympathy and understanding in psychotherapy had showed new possibilities for the man, which hadn't seemed to exist before. Using the therapy relationship itself as a tool for change, the man's relationship with himself and with others was reworked. He learned that he was not stuck, after all; that he could do things a little differently. For the first time in his life he felt able to allow others close enough to be friends with them. As he came to the end of therapy, he noticed an unprompted urge to be playful and to seek enjoyable, healthy things. He had much catching up to do, having missed out on youth, and he really wanted to enjoy it. He also dared look at others and himself without fear of punishment and shame, for the first time.

So this is part of what can happen in psychotherapy, between the people who are there. If we have been psychologically hurt in some way, and other people have knocked us down, or if something went wrong as we were growing up, psychotherapy and mindfulness, separately or together, can help us to walk again. Despite what has happened to us, regardless of what the harsh voices inside or outside our heads are saying to us, and no matter how difficult the challenge sometimes feels to us: we can get back up. Luckily we humans are made of pretty sturdy stuff. Given the chance, the psychological system will reset itself. Psychologically speaking, we can learn to walk again. We may stumble, we may fall. We may make our mistakes, as all people and living things inevitably do, but we can recover. And we can eventually, with the help of others, walk on with dignity, face the challenges of life and enjoy at least some of what it has to offer.

Increased awareness of the underlying issues beneath our day-to-day defences however, often brings some regret. People regret what others have done to them in the past; or, having had certain experiences at others' hands, they regret mistakes they themselves have later made in living. We may also become aware, perhaps through psychotherapy, of the ways in which we have acted unreasonably, perhaps not knowing better, or have treated others badly in the past. Often people feel each of these things; but reflecting on them, with the help of others, can help to prevent recurrence.

I'm sorry to say that I have also treated people pretty badly, and pretty mindlessly, sometimes myself. Having felt an early sense of threat from others, and having experienced rejection from others later on, I tended also—to guard my morale and to keep the criticized person at a safe-seeming distance—to be harshly critical of, or horrible about others. While this habit was sometimes amusing to people in social situations, it was also destructive. Unsure, deep down, of myself and my place in the world I would target, then attack, others' apparently weaker characteristics so as to strengthen my own position. Threatened by feelings of low mood and shame, my mind attacked vulnerable parts of its environment; but as so often—or perhaps always—this cycle was self-reinforcing. My nastiness towards others and rejection of them, driven by my own sense of insecurity, served to keep them at a safe distance. This prevented me from acquiring information that would help me change my perceptions of myself and of others, and eventually coming to accept both much more.

At times when I behaved mindlessly like this, I was semi-aware that it wasn't right. It didn't feel good, inside me, when I was doing it. I wasn't aware of why I acted like that. Now I'm aware of some of the psychological patterns involved, and the emotional consequences for others and for me, I regret the hurtful things I did and said. Now I say fewer horrible things, and am much less judgemental about other people; and I'm also less critical of myself, most of the time. This way of life feels so much better, much more secure and much happier. I'm glad to be part of a world that contains so many different and interesting people, with so many different and interesting things to say.

Ending Therapy

In the third, final phase, as the agreed end of the therapy approaches, the two people, client and therapist, can together identify and build on the gains made. Often, whether or not they have been practising mindfulness, the client will be more aware of the psychological reasons for their original difficulties—although original symptoms and their underlying psychological causes may appear on the surface to be different. A person who is very worried about cleaning the house, for example, rubbing their knuckles to the bone, may *really* be worried, deep down, about her marriage. Did she marry the right person, forty years ago? Does she want to stay with them now? Very often also, the people have already begun to make changes in their lives, doing things in different, less destructive ways—and are feeling better for it. They can also look ahead to their future life without psychotherapy. For some people this brings relief; for others, the prospect of independent coping brings real and very understandable concerns. How will they cope? What will they do? If there's a problem, to whom will they be able to turn? To which I will often reply, perhaps they might ask a friend?

But like the other interactions within therapy, these reactions can be considered and reflected on before the work actually ends. So in one way the psychotherapeutic relationship, while artificial in some ways, is reflective of much human contact. Similar basic feelings generally often emerge. Excitement and novelty at the outset; familiarity, friendliness, and increasing depth later on; and sadness at the close, as the therapeutic relationship between therapist and client ends.

Sometimes we may also feel sadness about ourselves, about others or about our lives; or about the time we have lost living our lives in negative, but understandable ways *after* psychotherapy. When we realize what has happened, and what we have been doing to ourselves, we may be quite shocked.

Looking back on my own life I see, with regret, how deep and hidden feelings of insecurity affected so many of the choices I made and what I did with my time. I lived so much of my life seeing personal and professional threats where they really didn't exist—and that was mostly because of my early experiences. So often it really felt as though jobs, projects and relationships would fail unless I immediately took drastic action to stop that happening. This drastic action then seriously reduced my quality of life overall. I lived my life on 'red alert', although there wasn't an emergency anywhere in sight. Most of all perhaps, looking back, I feel sad about the opportunities I had but didn't make full use of, simply because I didn't feel safe, or that my needs would be met unless I worked myself to the point of exhaustion. I could have got much more out of being at school, at university, and in the first years of my working life; but I was so fearful of being thrown out or somehow criticized for not being good enough that I did almost nothing else but work—to the point of making myself ill—all the time I was there. Because of the psychological procedures I was following, I missed getting to know many different people and many things much better. And overall, from my position now, I'm sorry that it's taken me over 30 years to learn that I can be *safe*. Despite what I might sometimes feel, I'm *hardly ever* under attack, or threatened by others; in fact, I'm free to take life much more easily, to look around—even to be playful: to enjoy myself. No one should have to feel like that in any way— feeling themselves to be distinctly sub-standard and almost constantly threatened. But a lot of people still do, even though the realities that caused the issues in the first place are long gone.

Knowing all the above, I really wish that someone could have seen what was going on and could have helped me to change. It makes me even more sad to think that if I had stayed for longer in therapy over fifteen years ago, many of these issues could have been resolved then. Whatever I do and think now, that time has gone and I can't get it back.

Yet more happily, now that I'm more aware of these self-reinforcing patterns and their psychological origins, they are much reduced in force. I've also come to accept that these difficult things really happened in my life. I felt the feelings; they felt bad at the time—sometimes *really bad*— but they did not last for ever. To a great degree, partly through therapy, the help of others and reflection on them myself, I've learned to accept them and to begin to let them go. Having had some issues to begin with, and having been through the therapy experience myself, I feel I've got closure on the most pressing psychological problems that I faced as an adolescent and young man. I used to feel that I was worthless in some particular ways; I now know that I'm good enough as I am.

* * *

In a simple way, therefore, and all being well, each psychotherapy has three stages: a beginning, a middle and an end. But there is something special about the joint environment between the two or more people present. It is there, in that precious space where feelings change between people, that our darkest-seeming secrets can be shared, where the light of human sympathy and understanding can shine, and where hope may eventually be rekindled so that psychological change can begin. In other words psychotherapy, criticised by some who don't know any better—possibly unfortunately for them and those who are close to them—offers a model for more compassionate, deliberate, reflective relationships between ourselves and others. Ultimately, 'Our shared belief is that a positive therapeutic relationship is an interactive engagement of two equals sharing an important and life-changing experience.'[9]

So taking some of its qualities together, and whether or not it includes the practice of mindfulness meditation, psychotherapy, in the light of psychological theory, encourages us to be more aware, conscious or 'mindful' of how we live our lives. Like the practice of mindfulness, therapy encourages us to consciously look in a kindly way on ourselves, our lifestyles and each other. Again like mindfulness, where the accent is put on self-awareness, therapy can also in effect help us to shift to a different, less driven and defensive mode of being,[10] to relax and in doing so find more space in our minds to be aware and to make good choices. This has the advantage that we become more conscious of, and so in a sense psychologically distanced from, our feelings, thoughts and actions. In time, instead of simply feeling unpleasantly pressured and driven by powerful thoughts and feelings that demand us to act in certain ways, maybe to feel safe, we can consider other and perhaps more beneficial options—and from a more relaxed, psychologically whole point of view.

Over time in therapy, especially when aided by mindfulness, the content and quality of our thoughts and feelings can change. With a little help and guidance from

9. Shapiro, F. (2005), 'Foreword'. In: M. Dworkin. *EMDR and the Relational Imperative: The therapeutic relationship in EMDR treatment.* New York and Abingdon: Routledge: xiii.
10. Teasdale, J., Segal, Z. & Williams, J.M.G (2002). *Mindfulness-based Cognitive Therapy for Depression.* New York: Guilford Press: 93–94.

others, they can move, together with the inner voice that we may perceive, from being demanding, destructive and pressurizing ('Get on with it, you idiot'; 'I've been *so stupid'*), to kind ('I'll feel better if I give myself a break now'; or 'It's OK for me to have these feelings'). Because of this, people who have often felt very 'trapped' by their lives and confronted by a limited number of choices—or just one choice that is less than enjoyable—find that, via psychotherapy or mindfulness work or a combination of the two, they are actually free to do something else that they want to do more.

Often such a choice can seem unthinkable to begin with; but looking back it can seem completely straightforward. It might be OK if you work 40 hours a week rather than 70. If you tried this you might—just might—find that *you are good enough as you are. There is no state that you have to achieve.*[11] This is a central compassionate message of psychotherapy, and indeed of mindfulness meditation. Some of our basic assumptions about ourselves are frequently not quite right; indeed, tragically they are often very wrong. This is virtually a psychological law: the assumptions or thoughts of anyone who is anxious or depressed might be usefully corrected in a compassionate, positive way. We *can* be good enough as we are. No amount of self-criticism, self-punishment or compensatory activity—while it may temporarily feel partly good and right—can really ever help to correct the original negative assumption about the self. But we can, in a sense, swiftly begin to redeem ourselves and our lives if we realize that of all the things in the world, only the practice of kindness, to ourselves and to others, has a chance of giving us back the life and time many of us lose in suffering.

Where's the Evidence?

Psychotherapy, or treating one another and ourselves mindfully, may sound persuasive to some of us—but is it really effective, and how does it work? A large amount of rigorous scientific data of many kinds exists to suggest the benefits of psychotherapy for people of all ages, including children and older persons.[12] Sometimes, indeed, the measurable benefits of psychotherapy equal or exceed the effects of taking medication alone.[13] There is so much data supporting the treatment benefits of psychotherapy, in fact, that it is beyond reasonable doubt that it is helpful for many psychological problems, including feelings of anxiety, depression, panic, psychosis and post-traumatic stress. Just take the example of depression, which produces extraordinary personal and family suffering as well as social burdens, including increased use of social and medical services coupled with absence from work. A number of high-quality scientific studies have compared the effectiveness of one well-established

11. For this phrase, I am indebted to my colleague, the mindfulness instructor Michael Chaskalson.
12. Roth, A. & Fongay, P. (2005) *What Works for Whom: 2nd edn.: A critical review of psychotherapy research.* New York: Guilford Press.
13. Hollon, S.D., Thase, M.E. & Markowitz, J.C. (2004). Treating depression: pills or talk. *Scientific American*, 35–39. **Volume no.?**

form of psychotherapy, cognitive behavioural therapy (CBT), with antidepressant medication. The 'essential finding' of these studies was that CBT was just as effective as the medication in treating depression—even when doctors were free to prescribe the antidepressant of their choice.[14] Furthermore, it is typical that 50 to 70 per cent of people with depression no longer meet diagnostic criteria for that issue after treatment, according to standardized and scientifically validated measures. A similar picture of effectiveness emerges with other psychological issues and other psychological therapies, to greater or lesser degrees. Even quite new psychological treatments, like eye movement desensitization and reprocessing (EMDR), have quite large amounts of research data to support them.[15] But what is it, exactly, that makes psychotherapy so beneficial and so effective? There are various views on this and, as might be expected, different psychotherapies can offer different benefits; but it may be that psychotherapy offers something that is essentially human. One person's pain can be eased by another person's help and psychological presence.

To begin with, the very act of talking about one's difficulties to someone else, or emotional disclosure, is beneficial and often helps. Connecting with another person in this way has various positive effects. Disclosure of our deepest thoughts and feelings about stressful experiences, anxiety or depression eventually helps the difficult feelings to dissipate. Disclosure also improves people's perceptions of their own health. They report fewer physical symptoms such as headaches, and consult their doctors less often, even about existing illnesses.[16] Then again, disclosing one's feelings to another person can boost immune-system functioning. Shortly after episodes of emotional disclosure, people show various improvements in their immune systems, including more natural killer cells.[17] Against this, suppressing thoughts about traumas can lead to reduced immune–system functioning.[18] Talking or writing about difficult times in a meaningful way—trying to understand what has happened and why it has happened—can help us to integrate the issue into our lives.

In fact, talking or writing about our experience—creating stories or narratives about it—may be essential. By doing this, the storylines of our lives can be connected with verbal and non-verbal expressions of emotion. Different brain areas, including the left and right hemispheres and cortical and sub-cortical areas, are most probably involved, working together in self-reflection. In this way, and through psychotherapy, a comprehensive narrative structure provides the organizing, executive parts of the

---

14. Craighead, W. E., Hart, A.B., Craighead, L.W. & Ilardi, S.S. (2002). Psychosocial treatments for major depressive disorder. In: P.E. Nathan & J.M. Gorman (eds.). *Treatments that Work: 2nd edn.* New York: Oxford University Press: 245–261 (248–251).
15. In this case, for PTSD. For a critique of this data, see: Mollon, P. (2005). *EMDR and the Energy Therapies: Psychoanalytic perspectives.* London: Karnac: 253–269.
16. Pennebaker, J.W. (1999). Writing about emotional experiences as a therapeutic process. *Psychological Science, 8,* 162–165.
17. Booth, R.J. (1997). Changes in circulating lymphocyte numbers following emotional disclosure: evidence of buffering? *Stress Medicine, 13,* 23–29.
18. Booth, R.J. & Pennebaker, J. (1998). The immunological effects of thought suppression. *Journal of Personality and Social Psychology, 75,* 1264–1272.

mind with the best possible chance of overseeing and coordinating our physical and psychological functions. There can be 'feelings about thoughts, and thoughts about feelings'.[19] Connections about their responses in certain situations can be made by the person in ways that have not been made before—even in what were previously considered by the person as difficult or stressful situations.

The actual accepting, kind presence of another person, the psychotherapist, may be important in itself, as noted earlier. This is suggested by the frequent finding from psychotherapy research that, regardless of the specific therapeutic technique used (whether CAT, CBT, EMDR or another method), it is the quality of the relationship (or the 'therapeutic alliance') that is the most important factor for the outcome of the psychological work. Because of this finding some people have been sceptical about the actual benefits of all psychotherapy. They argue that because the therapeutic alliance affects many or all types of psychotherapy, psychotherapy itself may have little to offer—as though 'it can't be that good'. On the contrary. I believe it is mainly the quality of the human presence with us that can help to restore us, and each other. Kindness changes minds.

And as you might expect, psychotherapy affects the brain, and brain activity, in beneficial ways. While it was once believed that the adult brain was not able to change, it is now known that within certain limits the healthy brain remains changeable and 'plastic' at any age. Plasticity reflects the ability of neurons to change how they behave and connect with each other, in response to shifting environmental demands. This functional reorganization occurs at a greater level, and faster, than previously thought. Changing environmental demands can encourage changes in brain function and, in the case of psychotherapy, new emotional learning.[20] It is very likely that while extreme stress prevents new learning and brain growth, mild to moderate stress stimulates brain growth hormones, leading to increased production of brain cells in areas involved in learning. One benefit of effective psychotherapy is that it allows the affected person to gradually face mild stress—as difficult feelings and areas of experience are touched on together—but within a safe environment, in which feelings of safety and challenge or mild stress can be alternated. Such possibilities for change and relearning offer hope for recovery.

There is also specific neurological evidence of the impact of psychotherapy. Studies using positive emission tomography (PET) imaging show that people experience significant changes in metabolic activity in the right orbitofrontal cortex and its subcortical connections as a result of successful psychotherapy.[21] Evidence is emerging that specific psychological issues, and the positive changes that occur in psychotherapy, are connected with certain brain areas. To take one example, a key

---

19. Cozolino, L. (2002). *The Neuroscience of Psychotherapy: Building and rebuilding the human brain.* New York: Norton: 35–36.
20. Ibid. 296–299.
21. Schwartz, J.M., Stoessel, P.W., Baxter, L.R., Martin, K.M. & Phelps, M.E. (1996). Systematic cerebral glucose metabolic rate changes after successful behaviour modification treatment of obsessive-compulsive disorder. *Archives of General Psychiatry, 53,* 109–113.

brain area thought to be involved with obsessive-compulsive disorder (OCD) is the orbitofrontal cortex, parts of which are linked to recognition of contamination and danger. In OCD, a feedback loop may be set up that results in parts of the orbitofrontal cortex being overstimulated. Brain scans have shown, however, that reduction of OCD symptoms is correlated with decreased activation of this brain area. Furthermore, these positive brain changes are similar, or even the same, whether the person is treated with medication or psychotherapy.[22] Similarly, improvement in the symptoms of people with social phobia is connected with reduced blood flow in amygdala-limbic circuits, notably in the right hemisphere.[23] Finally, activation of the left hemisphere of the brain through sensory stimulation produces greater self-serving attributions, and positive emotions. Relative left frontal activation may be linked to reduced psychological problems and, in particular, may produce a lower risk of depression.[24] There are similar positive results for the benefits of mindfulness.

In view of the above evidence for the actual neurological benefits of psychotherapy, it is also possible or likely that the caring, supportive, yet safely challenging environment provided by the therapist has a direct and beneficial impact on the brain's new learning, and reinforcement of this learning. Contact with the kindness of the psychotherapist, and becoming more mindfully aware of what is happening in one's life, may trigger greater production of such endorphins as dopamine, serotonin and norepinephrine.[25] These, in turn, may well again support neural growth and plasticity in key parts of the brain as part of the process of change.

In other words psychotherapy and mindfulness, separately or together, where people consider new ways of being, actually seem likely to have a demonstrable, neurological impact—helping the brain to repair itself. Given the mind–body link, and the importance of our feelings for our overall well-being, perhaps this should not surprise us.

* * *

In the light of the above, the curious predicament of humanity is clear. Brilliant though our minds are, their limitations predispose us to attend above all to ourselves, as we consciously and unconsciously seek a sense of balance, or homeostasis, as part of the processes of life-regulation—and survival. While the kind of care and attention with which we provide ourselves depends on many factors, including our earlier, learned experiences, our acknowledgement of others' needs is usually small, except when it

---

22. See Cozolino, L. (2002). *The Neuroscience of Psychotherapy: Building and rebuilding the human brain.* New York: Norton.
23. Furmark, T., Tillfors, M., Marteindottir, I.,Fischer, H., Pissiota, A., Langstrom, B. & Frederikson, M. (2002). Common change in cerebral blood flow in patients with social phobia treated with citalopram or cognitive-behavioural therapy. *Archives of General Psychiatry, 59,* 425–433.
24. Tomarken, A.J. & Davison, R.J. (1994). Frontal brain activation in repressors and nonrepressors. *Journal of Abnormal Psychology 103(2),* 339–349.
25. Cozolino, L. (2002). *The Neuroscience of Psychotherapy: Building and rebuilding the human brain.* New York: Norton: 300–301.

suits us or those we know and love. But our psychological development—indeed our happiness—through life depends in many ways on others and on our relationships with them. In childhood, in adulthood and in later life, as well as helping ourselves we can do much for others.

The effectiveness of psychotherapy, I have said, rests largely on this interdependence and the quality of our interactionality. Our relationships and interactions with others throughout our lives can profoundly affect how we feel, and our level of well-being. If we are treated badly and mindlessly by others, our psychological and physical health may be reduced for years, or even decades afterwards. But where such problems exist, close, mindful, positive contact with others—of the kind that occurs in psychotherapy—can have a powerful redeeming and healing quality. The psychological difficulties and their roots may be recognized; fear—often fear of others—can be acknowledged and reduced; and new possibilities for change may emerge. Other people may harm us; but they can also, if we dare allow them close once again for just a short time, offer us hope. Similarly we may ourselves, by offering our presence, offer hope to them. The spirit of kindness and mindfulness between people—no matter who they are, no matter what colour their skin, no matter what they look like or where they come from, and no matter what they do—can kindle new life and new love. At any moment we can help each other, and ourselves, to be.

Given what we know about psychotherapy, mindfulness and their uses, maybe our greatest ground for hope is our massive ability to learn—and still more crucially, to learn from our mistakes. It was the great Russian psychologist Ivan Pavlov we again have to thank for this insight. And it's not just human beings who are equipped for change, of course; even the humble fish—so often the butt of jokes about its dullness—is actually able to make new and important long-term memories and behave accordingly.[26] Similarly, I see people every day who, in the light of a little aided self-reflection, and working outwards from the secure base of mindful therapy, learn new ways of living and being. On a bigger scale, with the development of psychology human beings have learned to help themselves and others. From this perspective, psychology itself can be seen as a tool for enhanced human mindfulness and self-reflection: a way of holding up a mirror so that we can see ourselves and what we do. It is because of our power to learn and change that, despite all evidence to the contrary, I am eternally optimistic about humanity. The history of human civilization suggests that we, too, can integrate new information, rethink and, if you like, re-feel. Our evolved ability to *recognize our psychological mistakes* and *learn from our psychological experiences and then behave differently* means that hope does spring eternal.

So one humane response to humanity's predicament in living with each other in a world that is shared is simple, as I shall suggest in the rest of this book. On the basis of our own lived experience, and some of the available psychological evidence, we could reflect just a little more on how we ourselves, and other people, might be feeling.

---

26. Brown, C. (2004). Not just a pretty face. *New Scientist, 2451*, 42–43.

Growing just a little more mindful like this, we could reflect on our own psychological limitations and error and acknowledge our own humanity and that of others, however imperfect, releasing us all from the pressurizing, negative illusion of human perfectibility. Where might such reflection lead?

In 1892, William James put this memorably:

> We have unquestionably a great cloud-bank of ancestral blindness weighing down upon us, only transiently riven here and there by fitful revelations of the truth. [...] Our inner secrets must remain for the most part impenetrable by others, for beings as essentially practical as we are, are necessarily short of sight. Cannot we use our sense of our own blindness to make us more cautious in going over the dark places? Cannot we escape some of those hideous ancestral intolerances and cruelties, and positive reversals of the truth? [27]

I believe that with a little modern, mindful psychological awareness, and just a little conscious effort, we can. In the next few chapters we'll explore what it can mean to look at some of the 'dark places' in our lives. I'll try to give you a sense of what it's like to have effective psychotherapy, with or without formal mindfulness practice (depending on whether it is appropriate), when people and their feelings change in positive, useful ways, during and after personal contact with a psychotherapist.

---

27. James, W. (1899). What makes a life significant. In: W. James. *Talks to Teachers on Psychology: And to students on some of life's ideals.* London: Longman, Green: 265–301: 268.

6

Mindful Treatment of the Younger Person

No one ever keeps a secret so well as a child.
Victor Hugo

Where children and young people have suffered and been ill-treated by others, the practice of mindful kindness towards them, perhaps as a part of therapy, may help them recover. Often, since children and young people are still growing physically and psychologically, their recovery may be surprisingly swift. With just a little help from others, they often regain their psychological balance.

While all children and young people are sensitive to their psychological environment, depending on their temperament, the younger the child, the more sensitive[1] they are to what happens to them and how they are treated by the people in their lives. Even before children learn to talk the young mind responds swiftly, and sometimes drastically, to changes—with good reason, since the child, as an evolved organism and living person, needs to survive in a potentially hostile world. If the child perceives that danger exists, then that lesson needs to be learned quickly and danger avoided in future.

With young children and young people who have learned such lessons early in their lives because of being hurt or being in danger, we ourselves may need to listen, carefully and mindfully, to hear what is wrong: how we may be of help to them and kind to them. But as with most or all people of any age, if we ask them in the right way, and give them space and time to talk, they will often tell us how they feel: why they are feeling this, why they are feeling that.[2] Once this process has begun, children and young people, like the rest of us, often come to feel better and safer—more ready

1. See Cozolino, L. (2002). *The Neuroscience of Psychotherapy: Building and rebuilding the human brain.* New York: Norton: 78–80.
2. Carr, A. (1999). *The Handbook of Child and Adolescent Clinical Psychology.* London: Routledge: 450. See also Gottman, J. & Declaire, J. (1997). *Raising an emotionally intelligent child: The heart of parenting.* New York: Fireside / Simon & Schuster.

to explore themselves, their environment and their lives. This was the case in my discussions with children and young people below. In some cases mindfulness was used directly as part of treatment, in some cases not; but in each case, each person became more mindful of the psychological suffering involved, and its causes.

And one final thing. In the cases that follow, while I use terms like 'anxiety', 'depression', 'eating disorders' and 'obsessive compulsive disorder', let's not get too hung up on them. The scientific case for the differences among these things (if indeed they are 'things') is at best unclear.[3] For one thing, have you ever met anyone with an eating disorder who wasn't depressed as well? Or a person with obsessions and compulsions who wasn't anxious? No? Nor me. Such people are as rare as unicorns, and when we're clinically unhappy we tend to have a unique group of noted problems, so don't worry too much about these loose names of the collections of symptoms. It's the symptoms themselves, the story they begin to tell, and above all the *person's feelings* that we're really interested in. After all, it's how we feel at any time that matters to us most.

Don't Panic! Feelings of anxiety in Simon, a 7-year-old boy – 12 sessions

I met Simon when he was 7. When he came into my office, a small, slight boy, he looked serious, tired and worried—not how you want to be or how you want to feel when you're so young. Simon came with his mother, Dawn, and his father, Gary. Simon also had a younger brother, Matthew, who was aged 5. Just looking at the four of them here with me, I felt concerned. It looked like a serious matter. What was the problem? The problem, Dawn explained, was that for the last few months Simon had been unhappy about going to school. Often when he was there in classes he'd feel both dizzy and faint—so much so that on some occasions he'd feel he had to leave the class and get some air outside. Understandably, everyone was concerned about Simon's dizziness. The family had been to the family doctor, but she had been able to find no physical cause for the problem. Looking at Simon sitting there opposite me, I felt for the little guy, who understandably seemed bewildered as he looked around my office.

My first impression was of a young boy who in some way felt helpless, or powerless, to deal with events in his life. Often, or perhaps always, children's own feelings and responses are the most important, despite how much others around them might care, or what they might say. So after Dawn's explanation of the situation, I asked Simon what *he* felt. He said that sometimes at school, in class, the feelings came. How did they feel? Bad. When exactly did they come on? At times when the work in class was more difficult. That's understandable. What helps Simon? Leaving the class, and getting some air. Great; that can help—except that sometimes the bad feelings had led to Simon missing school on some days. This was a pity, especially since, as Dawn explained, he was doing really well in some subjects and had some

3. Bentall, R.P. *Madness Explained: Psychosis and human nature.* London: Penguin/Allen Lane.

good friends there. He also got on well with his younger brother, Matthew, even though it had taken a little time for the older boy to get used to having a little brother in the house. He didn't sound as though he had much fun, though. He wanted to play football, he said, but didn't feel confident enough to be with the other boys. Instead, her preferred to spend time alone, playing with his soldiers.

I wondered if Simon could tell me a little more exactly about the bad feelings: what they actually felt like. He said that they were 'scary, like something really bad is about to happen', with funny feelings in his head and stomach. I felt for the boy when he was saying this. These were feelings that he couldn't understand, and that felt really unpleasant. In order to help us all see the situation more clearly, and to help show what had been going on, I asked Dawn a little more about the family's background. While Dawn talked, the two little brothers played in the corner of the room.

Dawn explained that she and her younger sister themselves had had a difficult start in life, many years before. They had been raised by a father who was a powerful, controlling and critical man at home, and a warm mother who had never felt able to stand up to her husband. Often, Dawn's father's harsh words and harsh ways of being affected the rest of the family. Dawn said that largely because of him she grew up with 'low self-esteem'—often being critical of herself, as she described it. One result of this was that she felt she underachieved at school, and left too early. Another result was that like many people who have a difficult early emotional start in life, she found it hard to make good choices when it came to partners. Feeling low in herself, and as though she didn't deserve to be treated well, she married Gary, who was her first boyfriend. Gary was rather like Dawn's own father. Dawn was sure that she was loved by her husband, and at first things went very well; but around a year or so after their wedding, his habitual criticism of Dawn turned to violence. Because of his possessiveness, the couple would often have late-night rows after he had been out drinking. Perhaps himself feeling insecure about whether Dawn actually loved him (she did), he sometimes attacked her as well as shouting at her, pushing her across the room, even hitting her. The neighbours could hear what was happening, and demanded to know that it would not happen again. But Simon could also hear. Eventually, with the help of a girlfriend, Dawn came to see that Gary needed help. Fortunately when he was sober Gary came to see this too. He got some help with his anger. Things were so much calmer, Dawn said. Gary took better care of her, Simon and Matthew; indeed, he was there with her to show it. So, since life at home had calmed down over the last few years, why the worries for Simon?

At first, understandably, Simon did not want to talk about what had happened, or how he felt. It's normal for a young boy or girl to feel like that—to feel a bit shy, and to find it hard to talk about difficult or scary feelings. But gradually, with some encouragement and over a few sessions, he came to feel comfortable enough to say what he had been feeling, at important times during his development.

He began by saying that he loved his father very much. But I wondered how had it been for Simon when his mother and father, mum and dad, weren't getting on so well as they had done. I wondered what he used to do at the difficult times. As we began to talk about these difficult periods, I could see Simon's body language change. His breathing became visibly faster, his face more stern, and his eyes began to check around him. Understandably, feeling more anxious as we addressed memories from this past, he was scanning for signs of danger. I felt I wanted to protect this little boy and help him to feel more safe, which was far from how he'd been feeling.

'At the tricky times, Simon, what used to happen?'

'I could hear mum and dad shouting. I was hiding in bed to make the shouting go away; but it wouldn't.'

I wanted to hear how that had left him feeling, so that he could begin to make the connection between the past and the present fears, and be mindful of them. He looked at Dawn, and Gary particularly, before answering, perhaps to check that it was safe to talk and safe to say how he felt. It was both.

'Scared.'

That was all he could say right now, because of the feelings that were coming up. I noticed the trembling in his voice, and the fact that he was shaking a little. Dawn saw that he needed some reassurance, so she reached out to hold Simon as he talked. They both had tears in their eyes. I wanted to make this situation feel as safe for Simon and his family as possible, so he could come to say how he was *really* feeling.

'It's OK to be scared,' I said. 'It was a scary thing for you then. You were there, all alone, not knowing what was happening to your mum and dad. Maybe as well as being frightened for yourself, you were worried about them being all right.'

'I was.'

'And maybe you felt that something really, really terrible was going to happen to them, or to you. Or both.'

'I did. I didn't know what, but I did.'

The emotional point, the feelings that were troubling him, were clear. This little boy had been very scared. But with these difficult things happening, and the difficult feelings that came with them, who had he been able to tell? Again Simon checked out both his parents' faces before answering, as though again making sure that it was somehow safe to answer.

'Nobody. No one.'

Understandably, with the sense of fear in the house, with him hiding in bed with his eyes shut and the sheets pulled up over him to keep out the noise of the arguments and fighting between his parents, and Dawn having been taken up with understandable thoughts of getting away from her husband, Simon had felt there was nobody for him to talk to about how he felt. So he had kept all his feelings to himself. This was difficult for him.

I was glad that Simon was beginning to talk now. The atmosphere in the room had changed. There was a sense of relief that I noticed—as though, at long last, the truth about Simon's feelings had begun to come out. He had been frightened by what he had seen and heard when he was about 4, and too frightened to talk about it. I felt it was important to help him feel safe enough to talk now, and to have people—the most important people in his life, his family—hear what he had to say, and listen kindly to him with their full attention.

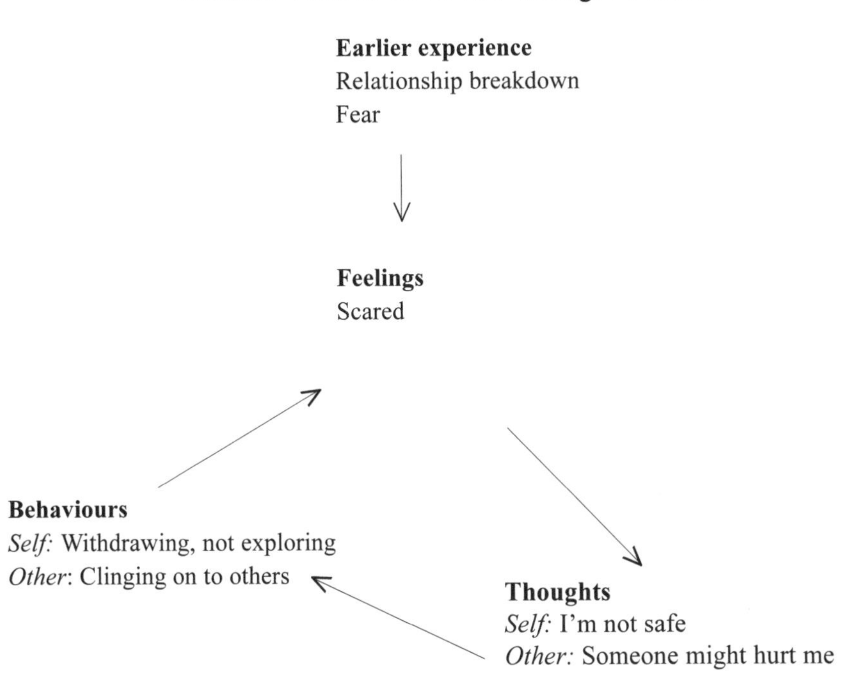

Figure 6.1 Simon's formulation

'I wonder, Simon, if the feelings that you've been having at school—and maybe this is a really big question—are a bit like the feelings you used to have during the hard time?'

He nodded; then he said, 'Yes. It feels just the same. I was worried Mummy was going to be hurt.'

I asked him whether he had this worry at school during the dizzy times, too, and whether this worry had also made him want to come home and make sure she was safe.

'Yes.'

As you might expect, these things were difficult for Simon to say; they were also hard for Dawn and Gary to hear. Understandably both initially felt much guilt, and Dawn quickly began to blame herself for not taking better care of her son at a time when he needed her most. She also wondered if she had picked the wrong man to marry—or that's how it felt sometimes. This, too, was hard to admit, and she felt bad and guilty about this also—that she had put her boys through such difficult times as well as herself. But Dawn did admit it, and began to live clearly with the real feelings. And then there was Gary: listening to what was being said, he clearly felt upset and said repeatedly, and in front of the whole family, how sorry he was that the problem had happened.

By this time in therapy, after three sessions or so, we had reached an important destination. Simon had been brought to me by his parents because of difficult feelings that he had, mostly at school. These had led to his wanting to leave school and come home to be with Dawn, where he felt safer. Talking about the worries over a number of weekly sessions with the whole family showed that there were some good, understandable reasons for Simon's feelings. At a young age, unfortunately like too many children, he had seen and heard shouting and violence between his parents. To such a child, especially one who is sensitive by temperament, this can be very disturbing and frightening. Because of these times—even though they were not frequent—they had left Simon with powerful memories and sometimes feeling insecure. So while his brother Matthew appeared not to have been affected in the same way, at periods when Simon might be expected to feel stressed or vulnerable, as at school, the worry came up, bringing strong feelings with it.

In making the link between the present symptoms, the bad feelings, and their origin in Simon's early experience of great fear, we prepared for the next stage of therapy. This was gently helping him to explore the feelings still further—to get used to feeling them, little by little, and seeing how they changed through the day. Together we noted that sometimes the feelings *were* there, but sometimes they weren't. Understanding the bad feelings, seeing how they could change and getting used to them gave Simon more confidence over the week. He was also helped by clear reassurance from Dawn and Gary, who said, and showed, how much they cared for Simon and how safe he could be from now on.

Over the sessions I could see and feel how Simon was becoming more confident, smiling more—rather than looking so serious—and feeling safer. This was clear, for example, by his playing more in our time together, rather than talking and moving in more restricted, rigid ways. The freedom in him was wonderful to see. During our sessions Simon's experience of him, and his family's experience of himself, changed significantly. From being a serious-minded, fearful boy, he came to see himself more as a playful boy with just a few fears; in fact, the whole family became more playful and humorous as the atmosphere lightened. Simon played more football with friends out in the street, as he'd always wanted to do. He was spending less time playing alone; and sometimes he and Gary would play together: father and son. They both enjoyed this.They did things together more, like going bowling, and enjoyed doing so. And Dawn, who had been feeling guilty and had been blaming herself so much for what had happened, came to see that actually she had done the best she could at the time. She saw that it was her relationship to her own parents—and her critical father especially—that had led her to be attracted to, and settle for, the way Gary had initially treated her. This wasn't her fault. So gradually she began to view herself, and the decisions she had made, more kindly with regard to Simon's problems. Like most of us, most of the time, she had done her best to cope in the circumstances in which she found herself. No fair-minded person could reasonably blame her for that. And Gary too had honestly faced up to what had happened. He explained, in an emotional family session, how he had been frightened by his own father, and how this made him insecure. He had originally been afraid that Dawn would leave him, and had covered up his insecurity with alcohol-fuelled anger.

So while Simon's early experiences of feelings of danger and fear at the hands of others may have left him a little more vulnerable to later worries, and led him to try and escape or avoid the feelings when certain triggers appeared, he had recovered to

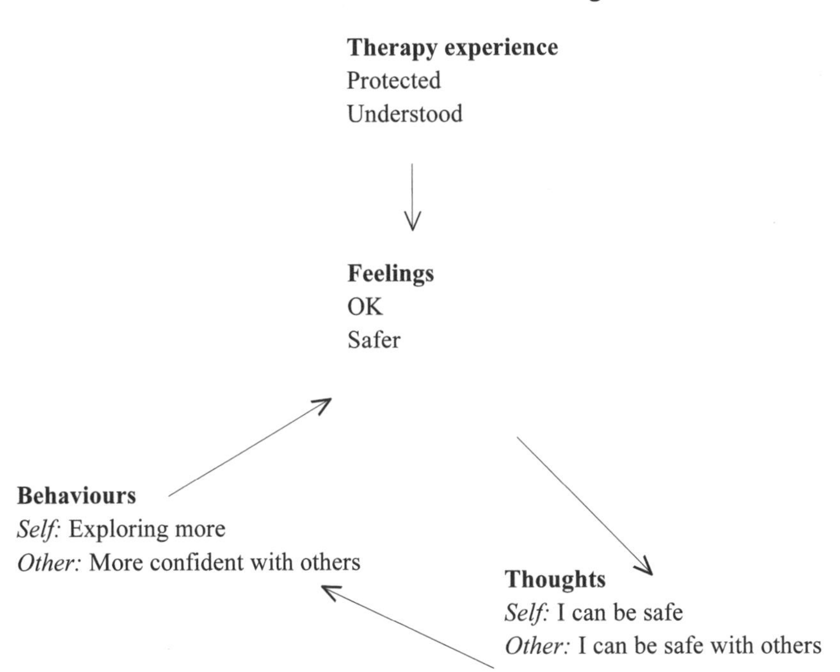

Figure 6.2 Simon's formulation at the end of therapy

a great degree. With some kindly help to explore and begin to understand his feelings and their origins—so becoming more aware and mindful of them—Simon had come to feel safer, and was now more free to enjoy himself and his young life.

Simon's feelings had changed. He knew the psychological reasons now why they had begun, and what they were for—to tell him about the danger that he felt he had been in; but now they didn't seem so unbearable after all. Being clearer about what had happened when he was younger, he could now tell more effectively when he was *really* in danger (which actually wasn't very often), and when he wasn't (which actually was very often). He also agreed that it would be a good idea to tell Dawn or Gary how he was feeling, at tricky times. Understanding more about the problems, they were both keen to help. Naturally we were all really pleased about that, when the time came for the family to leave therapy; and as often happens, we were all sorry to part from one another.

In Simon's case difficult, fear-inducing early experiences led him, as quite a sensitive boy to begin with, to try and get out of worrying situations or avoid them completely. Sometimes, though, children who have been badly treated earlier in their lives can react very differently. In certain children, difficult feelings can produce very different behaviour and responses. At worst, the results can be chaotic; and before the problems have been properly understood, it can seem to some people as though the child deserves to be told off, or punished, and somehow 'put right'. This was so with Lisa.

Punishment, Please! Severe behavioural problems in Lisa, a 10-year-old girl – 10 sessions

Lisa didn't come and see me; I always went to see Lisa. This was the kind of case in which everyone had given up. Everyone felt that they had tried everything.

I first visited Lisa at her home with her aunt, Sarah, and her brother, Michael. Sarah had, she said, no idea what to do or where to turn; Lisa had been so difficult, especially at school. 'She brings,' Sarah said, 'chaos wherever she goes.' I looked at Lisa, sitting on a chair next to them. She looked innocent of any wrongdoing. OK, what was happening? Where?

At school Lisa was getting into serious trouble almost every day that she was there: so much so that she was currently under threat of having to leave, which would have been a disaster for her socially. She was disruptive in lessons. She would interrupt when the teacher was trying to talk to the whole class. She would interrupt other children either when they were trying to talk, or when they were busy trying to concentrate. At quiet times in the class, she would often throw pencils and paper around the room so that no one could get anything much done. When things reached their worst (as they did on most days), Lisa would be sent out of class to be talked to severely by a senior teacher. This talking-to had the brief, temporary effect of making her quiet; but then, just minutes later, the problems would restart. Quite often she'd make pretend calls and take pictures with her mobile phone.

At home Lisa was very different. Sarah said that she was as 'quiet as a lamb', and never caused any trouble—even with Michael. She came home from school on the bus, helped to feed the cats, then went to her room. She never shouted or swore, as she was said to do at school; all had been going smoothly. Lisa had been with Sarah for almost two years and had not given her any trouble; but recently Sarah had been shocked to hear about the trouble at school. As Sarah explained this to me, Lisa whistled and played with her hands. Clearly, she didn't like to hear these worrying things being said about her and her life. It really looked as though the talk was making her feel insecure; I had heard enough for now. I needed to see for myself what was happening with Lisa at school. I asked her permission to come and see her there, which she gave.

It took ten seconds for the trouble to start. The teacher, with a classroom of twenty children, had just begun to talk. Ten seconds later Lisa began to sing loudly, directly into the ear of the boy next to her. She did this for over a minute, ignoring the instructions of the teacher to stop. When she had finished singing she began to pick up a packet of pencils and throw them at other children, who ducked gamely out of the way. She picked up her mobile phone and took some pictures of the classroom, with some of the children laughing. Despite some of her behaviour, Lisa was clearly liked by many of the other children—and on this performance I found it easy to like her myself. She was creating a lot of disturbance in the classroom. In academic terms, she was achieving little except the destruction of the teacher's aims and the distraction of herself and other children. As happened on many days, Lisa's distraction of others was so bad that she was sent by the class teacher to the headteacher of the school as a punishment. She had her head bowed, but still had a half-smile on her face as the teacher shouted at her, 'Get out!' Even though she was smiling, I felt sad for Lisa. Being with her there, I wondered if somehow she had got what she wanted, but that she was also trying to escape from something, or avoid something. I found her where she was sitting, next to a table and alone outside the head's room. I wondered what had happened for her in the classroom.

'Nothing.'

Lisa did her best not to look at me. The ceiling came to look very interesting for her. I wondered if something had upset her. She raised her voice, almost to a shout.

'*No!*'

I felt that with the force of this answer Lisa might have been trying to keep me away from a difficult feeling that she would rather have avoided. Sensing that these were really hard feelings for her to talk about, I was particularly gentle in what I said, and how I said it. With a little more prompting, Lisa was soon able to say that she was actually really worried about being in class. Clearly this was not the impression that her behaviour gave to others. What was she worried about?

'I can't read. I'm stupid, and everyone will think I'm stupid.' As she was saying this, her head sank towards her chest with feelings of shame. I comforted her. We also wondered, together, whether other children had said hurtful things to her in the past. There was a long pause. Lisa looked out of the window.

'No. No children said anything.' OK. So was there anyone else who said hurtful things?

'My mum. My real mum.'

'That must be really hard,' I said, 'if your mum says bad things to you.'

We agreed on that. I wondered if Lisa could remember the kind of things her real mother used to say.

'Some things. She used to call me a lazy cow sometimes. And stupid. She said I was stupid. But a lot of it was when I was little, so I don't know.'

This sort of talk was hard to listen to; but Lisa's less positive behaviour began to make more psychological sense to me. As anyone would do, feeling threatened by a situation—in this case at school, in class—Lisa took evasive action. This was her disruptive behaviour, which got her out of one kind of trouble (the feelings of shame and stupidity) but into another (with her teachers and headteacher). I needed to hear more. In particular, I needed to hear more about Lisa's early life with her real mother and father.

Back at the family home on another day Sarah, with regret, explained about Lisa's real parents. Sarah's older brother had been called Jack. There were some complications at his birth and it was felt he might have sustained some subtle brain damage that affected his development. He had grown up with many behavioural difficulties and had run away from home at fifteen, keeping in touch only sporadically. On his travels Jack had met Daisy, who had come to the area from the US when she was a toddler with her parents, before they had broken up. They had been young—teenagers—and had lived locally. Neither was working and both, drinking too much and taking drugs, had a chaotic lifestyle, with frequent arguments and fights between them. They struggled to take care of themselves, let alone anyone else. When Lisa arrived the couple separated permanently. Jack was not interested in having a child, and left Daisy. The last time he had been heard of he was living in London. And Lisa's mother, still very young herself, resented having to be responsible for her daughter, which led her to neglect Lisa. Sometimes there was also physical abuse; when she got angry, Daisy would often burn Lisa with cigarette ends. After a few months, with Lisa at the age of around 8, the situation became so severe that drastic measures were needed and she was removed from her mother and taken into care. Eventually she came to live with Sarah, who had always taken an interest in Lisa and Michael.

It was moving to hear this story. This apparently bad, naughty and disruptive girl had had very strong psychological issues to deal with. It was clear that she had been verbally abused, as well as emotionally and physically neglected. She had also had very little early caring contact from either parent and, at a young age, had all but lost contact with them. These difficulties had also made life early on in school very hard for Lisa; feeling upset so often, she had not learned to read and write as she could have, and so her academic skills were not as developed as they might have been. Lisa was in the family kitchen looking after the cats while I was, with her permission, hearing about her life. All of us there felt a lot for this troubled girl. Lisa returned to the room. I said that although the problems at school were difficult, there were—as always—some psychological things that we could try together. The formulation of the problems looked like this:

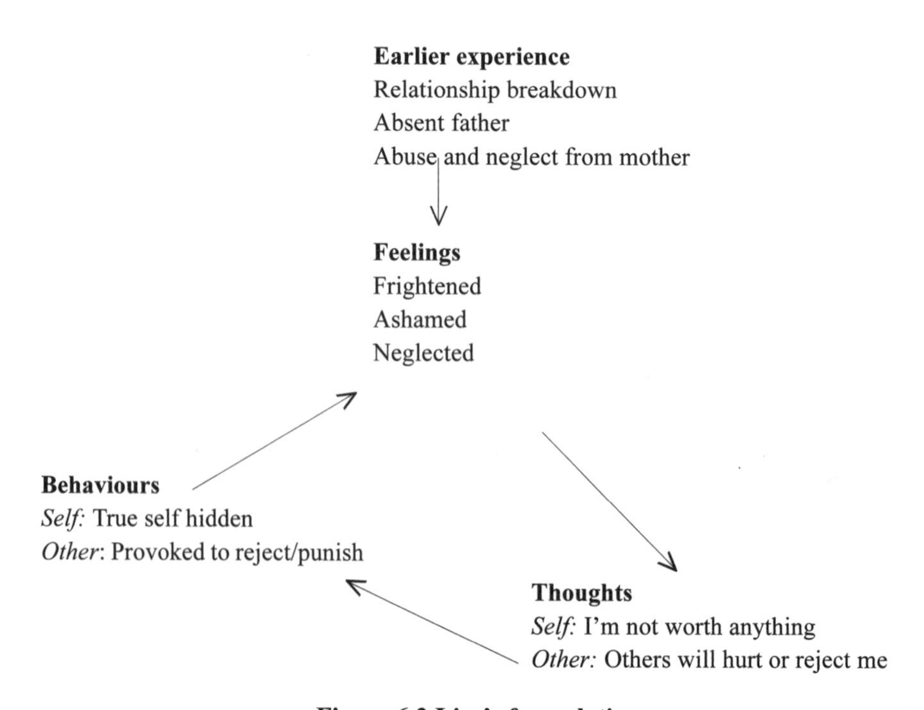

Figure 6.3 Lisa's formulation

Somehow we needed to work out how Lisa could feel better and maybe safer in herself, and so not need to be disruptive at school.

First, since Lisa had been affected by the verbal abuse from her mother, she and I alone spent some time talking about that. This, as you'll be able to imagine, was hard for Lisa to do. When we got anywhere near her memories of this I could see her fidgeting, not wanting to talk or even think about what had happened. The memories of her mother's behaviour were painful, and they seemed to bring up in Lisa a strong sense of shame. Her mother's words and actions had led her daughter to feel ashamed of being herself. I didn't want her to feel that way any longer, so in talking about the feelings we were clear in naming them, and how they felt. Lisa, who often became tearful in these sessions, said that they made her feel 'dirty, like I'm not worth anything'. We also made very clear that while Lisa had had these powerful experiences that had affected her, they were in the past now. We observed together that people around her in her life now were very different from that. Sarah, we agreed, was very loving to her. She had good girlfriends whom she liked, and who liked her, at school; and despite all that had happened, she liked her teachers. In this way and over time, the force of her mother's original, terrible words to her—having been repeatedly remembered—became understood and accustomed to, to be a little reduced in their effect.

Second, with permission from Lisa and Sarah, I went back to school to speak to her teachers. Being kind people they were keen to hear how they could help, and to know how she was feeling—not least because if Lisa was doing better in class, the whole class would very probably run more smoothly. I needed to explain a little about Lisa's background and what it meant for her psychological set-up. After Lisa's start in life, which involved great insecurity, I explained, she would be quite likely to feel more insecure than the average child, particularly at times of stress. It was likely that these feelings of insecurity would be triggered by any difficulties at school, and that these would make her behaviour worse if nothing was done about them. Because of her past history of being criticized and abandoned, Lisa might very well feel very alone at difficult times—as though she had to cope by herself and no one was there for her. We could help her to deal with the feelings better, I said, if she could have her mobile phone on her—which had often been confiscated, so that she could call Sarah for reassurance. We also made sure that Lisa had a picture of Sarah on her phone that she could look at during anxious times. We also agreed that before school, and at any time during breaks in the school day, Lisa could go and call her aunt for a little encouragement and reassurance. Over time, Lisa might well come to learn that despite her expectations it was possible that other people could be there for her, and could care for her.

Third, we talked at home about Lisa's feelings and whether she could have a little time each evening after school to talk about what had gone on, and how she had felt at different times in the day. For a girl like Lisa, who had had such a difficult emotional start in life, such a period devoted to thinking and talking about feelings, and how they had changed through the day, promised to help her gain just a little more control over them. For when we are more aware of our feelings and how they arise, we are in a better position to manage them ourselves. We all agreed to this. So together we experimented with a new plan. Given the level of abandonment, anxiety and shame that Lisa had experienced from an early age, and her difficulties in managing her emotions, we tried together to help her learn these skills.

How did everyone get on in this case? Things gradually started to settle down in Lisa's life. Most obviously she was calmer at school, less disruptive in class and more able, gradually, to manage her feelings for herself. This meant that she, and others around her, were more able to concentrate on what they were doing. She had made good use of opportunities to talk to Sarah at difficult times; in particular, she liked to go and talk to Sarah before school started. Lisa said it helped her 'cool down' before the start of lessons. Even better, people at school were noticing the difference in Lisa. At home, Sarah was also very pleased. She was very happy that Lisa was better behaved at school. She saw that, as a young girl, perhaps Lisa had been a little too well behaved when at home. Instead, she realized that it was to be expected that Lisa would sometimes be a bit boisterous, or might even swear about some things. This—the liveliness of youth, she now saw—could also be a good sign, provided it did not go too far. We talked about it, and together took it as a sign that Lisa was now confident enough to be more like her *real self* with Sarah. And Lisa, settling down both at school and at home, was becoming much more herself: happier, more lively and gaining in confidence. I watched in the playground as she interacted happily with others. Compared with when we first met she seemed to be allowing herself to be much closer to others, and them to her, than before. More able now to see the hurt and feelings of shame from the past as actually *being* in the past, Lisa was able to be less defensive around others and less attacking of them. Her mobile phone was used much more for social rather than disruptive purposes.

When we parted, it was clear that there could quite likely be some difficulties in future—for example when Lisa became interested romantically in others, which was only a few years away. She was already getting on well with boys. Managing such relationships, and the powerful feelings that they bring up, was likely to become an issue for her; but there had also been some significant changes that had made a difference in Lisa's life now. Above all, feeling more positive about herself, she no longer felt as though she needed to invite punishment and rejection from others. Her view of herself, and others' views of her, had changed from being a 'problem girl', to a 'girl with some problems', and then to 'a likeable girl who is good at things'. This recognition of her personality was a significant step. She was looking forward in life now, not back: she sometimes tried different activities after school, like horseriding, which she really began to enjoy. The psychological cycles maintaining her problems had begun to switch around a little. There were positive signs.

So, having had a very problematic early experience of care that involved abandonment and emotional abuse from her mother, as well as the effective loss of her father, leaving her with deep worries about whether or not she could be safe and whether she was shameful or not, Lisa came to see herself and her world in a different way. She had responded to the kindness of others—her aunt and teachers especially. Their gentle, patient presence and their input in being prepared to listen to her concerns

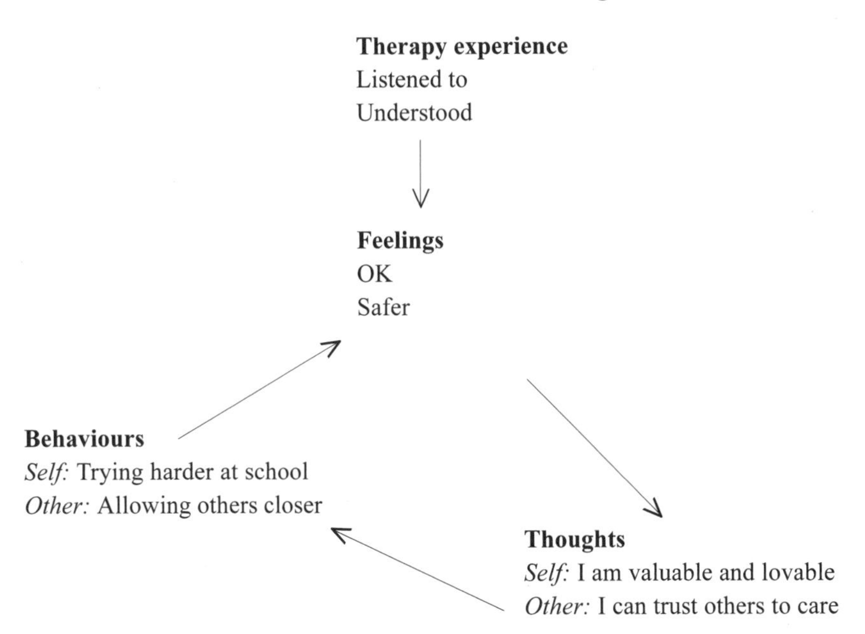

Figure 6.4 Lisa's formulation at the end of treatment

had given her the message that she could be safe: that people can behave differently—even though we might not automatically expect them to—and that she didn't have to set herself up to get hurt, punished or rejected by others over and over again. Once her underlying feelings had been addressed and her sense of self began to improve, her pattern of behaviour could start to change for the better. For all her difficulties when we first met I liked Lisa a great deal, and cared about her. I often wonder how she is getting on now.

* * *

In general when working with a person psychologically, the younger or the more dependent they are on others, the more other people will be closely involved with their psychological care. Consequently my work with Simon and Lisa, quite young children, required that their families and schools were involved. As people mature and become more independent they can be treated individually, often without the help—or even in some cases without the knowledge—of other people in their lives. In such cases it is partly the kindness and skills of the therapist that can be important to enabling change in the adolescent or young adult; but a similar psychological principle still applies. Early psychological damage sustained from others can often be undone only by later care from others.

A Grief Delayed: Anorexia and anxious feelings in Steve, a 16-year-old young man – 16 sessions

It was quite hard to tell from just looking at Steve that there was anything much wrong with him, or that he was, or had been, suffering greatly. But he was clearly over-thin, and when he spoke, in quite a brisk way, it was clear that he had had some significant psychological issues to cope with in his young life.

Steve explained that, like many people with eating disorders, he had been under the care of various doctors, including psychiatrists. Over the last year his weight had been so low that he had been admitted to a specialist eating-disorders unit in a hospital, where he had been helped to put on weight—which he found very hard to do, since he felt less comfortable like that. His weight had been more stable recently, he said, but he remained under the care of a dietician. But while his weight had improved and he had been able to return to school, he said, his mood was 'bad'. He said that he felt anxious and depressed 'all the time'—which I doubted, since even when people feel low there are patches of the day, or week, when they feel a little better. I wondered if there were any times during the week when he felt particularly bad.

'When I go out.'

'What happens then?'

'I feel terrible. I'm walking about, maybe along the street or into some shops, and I feel like shrinking away. It feels as though everyone is staring at me.'

This is quite a common fear among people. We naturally feel anxious about how others see us, and some of us, if we are a little more sensitive or are under stress, can feel this rather more acutely at some points in our lives.

'What do you feel might happen?'

'It feels as though all the people are looking at me, criticizing me, judging me.'

'And what might happen? What might happen if they saw the real you?'

'They'd see straight away that I was a bad person. Then they'd reject me, and push me away. They'd have every right to.'

By now it was clear to me that Steve was struggling psychologically. His view of himself was strongly negative—so much so that he had been very controlling of his diet, and very strict with himself regarding what he ate and what he did in terms of his exercise routine, which involved swimming in the morning and running in the evening. But, as a sensitive young person, he was also fearful of others' views of him. Understandably, this had led him to avoid social situations, so that he began to lose contact with friends he had previously valued. Naturally, this had made his mood worse recently.

I was beginning to feel much compassion for this likeable young man who, it seemed, was spending much time being hard on himself rather than enjoying himself, his friends and his world. I was wondering how he had come to feel this way. In particular, I was wondering how he had come to feel so desperately threatened that he had to do all these things in order to feel OK, and how he had come to see others as being so critical and threatening to him. It was time to explore, ever so gently, his earlier experiences.

When I asked about his relationship with his parents, Steve smiled. It was as if to say: 'What's the point?' He explained that until he was seven he remembered being happy at home with them, feeling secure and cared for; but then trouble began between his mother and father. He described his father as a large, dominating man. He had been a successful IT consultant for many years and was, Steve said, hugely ambitious—a driven man, who believed that by providing for them financially he was doing all that he could do. Steve's mother, on the other hand, was a teacher. She too was often busy now, although she had taken time out from her career when her children were small. Difficulties in the marriage arose and, from Steve feeling safe and secure up to the age of seven, after that he felt very different. That was when his brother Adrian, two years older than him, was hit on the street outside the family home by a passing car, and died on the way to hospital.

Understandably, the family found it difficult to cope with such a loss. Steve said that he wasn't aware of much sadness being expressed by anyone, but in the aftermath of the accident he remembered loud arguments between his parents. The level of tension in the house increased: so much so that even when he was young Steve could feel it very clearly. He had memories of his father's angry face when he was shouting at his wife, and sometimes at the rest of the family. Steve found this very upsetting. He felt that he was 'never the same after that', as though something had happened to him internally. I'm sure that in a way he was right.

It was at this time that he began to be more selective about his food—willing to eat some things but refusing to eat others. At first his behaviours were mild; he counted calories on some foods. Over time, though, things became worse. Steve, feeling the stress from home, was already struggling at school, and life there was made worse by bullies. He was sensitive, not as confident as some of the others, and he suffered for that. He was taunted by one group of boys for being 'a wimp'. Looking back, Steve felt that these words, repeated again and again by his tormentors, pushed him beyond his limit. It was then, at around the age of 13, that he began to diet seriously. This meant that as well as cutting down drastically on calories—taking in only 100 calories per day, just a fraction of what he needed for healthy growth—he also began to exercise hard to work off the excess weight that he felt he carried. Naturally, his parents were very worried all this time; but as Steve acknowledged, there was little or nothing that they could do as their son wasted away in front of them. Steve's control over himself had itself got out of control, and his life became more and more restricted. For a while his weight had improved; but then recently his psychological health had dipped again. This had brought back his negative feelings, and his need to diet and perform his food-related rituals, with much greater force. That was shortly before we met.

As I said to Steve, he had already said enough to make clear what the key issues were. I wanted to be more precise about how he had felt, as a young boy, about the loss of his brother, about the bullying and about his father's behaviour. He was clear about this.

'I was terrified; terrified. I think I was frightened that both mum and dad would leave, and that I'd be left somehow alone, with no one to be there for me. And there was Adrian's death; we never talked about that.'

I wondered whether these fears were the basis for his rigid dieting; they were both a way of controlling what seemed to his young self the only way of managing a very uncontrollable-seeming situation. It felt to both of us that this explanation made sense. As a very young boy, he had been sorely frightened by what had happened to his happy home. Previously he had been the kind of boy who enjoyed being close to his mother, often clinging on to her, but after the terrible loss of his brother he said it felt to him as though his world had fallen apart. Maybe his dietary control was really his way of keeping himself together: his way of feeling safe in himself when the world that he had trusted seemed to be falling down around him. At times of increased stress—like during the bullying that he endured—he resorted to these habits as a way of making himself feel better. But I got the sense that Steve had had enough of those habits, and that he was keen to change what he did and become happier. We agreed that this was the case and that we would see what, if anything, psychological therapy might do for him. Most of all I felt that as a fragile-looking person, Steve needed a safe place with a kind person to help him begin to work out, and work through, what had happened. Since the problems had been around for some years, we set our expectations low. This made it easier for us to be pleased with any positive results that we might get. Our sketch of Steve's formulation was the following:

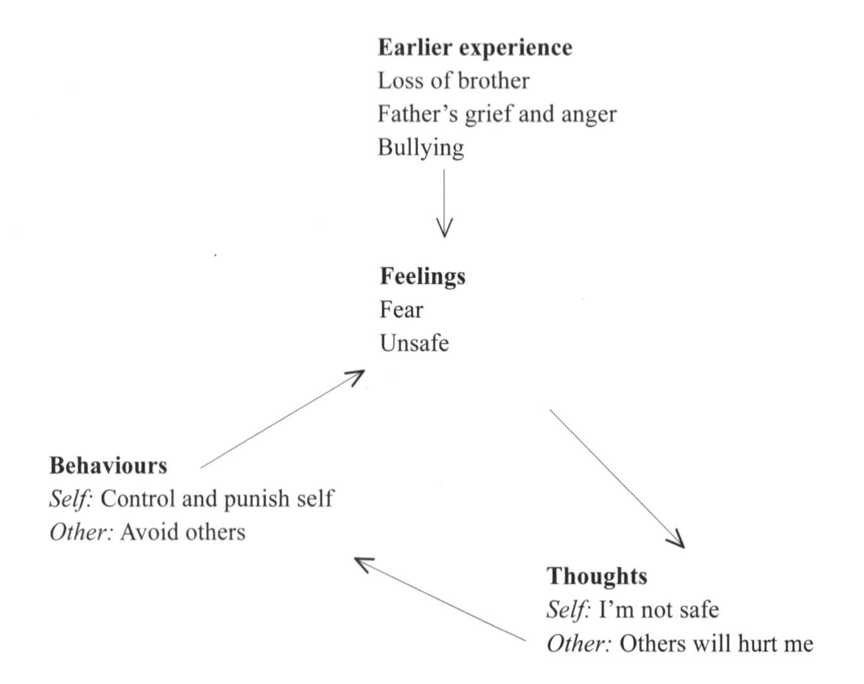

Figure 6.5 Steve's formulation

We met a number of times in my office, and together we did some important things. The first thing we did was some mindfulness work. I encouraged Steve to simply do a little mindful breathing each day—15 minutes a day to begin with. Initially Steve was sceptical, and couldn't see the point of this, but with time he was able to tune in to his thoughts and feelings more. We then used mindfulness as a basis for what followed.

We explored next the underlying feelings that Steve had about what had happened when he was small and growing up. He said that he had never been open with anyone, perhaps even himself, about how frightened he had felt as a small boy after Adrian had been snatched so suddenly away, and the atmosphere in the house had changed so drastically. When Steve was recalling these events it was easy to see his younger, fragile self, buffeted by family storms over which he had no control. When he was talking like this his voice changed, becoming by turns quieter—talking like a whisper—and then, as his level of upset increased, broken with distress. However as we did this we both had a sense that what had happened was being put into its historical context, as something that had been but had now gone.

Also as part of this process, we explored his feelings about his brother, mother and father. For the first time Steve began to get in touch with feelings of loss for his brother, and anger at his father. This was a painful process. With regard to the loss of Adrian, Steve came to see how much he really missed him—and missed him not just in the past, but in the future that they should have had together. Reflecting on this grief led Steve to sob for his brother in a way that he felt he had never sobbed before; and with regard to his father, previously, he had felt frightened of him for much of the time. Now, in hindsight, Steve could begin to see some of the psychological effects that he had had. He and her mother had not only been frightened of him, but he had little of the sense of protection and safety that one might expect from a 'good enough' parent. Steve came to see that after the loss of his brother, his father had showed signs of not coping. He had bottled up his grief, which then came out as anger. So eventually, instead of the family home being a place where Steve could feel safe and learn to explore, he felt unsafe, and became—with his dieting—a prisoner. He was *his own* prisoner. In that way he would not have to venture out into the dangerous-seeming, risky-seeming world outside. As we talked about this, Steve got in touch with his anger at his father. Whereas previously, he had viewed him with great respect, now he came to view him differently. In fact, as a father he had let him down; he had behaved selfishly in many ways after the death of Adrian and this had left his son with serious worries about himself and made it much more difficult for him to develop healthily. From this perspective his eating problem was a way of asking for help to deal with difficult feelings.

Finally, using techniques from cognitive behavioural therapy and mindfulness, we took care to help Steve to become mindful of his distorted thought-patterns about his diet and food. Like many, maybe all people with psychological eating problems (and of course I was one), Steve's judgements about food needed reflection. Was it really true, for example, for him to say that by eating just a bite of a bar of chocolate, he would definitely get 'fat'? Maybe not. Was it also true that if he ate one 'bad' thing (like a small biscuit), he needed to use laxatives to get rid of any excess weight? Maybe not. So over time, by working together we were able to be more mindful of some of these threat-related thoughts and scale them down. Gradually Steve's thinking about food, its effect on him, and his body-image became more balanced. He began to see that he was OK as he was.

And in our work together, was it OK for Steve to get in touch, in the safe environment of therapy and with me as a kind, safe person willing to listen, with these long-hidden negative feelings about the loss of his brother and the bullying he had endured at school? Surely it was; and not surprisingly, as we contacted his original fears and talked through his experiences, his anxiety and depression began to lift. One sign of this was that he began to act more spontaneously with friends at school. I'd hear about fun times that he would have with friends, and trips, maybe to the cinema, that were being planned. We talked about this, too—and these things felt good to Steve. At the same time, we noticed together that his need rigidly to control his diet seemed to be dropping significantly. He couldn't explain why, exactly; it was 'just a feeling'. I wondered whether Steve was feeling a little safer now than perhaps he ever had. Equally, his relationship with his mother improved, which he described as feeling more open, more adult and more respectful. We talked about this in a family session, with Steve's mother present. She acted as a witness to Steve's progress, and felt that both of them were benefiting and feeling more relaxed.

Interestingly, too, Steve said that over the weeks his view of me—and so of himself—had changed in a positive way. He began to be noticeably more assertive with me—as though he was staking out his territory as a person, sometimes contradicting and interrupting me, being in conflict with me: but within healthy limits.[4] As I said to him, this was pleasing, because what it meant was that in our work he had begun to undergo the key process: looking at the losses the family had encountered, but denied; and that of beginning to make his own decisions and to begin to live his own life.[5] For all of his existence so far he had been living in the shadow cast by loss of his brother and its effect on the family. Now, we had the feeling that he was moving, slowly, towards the light.

I saw Steve some months after our sessions, just to check how he was. There had been some bad days: in recovery from psychological issues, we expect this; just like a physical wound that we are recovering from, we may be rather tender for a while. For the most part his changes had been maintained, and actually built upon. His weight had stabilized, and best of all, he was now able to go out with his friends to the cinema and into coffee shops; whereas before, feeling frightened and ashamed of himself among others—literally not wanting to be seen—now he had begun to hold his head high. At times, he said with a broad smile, he was pleased to be himself now, and pleased to be alive. Together we had freed Steve from his self-imposed prison, which had protected him from earlier, underlying fears—past dangers that were long outdated. I was delighted for him because of his progress, and I really wanted him to be able to go off and enjoy his life. But naturally, what *I* wanted wasn't the issue: it

4. Apter, T. (2002). *The Myth of Maturity: What teenagers need from parents to become adults.* New York: Norton.

5. Szmukler, G. & Dare, C. (1991). The Maudsley Hospital study of family therapy in anorexia and bulimia nervosa. In B. Woodside & L. Shekter-Wolfson (eds.). *Family Approaches in Treatment of Eating Disorders.* Washington, DC: American Psychiatric Association.

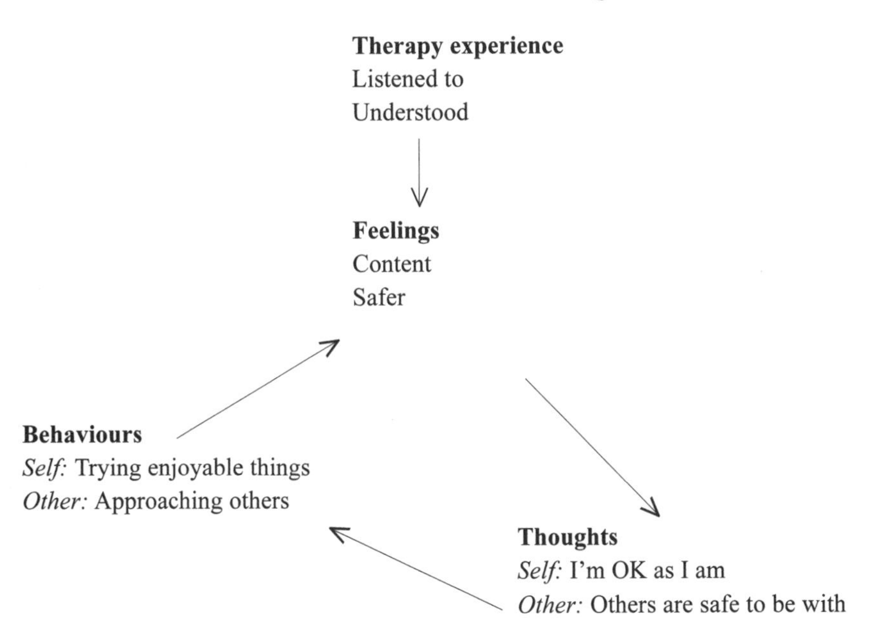

Figure 6.6 Steve's formulation at the end of therapy

was what he wanted that counted, and his mindfulness work was still helping with this by allowing Steve to get in touch often with what he was feeling and what he wanted for the present and the future.

Down on Yourself: Feelings of anxiety, depression and self-harm in Matt, a 19-year-old young man – 24 sessions

Unlike the young people I have mentioned above, it was clear on first meeting Matt that he was a deeply troubled young man. He looked uncomfortable as we were walking to my office, and once we were there he struggled to make eye contact with me, preferring to look away into the corners of the room. As we began to talk he crossed his arms and legs. This gave me the feeling that he maybe thought I might want to attack him, so defensive did he look. After the feelings he described, I could easily begin to see why.

Matt's life sounded to me so deprived when we met that I could understand if sometimes he was overcome with feelings of despair. Living in a one-room flat, without a job and having few qualifications, he worked in a factory making vacuum cleaners—not something that he enjoyed. When he wasn't at work, as he had only one male friend and no girlfriend, he most often stayed at home—and there he suffered with powerful feelings. These feelings were mostly of depression and despair; they were, he said, worse in the evenings. It seemed that they built up during a stressful day, and became very forceful by nighttime. I wondered what happened then.

'That's when the burning and cutting starts.'

Matt rolled up his sleeves to show me his arms. On each forearm, there were dozens of clear burn marks. Some looked fresh, others were clearly healing. I winced when I looked at them; I wondered what kind of terrible pain, internal or external or both, he must have been in.

'I don't know. I've thought about it a lot, but I don't know. It happens most nights.'

I also wondered what sorts of thoughts and feelings went with the cutting and burning. Matt hesitated and I sensed that he found it difficult to say—to begin.

'Really bad feelings. Really bad. So bad, you can't imagine. I think to myself that I'm completely worthless. I'm a failure in *everything* that I do, and I should be punished for it, that I should be hurt. Then, most often, the harming begins.'

I felt for Matt. I also felt for him because he seemed so lonely—so far from being truly cared for by someone else that he was able to burn and cut himself with no one noticing or trying to help. He had never had any psychological help before. He'd never asked for it. Why?

'It felt as though it'd be weak to ask for any help. I'm a man, aren't I? And men aren't meant to have problems like mine. We're meant to sort it out.'

We agreed on this, as on many things. Often men—particularly traditional-style, older men who find it hard to talk about feelings—find it very difficult to ask for psychological help and admit that anything at all is wrong.[6] This delay in seeking help means that quite often their psychological symptoms get worse than they need have had they been treated earlier. Indeed, I've done this myself. I could have been helped psychologically much earlier, and suffered much less, if I'd asked for help. So it was no surprise to me that Matt had found it difficult to come and ask for help, and had gone to his doctor only because he was absolutely desperate. It felt, he said, 'like the last thing I would do before I killed myself'. It was clear to me that for the time being we were both in deep water together, and that we would need each other to get safely to the shore.

Already, despite his slight defensiveness, I had a firm sense of liking Matt, wanting to care for him and help him, and wondering how he had come to feel this way about himself and perhaps about other people. I asked him about his parents. He didn't like this, and bridled.

'What about them? They're nothing to me.'

Unfortunately, as is sometimes the case when meeting people in psychotherapy, they were worse than nothing. Their activities had not left Matt with a neutral sense of himself. They had left him with a strongly negative sense of and feeling about himself. What had happened?

'They've always treated me like an idiot.'

How?

'Ever since I can remember. my Dad was always at work and never spent any time with me and my older brother. When he was there he used to hit me for anything

---

6. Cochran, S.V. & Rabinowitz, F.E. (2000). *Men and Depression: Clinical and empirical perspectives*. San Diego: Academic Press.

that I did, or didn't do. He gave me a real belting for that.'

I found this account quite frightening and quite repulsive, in fact —the idea of a normal, sensitive young adolescent being physically abused by a much stronger man, his own father. I noticed that when Matt was talking through these details, he was smiling. Sometimes people do this when they are emotionally 'cut off' from the pain that they have experienced. This incident was not isolated; Matt said that there many such times when he had been physically or verbally abused by his father, who sounded like a very unhappy man indeed.

'Whatever I did, at home or at school—whatever I said to him, I was 'stupid.' "Don't be so stupid"—that's what he'd say. That's what he *always* said. Nothing I did was ever any *good.*'

I began to understand from Matt that his younger self had been effectively battered by his father. He had been allowed little room to develop as a healthy individual; his needs and wishes had been crushed. What about his mother?

'She's all right: but like Dad, she's always been depressed. She works as a carer for next to no money, and she struggled to cope with Dad's anger, just like I do. She can't stand up to him; none of us could.'

'What about when you were really young? What was she like then?'

'Like I said. I think she was depressed after she had me. They hadn't meant to have me—or at least Dad hadn't—and she was in a bad way for a while, in and out of hospital with her nerves.'

I explained to Matt that it was possible that his mother's post-natal depression may have made it a bit more difficult for her to care well for him; and because of that it may have been more difficult for her to provide him with a good emotional start—skill in managing his feelings, in particular.[7] So with regard to both parents, Matt had had a difficult time. I wondered how school had been for him. Matt's gaze dropped again.

'I hated it, most of the time. They didn't find out until I was thirteen, but I was dyslexic. I couldn't read when all the other children were starting to. When I was about six, the teacher made us all get up, one by one, and read to the class. With me, the letters and words were just jumping all over the page.'

I could see Matt's face changing as he recalled this shame-producing incident.

'I remember everyone laughing at me. After that, I got out of school, and schoolwork, whenever I could. I left school as soon as I could. But not with any qualifications. Dad got it right after all. I was really stupid.'

By this time, I was feeling for Matt. It sounded as though he had very few psychological resources that could help him through difficult times like this one. He also explained that he had had one relationship with a girl, but that she had finished it because he found it so hard to say how he was feeling. She wanted emotional answers,

---

7. Goodman, S.H. (2003). Genesis and epigenesis of psychopathology in children with depressed mothers: toward an integrative biopsychosocial perspective. In: D. Cicchetti & E. Walker. *Neurodevelopmental Mechanisms in Psychopathology*. Cambridge: Cambridge University Press: 428–460.

but Matt felt most of the time as though he didn't even understand the questions.

'After a few months she gave up trying to get through to me. She went off with someone else.'

This sounded like a potentially difficult and painful experience; but again I felt that Matt's feelings were cut off. There was little clear sign of sadness that I could see. How did he cope with that?

'I didn't really. I was seventeen. Mum was depressed; Dad just got more and more angry at both of us. After an argument I just left, ran off. Went to stay with my friend, before I got the flat.'

And how was Matt feeling around this time?

'I began to feel worse. Much worse. I felt so bad about myself. I had already been burning and cutting, but now it got far worse.'

Why?

'It felt like there was no one who was there for me; no one to talk to. No one cared. When the feelings got really bad, especially at the end of the day, that's when I did it. I know I shouldn't do it, but it makes me feel better.'

As I explained to Matt, this is quite normal among people who self-harm. The cutting—if cutting is the method used—is often perceived by the person as relieving tension, making the feelings bearable again:[8] but often only for a temporary period before the next time the person's feelings seem to get out of control. I wondered if there was anyone else he could speak to about problems, when things got really difficult and the feelings were especially bad.

'There's only David. But he's busier now with this girl that he met. So no, not really. I don't have any contact with Mum and Dad—and the way they are, with Dad angry, going on at us all the time, that's got to be the best way. That's how it feels. As though there's really no one there for me.'

I felt that Matt was right. At the moment, at least, he had very little support. His experiences of being parented had been difficult, partly because he had not been encouraged to grow emotionally, especially by his father, and instead he had often had his confidence undermined by harsh, scathing criticism. His lack of confidence in himself had been further reinforced by his experiences of being shamed and humiliated at school, which had clearly stayed with him, and had made it hard for him to get on well there and succeed. So from a psychological viewpoint it was easy to see why, with less and less current support and having moved out of the family home, Matt, feeling low and hopeless in himself, should resort to hurting himself as a way of dealing with difficult and powerful thoughts and feelings. It felt to me as though Matt's problems were quite entrenched and quite severe. Where this is so, and where people may have incurred greater psychological damage earlier on in life, it is sometimes the case that slightly longer psychological treatment is indicated. We discussed this, and agreed to meet twenty-four times. That way we would have time

8. Huband, N. & Tantam, D. (2004). Repeated self-wounding: women's recollection of pathways to cutting and of the value of different interventions. *Psychology and Psychotherapy: Theory, research and practice 77(4),* 413–428.

to get a feeling of what the problems were, how they might be addressed, and give Matt some support as he began to experiment with psychological changes.

To begin with, we established that Matt's self-harming behaviour occurred in certain patterns. It seemed to occur at times in the evening when he felt he had nothing to do. That was when the desperate feelings set in. At one point we zoomed in for a close-up look at exactly what was happening in these situations and at these times. Together we realized that simply being alone was triggering many feelings in Matt. We saw that realizing that he was alone in his flat also led him to thoughts that, as he said:

'I'm a failure. No one loves me or cares about me, and I should be punished for being so useless.'

I reassured Matt that such powerful negative thoughts and feelings are quite

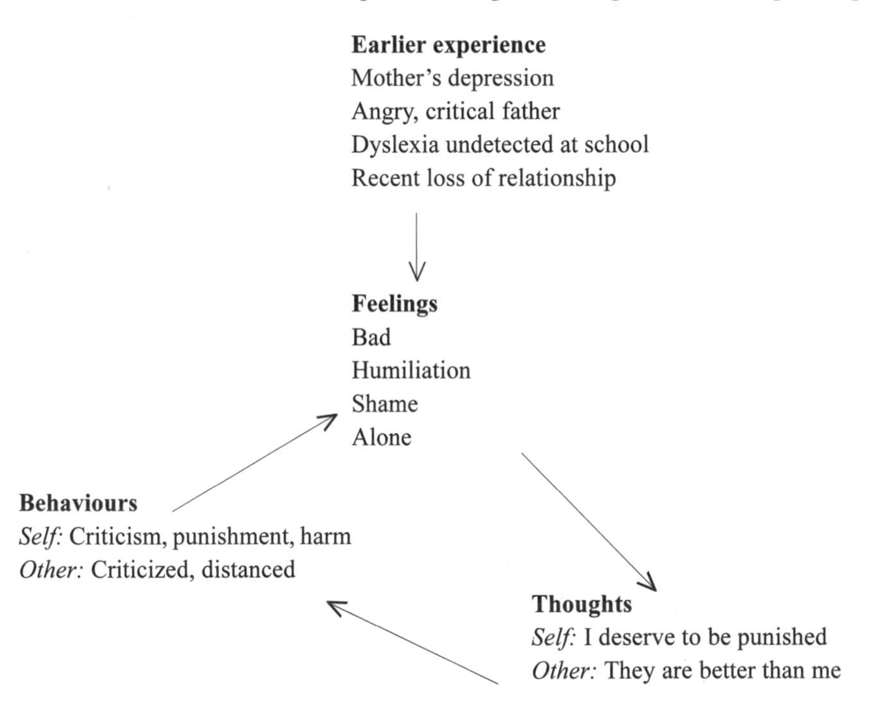

Figure 6.7 Matt's formulation

normal when we are feeling low; and encouragingly that like all feelings they can change—particularly when our lives begin to change, and the way we see ourselves and our lives changes. We talked about what it must be like for Matt to be in this psychological place. It sounded really lonely and hard, with little sense of hope or understanding. We agreed on that. But I also wondered whose voice we were hearing—saying that he was a failure, that no one cared, that he should be punished, and so forth. Matt considered this for a moment.

'It's my Dad's voice. It's very strong. In fact, I can hear him now.'

I wondered what it might be saying to him.

'That I'm stupid that I'm even here. That this sort of work is useless. And that no matter what we do, I'll never get anywhere.'

The voice was clearly vicious, as our internal voices can sometimes be. To begin with it seemed to be almost completely overwhelming to Matt; but over our sessions we gradually began to look at other alternatives. Matt could see, rationally if not emotionally as yet, that there were some possible answers to what this negative voice was saying to him. On reflection, it was not accurate to say that he was a complete failure. It turned out that there were certain things that Matt was proud of in his life, that he had accomplished. As a boy he had been good at sport, winning trophies at swimming. As a teenager he had taken time to help older people in his neighbourhood with household tasks that they were not able to accomplish by themselves. And more recently he had tried to help his friend the best he could, when the friend's relative had been gravely ill. All this, Matt and I were able to see together, was evidence that he was not the *totally* bad, despicable person that he had come to feel himself to be.

Matt could see these things and hear what I was saying; but he still said that he *felt* really bad at certain times. As part of this, his level of self-harm continued to be as high as it had been; consequently we took the work further, and moved closer towards his feelings.

This work was not easy for either Matt or me. It was predictable, given what Matt had experienced in his life, that he would not feel comfortable in close contact with me (as a man, like his father)—or perhaps with anyone. It was likely that the presence of someone too close to him might feel threatening in some way—perhaps acting as a reminder of the way he was treated by his parents. But although Matt felt like pulling away from me and the psychotherapy, remarkably he stayed with it; and with that act of courage by him the work took a new turn.

We talked about the relationship in the session *between us*. Matt said that to begin with it seemed to him that I was likely to be quite critical and dominating of him. Perhaps, he had thought, I might want to 'boss him about', or even hurt him in some way. We discussed this. Again, these feelings are quite normal if we have had less than ideal early life experiences; of course, I had had them myself. I also said to Matt that my intentions and my feelings were actually quite different from that. I cared about his well-being, and really hoped to be able to help him recover. Perhaps rather differently from his initial, automatic expectations, I was hoping to be 'there' for him during therapy and as he began to work through his feelings. I was planning, I said, to be there psychologically in a way that his parents—doubtless because of their own difficult feelings—were not able to be. I would be listening to him carefully, taking what he said seriously and doing my best to respond appropriately. Perhaps because Matt had had so little of this kind of psychological care before, we both experienced this as a moving conversation; and immediately after it the atmosphere in the room began to change. There was a sense that we were closer and more open emotionally. I took this as a good sign; such openness can often mean that the real feelings that people are concerned about are close by, contactable and, with help and time, changeable.

This conversation opened the door, over the next few sessions, to our talking about some of Matt's early experiences and how these had really left him feeling. Perhaps most prominently, he was able to recall how his father, on seeing Matt's school report when he was about eight, called him a 'stupid idiot' and, shouting, sent him to this room. Matt was able, with courage, to recall this vividly with me.

'I felt so frightened of him; so ashamed. I'd wanted him to be pleased with me, and to say that he loved me. But he shouted at me, and shamed me. I went to my room, and I knew then, for the first time, I wanted to die.'

Tears were streaming down Matt's face as he recounted this memory. My eyes were welling up with tears too. Was there anyone else he could have talked to about his feelings at the time?

'No one. I was alone. I hated it, but I was alone.'

Matt was still in touch with the powerful feelings of shame and isolation now; I could see that.

'Thinking back to that little boy who had been so hurt by his father, is there anything that he'd need? If you could go back now to help him, what would he need?'

'He'd need a big hug. There was no one there for him. He'd need someone to be there for him, and to just hold him.'

'Sure.' I said this in the gentlest way I could, so as to show how right I felt Matt was.

He was right, of course. He had felt terribly abandoned as well as shamed as a little boy—and this process had continued as he had grown up. Part of our work, as I explained to Matt, was to allow us to reconnect with some of those memories and the feelings that went with them, rather than pushing them away. This work was not easy; but over the twenty-four sessions, Matt was able to let me get closer to him. This allowed me, as it were, to extend a helping hand towards him, allowing him to grasp it and to be helped. It also allowed Matt to come to see that it was OK to help himself, when difficult and painful feelings arose. Previously, having learned from his parents that his needs were not to be taken seriously, he had pushed his feelings away. Gradually he learned to begin to accept them, and to begin to wonder what they might have been saying to him. As we discussed, it was possible, for example, that his low feelings in the evening might have been in part not a sign that he deserved to be punished (as he had believed), but that he might benefit from something else to do and other people to meet. Eventually, connecting with these feelings and coming to tolerate them more, Matt was able to begin going to a gym once a week. There he not only kept fit, which was good for his mood, but met some other like-minded people and made some social contacts.

Once Matt had begun to feel a little more confident in exploring his own inner world, rather than be terrorized by it, we did some mindfulness work together. By gradually experimenting, week to week, with mindful breathing, Matt found that as well as the negative voices deriving from the past that were in his mind, there were also other presences. He noted being aware of his own, more positive internal voice that, sometimes at least, would stand up to the voice of the critic. This we found encouraging; but also, being mindful, Matt felt able to tune in more to his body: so rather than feeling so split off from his physical experiences as he previously had been, he developed a greater sense of bodily awareness. One thing he noticed was that he felt healthy in his body, vigorous—which in turn helped to reduce his self-harm while also laying the foundation for the latter part of our work.

Towards the end of our sessions also, the bond between us developed so that we felt that we could trust each other. This was a curious feeling for Matt, who said that to begin with, especially, he had often expected me to be hard on him or criticize him in a psychologically painful way. He said that it was surprising to him that, as a man, I could be gentle and kind towards him, as well as talk about gentle, healing things like mindfulness: firm when necessary, but caring at all times. We talked about this and reflected that perhaps it was possible that different people behave in different ways. When we grow up with negative influences on us, we may instinctively assume that, for example, everyone will treat us badly or try to hurt us. One reason therapy can be useful is that it can act as a reminder that everyone, and every situation, is different and that we need not be stuck in one way of responding to others in situations, but can respond accordingly as the particular situation requires. In other words, psychotherapy can help us to be psychologically flexible, rather than rigid, which may well be of benefit to us in our essentially unpredictable lives.

By the time of our last meeting, Matt felt that he was more or less ready to experiment with new ways of living. As is often the case in longer-term psychotherapy, we had grown to have care and affection for each other. Matt felt that he could try to put some of what he had learned from our relationship into practice in his young future life outside therapy. The signs were good. His levels of psychological symptoms—his anxiety and depression—had significantly reduced, though had not entirely disappeared, at least for now. He felt as though he had much more energy and was better able to concentrate—also, his self-harming had all but ceased. How did he explain this?

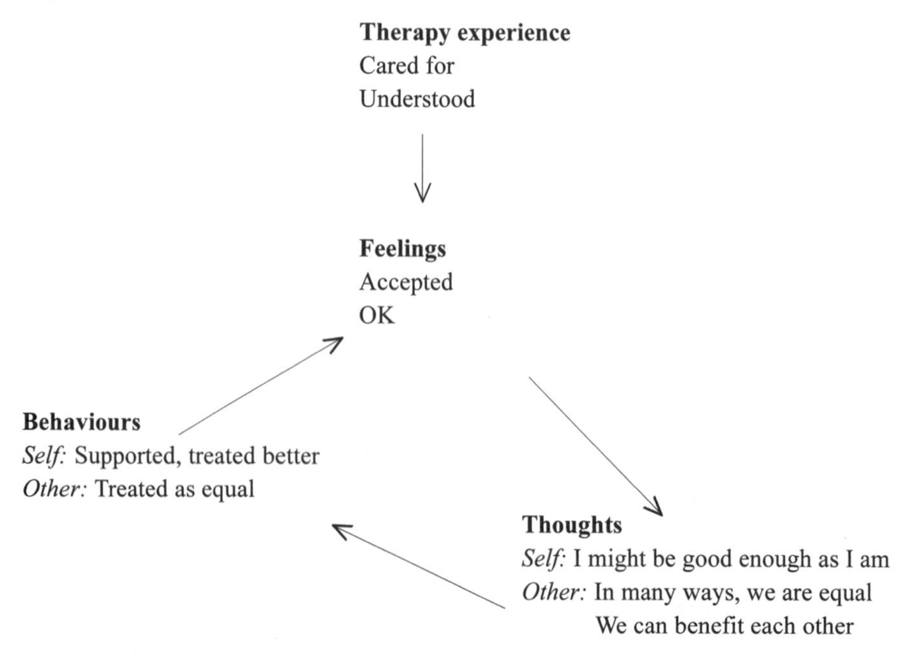

Figure 6.8 Matt's formulation at the end of therapy

'I can see now that what I needed was help, not more hurt. I'd taken such a hammering from Dad that I didn't know any other way, but coming here has helped me see that there are other ways. Just because I sometimes *feel* bad doesn't necessarily mean that I *am* bad.'

'What does it mean, then?'

'Well, it means that I have needs, and that I might need to give myself a little help while things are tough.'

As they were almost certainly sometimes going to be.

By the end of our work, we were both pleased that he was through. We had made good progress for now, and we were both looking forward to seeing how he got on with life. We didn't meet again, but some months later he rang to leave a message to say that he had started a job that he liked, that he had moved from his flat and was going out more. It sounded as though, from a position of feeling almost completely stuck in life, he had begun to move on—and I was really pleased to hear this. The critical, harsh and unforgiving voices within him that had emerged after his early life had begun to be replaced by kinder, gentler, firmer, more reassuring tones that put him and his well-being first. Compared with Matt's previous existence, such a psychological position was much more likely to lead towards health and his feeling good in a way that he had never done in his life—or at least not for many years.

* * *

Even more than the rest of us, children and younger people are sensitive to what happens to them—some more than others, depending on circumstances and temperament. As in each of the above cases, where children and younger people have been frightened, made to feel unsafe or hurt at the hands of others, they can derive significant benefit from psychotherapy of one kind or another, with or without formal mindfulness practice. Once the child has developed the ability to communicate, their feelings and meanings can be mindfully understood, connected with, and where necessary their suffering can often eventually be reduced. The creation of a safe space within therapy can finally allow the problematic feelings to be acknowledged, talked about, and worked through over time. As this gradual process of emotional acceptance and understanding continues, the feelings often lose their high emotional charge and become integrated into more healthy functioning.

When a child or young person has been affected in a negative way by their early experiences, it is important that they receive appropriate help. Early treatment, where psychological problems persist and do not resolve by themselves, can help to avoid further and perhaps deeper and more long-lasting problems later in life. Sometimes, though, psychological issues—a particular vulnerability—might not be identified when a person is young; having been quietly present for all of the person's life, they may come to the surface only in adulthood—sometimes when life has become more difficult for a particular reason. Such cases are discussed in the next chapter.

7

Mindful Treatment of the Adult

> A person should not strive to eliminate their complexes, but to get into accord with them: they are legitimately what directs our conduct in the world.
>
> Sigmund Freud

As an adult you, I—we—often feel as though we are *meant* to be OK. We're *meant* to have learned enough during childhood and adolescence so that we can cope by ourselves in the adult world, without the help of others: and cope more or less alone, no matter what we are doing or how we are feeling. Who needs to confide in others, and listen to them? Not me. That is what many of us believe, and it is the psychological rule by which we operate: so when things go wrong for us somehow, and we don't feel good or healthy for an extended period of time, it can come as a shock.

At such times, the kinds of feeling that we can experience may be unfamiliar—sensations of anxiety or panic, for example. Quite often it is difficult for us to accept these feelings—never mind what they might be trying to tell us about what has happened in our lives and how we are leading them. Whether we welcome them or not, such negative feelings may be a sign that some change in us is required, and that we too might benefit from good psychotherapy as adults. However, needing others to help us may make us feel uncomfortable, going against our views of ourselves as independent adults. These strong feelings, though—distress signals, in effect—may be a sign that indeed we do need others to help us, and that we cannot make it alone, whatever we may be trying to do. If this is so and we can temporarily let go of our pride as adults, allowing our hidden feelings of vulnerability to be aired and ourselves to be cared for, then we may benefit greatly.

In slight contrast to work with children, psychotherapy between adults takes place between consenting, mature people. Since both parties are adult, there is the potential for great freedom of feeling and thought. Nothing is off-limits. Nothing is too taboo. Desires, diaries, and dreams[1] can be integrated into the work and explored.

1. For a useful introduction to dreams, see Peters, M. (2005). *Dreamwork: Using your dreams as the way to self-discovery and personal development*. London: Gaia.

Any aspect of a person's experience can be usefully mentioned, interpreted and included in the shared, mindful understanding of the psychological issues involved. It is a wonderful gift, and one that is easily overlooked in the day-to-day practice of therapy: the sole aim of the work is that the person gradually comes to feel better.

Permission to Live: Feelings of depression in Alan, a 41-year-old man – 16 sessions

According to his letter of referral, Alan was struggling greatly with feelings of depression and wished to address the problems psychologically. I was interested to read that like many people he had often asked for a psychological approach to be taken but, for one reason or another, these requests had been declined by his GP.

When he stepped into my room, I saw that Alan had a striking, black, craggy face. It was obvious from the look in his eyes that he was a proud man, but one who had also suffered a great deal.

'I just get to the point, you know, when I feel so low that I wonder if it's worth going on'.

I wondered if these periods had any particular triggers.

'None that I'm aware of. I'm just tired of being so weak. I'm a strong man—always have been—and I despise myself for being so pathetic at these times. Then, when I begin to think like this, my mood dips even lower, and I start to think of ending it.'

'As we all would, in that situation.'

Alan looked sternly into my eyes. 'Do you know what I mean?'

'Indeed I do,' I said, not about to disagree with him at this stage. By this time I was wondering what it was underlying this behaviour, what was driving it: with the result that I myself was left feeling a little anxious.

Alan said that part of the problem was that his whole life had collapsed. As a younger man he had worked on the railway, and for some years had greatly enjoyed his career as a manager; but then the problems started. A junior colleague of his, he said, had been—from Alan's point of view—very unfairly picked on by a senior manager. Alan, being fair-minded, could not bear to see this happening. To try to stop it he got between the two men, with the result that the offending man was disciplined. This took over a year: but then the problems got worse. The senior manager began to try to bully Alan 'into submission'; extra work was forced on him, complaints about him were filed.

'Understandably, your stress levels were increasing.'

'Correct. I could have coped with that alone, I think. It wasn't racist—I'd been through some of that before; it was unpleasant, done by idiots, but I coped and survived. This was different. It felt more personal. At the same time my wife, whom I loved dearly, began to turn away from me. Our marriage eventually recovered, but it was a shaky time.'

Bad news. What happened then?

'I felt like I was cracking up; I mean, I *was* cracking up. I couldn't do anything I usually could—and I was a very good manager normally. I was in tears on the platform; I'd won company prizes previously. I tried to cling on, cling on: but I couldn't do it any more. They had the doctor examine me; he took one look and they sent me to hospital. Put me on medication. I never got back to where I was.'

This was a hard story to hear. Like many people I meet, Alan had seemed to have everything going well for him when he was struck by ill fortune. After his first stay in hospital and when he didn't recover quickly, he left the company. The couple moved to another part of the country to try and make a new start. But, he said, the feelings kept following him around even now, twelve years after the most difficult time. I wondered who was in Alan's life now, apart from his wife.

'No one. After what happened I'm not prepared to let anyone close to me any more. Not even my son. We don't see much of each other.' He was in his early twenties, had now moved away to London and seemed to be making his own way in life. In other words, Alan was quite lonely and spent much of his time brooding about how things had gone wrong in his life, how he felt he had messed things up, and wishing that they could be better—but not knowing how to make them better.

On getting to know Alan, I found him very likeable. In some ways he was a kind and tolerant man, which showed in the courteous way he treated me—keen not to make too much of a fuss, and to an extent looking after *my* needs. After hearing the story of the development of his symptoms, I was wondering why the difficulties with both his superior at work and his wife had left him in such a reduced, apparently weak and powerless condition, for over a decade. It seemed to me that there were likely to be other psychological factors that were involved. I wondered with him what his childhood was like. How were his mother and father? Were they psychologically available, present and warm for him, or were they different? Sometimes our experience with our parents is important for our later difficulties, sometimes not; in this case it was.

'Well, you couldn't imagine a more difficult man than my father.'

Alan explained that he knew that his father meant well; but in a faltering voice, suggesting the power of the emotion that he was feeling in the telling, Alan said that his father, a Jamaican who had brought his family to Britain in the 1960s, had been extraordinarily hard on him when he was growing up. He had been a mathematician, a man of the old school, and had overvalued correctness in family life as well as at work. His father, Alan remembered, had never been openly affectionate or warm towards him. Rather, he remembered being shouted at to 'tie up your laces properly' or 'shine those shoes', over and over again until the job, whatever it was and however unimportant it was, had been done to perfection.

'And how did that leave you feeling, when you were growing up?'

'Scared of doing anything wrong.'

Why?

'Because it felt as though if I did, the whole world would cave in. And I coped with that by always pushing myself hard and doing my best, especially for others.' I wondered how this left Alan's relationship with his father.

'Well, it should have been fine. But the problem was, by the age of fourteen I had the sense that I wanted to be an architect—my grades at school were good enough. But he didn't want that. He wanted me to do what he called 'a man's job'—like the railways. I wasn't sure about that. But then it happened.'

What?

'He died. I came back from school one day, and there were police at the front door, Mum in tears. He'd been hit by a lorry while driving. Complete accident on the lorry driver's part. There was nothing to be done.'

This loss of a parent for Alan was clearly a great one. How did it affect him? Alan thought about this for a moment.

'I never knew if I was good enough.'

That made good psychological sense, I thought. Since Freud, we have been aware of the potential psychological meaning of a man's relationship with his father, and of the personal complications that can result when this relationship is difficult or—as in my own case—completely absent. I didn't mention this fact to Alan for now, but I had it in mind. It struck me that we were a bit similar, both needing to work out what it meant to be a 'good enough' man, since there's no need to push ourselves too hard. We've nothing to prove to anyone.

At this time, though, I still couldn't *quite* understand why Alan had found life as a younger man so difficult.

'I felt, pretty constantly, that I had to prove myself as a guy. I went into the railways because I thought that was what Dad would have wanted. I was a black man in a largely white workforce, but that wasn't all of it And when I was there, I did as good a job as I could. Obviously, that meant looking out for others sometimes. I did that at home. Come to think of it, my wife, who I also looked after very well, said that I was running about for everyone apart from myself.'

And I wondered, why was that?

'In particular, Alan, was that because you had so little sense of yourself, and what you needed? And maybe, on top of that, your Dad left you with a sense that, as a person and a man, pure and simple, you were *not good enough*?' I said this compassionately, but felt that it might well be an important idea for Alan. He had tears in his eyes.

'In my own self, I'm never good enough. I'm weak. I feel like the weakling that he always said I was. Perhaps he was right about me after all. I remember when I was playing football in the park with my friends when I was about ten. He was watching. And the way he saw it, I just couldn't get it right. At first he was shouting, then he marched into the middle of the pitch and showed me how he wanted me to strike the ball. Everyone else was looking, and I just felt like dying of shame.'

Alan was moved to tears at this point, and I was moved also. Some of the basic things that a child needs—approval simply for being themselves—had clearly been denied him; instead he had been exposed to a withholding, conditional type of love.

One psychological result of this was that he, like many people, had often been striving in his life to be better than he was, because he never felt good enough in himself. We reached this conclusion—both happy and sad—together; it was a relief,

I think, for both of us. We felt that we had come closer to understanding some of the psychological origins of his worries.

Following this point in our work together, we took some steps forward. We achieved

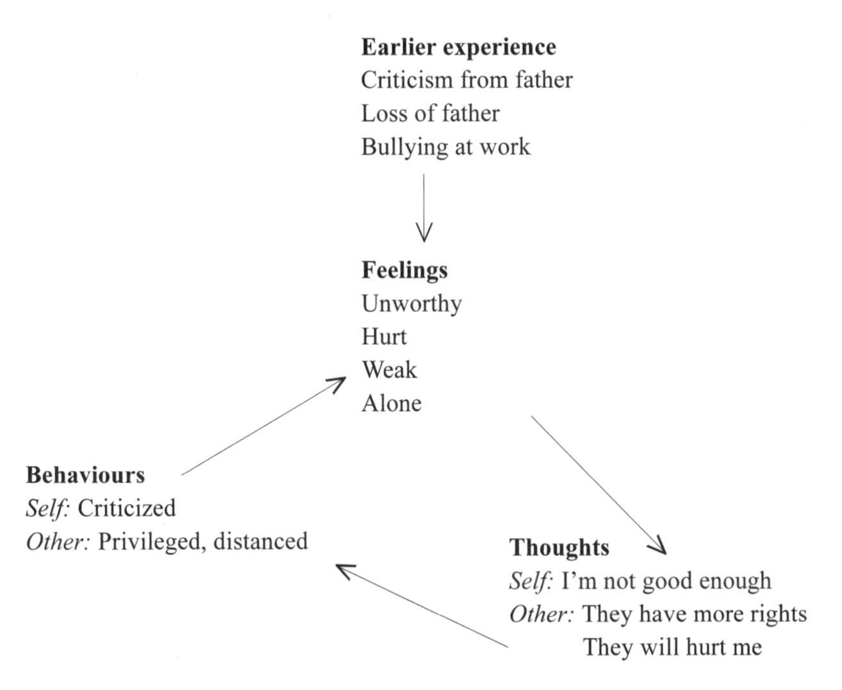

Figure 7.1 Alan's formulation

a little clarity now. Together we came to understand how Alan's patterns of relating—trying over-hard to care for others—had emerged; they had been a defence against, and a way of avoiding, his own feeling that he was unworthy of care and love. But like many people who behave in this way, his over-caring for others had led to his own downfall. We also became clear about his tendency to be very harshly critical of himself, and sometimes of others. Feeling threatened in certain situations, he would turn on himself or others, resulting either way in his feeling lower and still more isolated and unworthy of love.

In our therapy together we were able to consider the working of these patterns. To take his over-caring for others as an example, we were able to consider that Alan sometimes attempted to over-care for me—for instance by asking how I was feeling, when it was his feelings that mattered here in therapy. Similarly, I would note turns in the conversation when he would be very harshly overcritical of himself—or indeed would look sternly or critically at me, leaving me feeling momentarily slightly intimidated, as at the beginning of the therapy. In both cases we were able to wonder together whether these behaviours were really necessary, or whether for Alan, as an independent, adult man, they were redundant. Allied to this we were able to consider the underlying feelings that Alan most dreaded: the idea that he was simply not good enough, a failure as a man, a waste of time as a human being.

As you might expect, this was moving work—not least since we had both been short of fatherly support when we were growing up, and had had to some extent to develop our own masculine identities, as many men have to today. But difficult though this work was—and sometimes the tortuous nature of it was obvious to see on the lines of Alan's face as we talked—we made progress; and as is sometimes the case in psychological work, we both had a clear sense of the change that had quietly occurred. Alan summed this up well: 'Although my Dad died all those years ago, he's still been with me ever since, barking over my shoulder, saying that I'm not good enough. But now I'm starting to feel that his influence isn't so strong.'

Around this time in our work, we also talked about what it meant to Alan to be a man, including how it was to be aware of a whole range of feelings about himself. We looked at things he used to do and enjoy, like playing or watching rugby—even wondering if he could somehow get involved again. And we talked through some of his mixed feelings about his father—the love, the anger, the sadness and the loss.

'Can you be your own man?'

'I think I could begin to. I never thought I'd hear myself saying this, but I feel now that I can give myself permission to be who I want to be. I don't want to be an explorer or a dancer now, but if I wanted to that'd be OK. That wasn't true in the past. The old boy was holding me back.'

In contrast to some of his sad facial expressions during our sessions, Alan smiled wistfully. I had the feeling that together we had managed to lift a large weight from him. The atmosphere in the room had eased markedly since we had begun our work.

We had spent very little time, over the weeks, talking about his son, which was a sign of how overwhelming he felt his difficulties to be; but it was striking now that

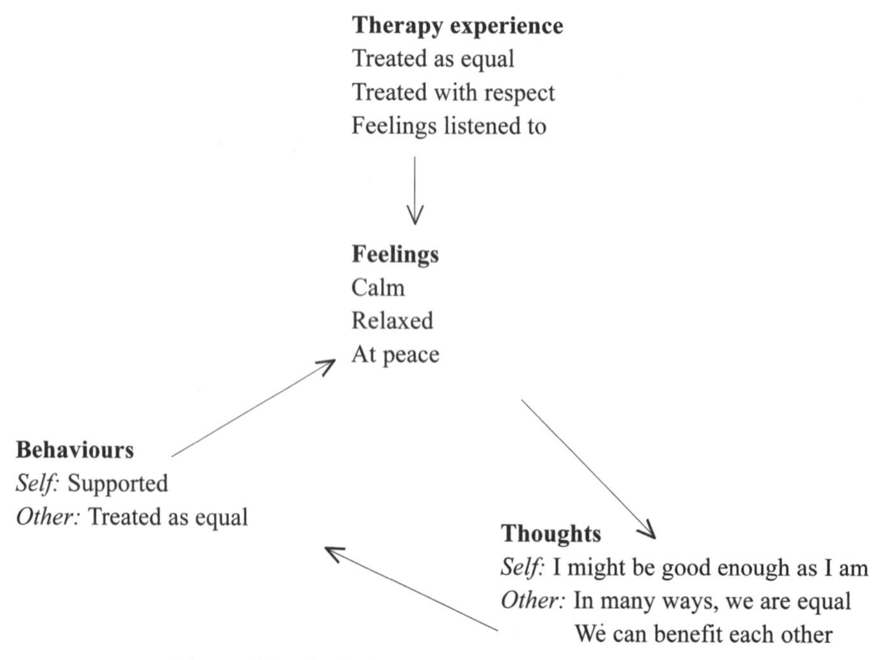

Figure 7.2 Alan's formulation at the end of therapy

Alan felt more able to be a good parent and a good father. He had come to feel closer to his wife. They both seemed to enjoy the contrast compared to how things had been before.

'I know more now what I'm doing with Lee. Previously, I was so confused. Who was I? Strong Dad, weak Dad, who was I going to be? Now there's no question: I'll be much more myself. I can say things from the heart now'.

Alan was ready to move on, and was looking ahead. I liked Alan a great deal, and was really pleased that we had helped to begin to change his persistent negative view of himself. By the time we had finished our work, Alan was feeling so good that he asked his psychiatrist to reduce the level of his anti-depressant; and I had a hunch that even on a reduced dose, he was doing fine. I also gathered that his relationship with his son Lee was closer than it had ever been—and looked as if it might remain that way. With me as a witness to the process, Alan had given himself permission to be the man he was, and was now ready to give his son permission —if it was required— to be the man he could be.

Betrayal: Feelings of post-traumatic stress in Hilary, a 47-year-old woman – 6 sessions

Hilary was a formidable woman to meet. While many people coming to see me for the first time are quite anxious, if Hilary felt that way she didn't show it. Instead, she asked about the design of the building in a manner that suggested she knew much more about it than I did, or ever would do. I noticed that I felt a bit intimidated, and a little controlled. She sat down briskly, as though she meant to do business.

'There's something very seriously wrong with me. There must be.'

'Why do you say that?'

'I'm a strong, capable woman. I have been for years. But recently I've just fallen to pieces.'

Hilary described strong feelings of anxiety, depression and panic. Sometimes the feelings were clearly linked to a trigger, like having to be in an enclosed space; but at other times feelings of terror seemed to rise up without any encouragement at all, leaving her temporarily paralysed with fear. Understandably this made her normal way of life difficult, if not impossible.

'I could just about cope with that; but then a few months after this all started, my sleep was affected. I kept having nightmares. Then, in the day, I was finding it increasingly stressful and, as I felt worse, I kept having bad thoughts that kept just popping into my head, uninvited. I try and push them away, but they keep on coming back. I feel like I'm at my wits' end. I can barely go anywhere outside now; I don't feel safe. It's as though something terrible is about to happen. That's how it feels.'

Hearing about this group of symptoms, including the nightmares and intrusive negative thoughts, I was wondering how the difficult feelings had seemed to start in the first place. Had there been anything of possible psychological significance that had recently happened to her? Hilary relaxed a little.

'Well, that's an easy one to answer. I'm a deputy head in a large state school, and I used to love my job—it had something different in it every day. But about seven months ago—June 21st, to be precise, I'll never forget the day—something terrible happened.'

'Go on.'

'It was after school. It had been a long, hot afternoon and the kids had been climbing the walls all day; there was an atmosphere in the school, you know? Sometimes you just get a feeling.'

'Yes, you do.'

'There had been trouble developing between two children and their families for months. Now it was all about to spill over into violence. A fight between two of the boys broke out, outside school. One of the older children ran back to inform the Deputy Head, David. We had got on very well up to that point. David, with another chap from the English department, went to see what was happening. By then, things had got much worse.'

I could see Hilary becoming more tense as she talked.

'By the time the two of them arrived, the fathers of the two boys had joined in—punching each other, hard. David and the other chap obviously wanted to calm things down and try to pacify the group. There were over a hundred children there, shouting and screaming. The police were called.'

'I'm with you.'

'The school receptionist had heard the noise and called me. I ran from my office, out and down to where the trouble was. Just as I got there, it happened. David had gone over to one of the fathers, in an effort to try to talk to him: but I saw a glint of light. I quickly realized what had happened. Quick as a flash, the guy had pulled a knife on David and stuck it in his chest. It's all a bit hazy after that.'

I wondered what else Hilary remembered.

'David fell to the floor, I think. He was clutching his chest. I knew that we had to save him, so we tried to stem the blood flow while an ambulance was called. All the kids around us were screaming. It was terrible.' It sounded it.

'For a while it wasn't clear that he'd survive. He was terribly pale, and his pulse was weak. I really thought that we might lose him. Everything raced through my mind.'

Hilary was moving anxiously, and perspiring with all these difficult memories from work.

'We were very lucky. There had been a hoax call close to the area—probably by one of our kids—twenty minutes earlier, so an ambulance was nearby. They pulled up, gave David oxygen and took him to casualty. He made it, but they said afterwards that it was touch and go for a while. He was off sick for 3 months while the wound healed.'

It sounded like a traumatic event to witness, but I wondered how Hilary herself had viewed it, and how she had felt.

'I'm normally the coper, the strong one: 'Hilary the Rock'—that's what everyone always says. That's how I was; that's how I got my job in the first place, and that's how I was afterwards. Right after the stabbing, in the following days, I felt very shaken, then things seemed to calm down. I just thought to myself: I've seen a lot of things in my life: car accidents; I had two miscarriages. But somehow I've always come through. I didn't think this time would be any different.'

'And to begin with, it didn't seem to be.'

'No. And that's how it stayed. The police were involved, the man was charged, the children settled down—though one or two took longer than others, and needed help from counsellors to do so.'

Fine. So that was that—was it?

'I heard a group talking about what happened. David was there, and I heard him say that he thought it was my fault that he had got hurt, that I had let him down.'

The disbelief was still evident on Hilary's face. I wondered how that had left her feeling.

'Within half an hour, I felt as though my whole system had shut down. I thought I had the flu or something. I had a school governors' meeting to go to, and I could barely stand up for feelings of fear and panic. I ran to the WC to be sick: and do you know, I really haven't felt right since. I was OK before that; but that's when the nightmares all started. All I see in them is violent images. I'm standing there, but often I have no voice and can't do anything about what's happening; and then in the daytime, particularly when I'm feeling tired and stressed, my head is filled with thoughts of what happened—of the violence: but also of what David did to me. We had been so close before.'

I needed to explore their relationship a little further. Hilary explained that for many years she had acted as David's mentor. He had wanted promotion, but lacked organizational skills. Hilary, using her own time in the process, had helped David to acquire these skills, allowing him to progress upwards within the school—as well as to apply for headteacher's jobs elsewhere, although he hadn't got one yet.

'That was it; that was it. I was so bitter about him and what he did to me. I'd not only resuscitated his career, I also helped to save his life. And then he stabs me in the back like that. It was devastating to me; it felt as if my whole world had caved in. If he could do that, what was the world coming to? We'd worked so closely, and I'd tried to do so much for him.'

Hilary's story of what had happened, and her symptoms, suggested to me that she was suffering symptoms of post-traumatic stress[2]—including frequent intrusive thoughts, and nightmares—that had been brought on by the incident and then the subsequent betrayal she had suffered. It seemed strange that her strong symptoms began only after she heard about her colleague's action. I wondered why this was.

'Well, call me a woman of the old school, but I've always thought trust was very important. When I was training as a teacher and beginning my career, we all trusted each other, pretty much. We looked out for one another and looked after one another.

---

2. See, e.g. Clark, D.M. & Ehlers, A. (2004). Post-traumatic stress disorder: from cognitive theory to therapy. In R. Leahey (ed.). *Contemporary Cognitive Therapy: Theory, research, and practice.* New York: Guilford Press: 141–160.

If one person was struggling—maybe with a particular child, or something at home, we'd try to help as best we could. That's the approach I've always tried to take, right throughout my career. Trust. It's been so important to me.'

'And that's why it seemed such a terrible blow when, after an event such as the stabbing, David seemed to betray you.'

'I think that might be right. That's when all the problems started—within minutes of hearing what he'd said.'

We now had a clearer picture of the psychological symptoms and their possible origins. There was at least one thread that ran through Hilary's life, and that seemed to be connected with her feelings of post-traumatic stress. That was her belief, beginning quite early on in her adult life, about trust and how trust was important to her. It was the catastrophic breakdown of trust that seemed to lead to the psychological difficulties.

Since the matter of trust seemed so important to Hilary, we spent some time talking about it and what it meant to her. This enabled us to do something that felt really important—to begin to trust each other a little and to develop the therapeutic relationship between us. To begin with Hilary showed clear signs of distress, being tearful in most sessions when we discussed how her trust in others had been damaged by what David had done; but gradually, little by little, her distress reduced and we were able to reflect together on part of her loss.

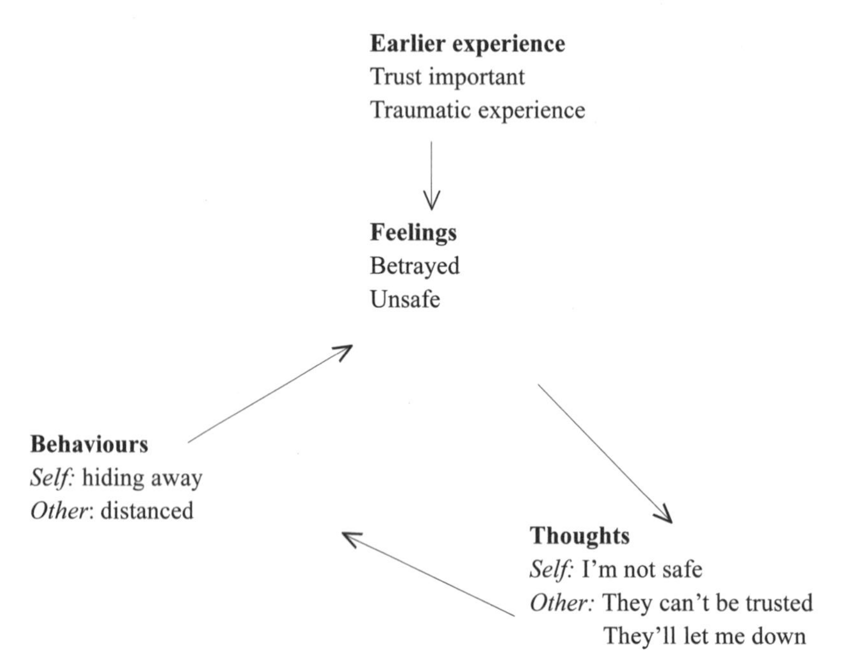

Figure 7.3 Hilary's formulation

---

3. For an excellent guide on mindfulness, including up-to-date references, see Kabat-Zinn, J. (2004). *Full Catastrophe Living: 15th anniversary edn.* London: Piatkus. For an academic view, see Hayes, S.C., Follette, V.M. & Linehan, M.M. (2004). *Mindfulness and Acceptance: Expanding the cognitive behavioural tradition.* New York: Guilford Press.

As part of this work of getting to know one another and coming to feel comfortable in each other's company, we practised a little mindfulness meditation.[3] In its most basic form, mindfulness can be very simple indeed—people are mindful of the movement and play of their attention. Typically, we are easily distracted and our attention shifts quickly from one area of our experience to another; but in mindfulness meditation people are gently encouraged to be aware of the subtle movements of their attention as it fixes on certain objects, thoughts or feelings—and then to let go of whatever their attention fixes on, to return their attention to their breathing and its rhythm. It often takes a little practice to get used to mindfulness, but very many people, including myself, find it useful from a psychological point of view. It can be used with many, if not all psychological problems providing it is used safely, so that people who might be at risk—perhaps the very anxious, or those experiencing psychosis—use it with caution, especially to begin with.

Hilary, like many other people suffering from post-traumatic stress, also found mindfulness helpful. After a couple of weeks of daily practice she found that her feelings of anxiety were a little less strong. She explained that the negative thoughts that intruded in her mind—from low-level worries about being outside and being safe, for example—seemed a little more 'distant' from her. This is a common experience for many people when they try mindfulness over a period. To begin with, before we become 'mindful', any negative thoughts and feelings that we commonly have can trigger in us great feelings of distress and suffering, but being 'mindful' of them, and gradually coming to accept the thoughts and feelings as part of our experience—whatever they are—can allow us to feel a greater sense of calmness and peace. This is the process that Hilary had begun. Naturally she felt good that she had gained at least a slight sense of relief from this part of our work, and I was glad about that, too. We had also accomplished our first task together—coming to work with each other and to trust each other just a little. But I felt that we could build on this foundation together, and take our psychological work further.

Since it seemed to me that Hilary's symptoms of post-traumatic stress were linked to certain key events and since, importantly, there was no other obvious history of trauma in her earlier life—nor equally importantly, certain signs of trauma-related functioning like dissociation (where a traumatized person goes 'blank' often, for shorter or longer periods) or self-harm—we decided that we would try to address some of her symptoms with some sessions of eye movement densensitization and reprocessing (EMDR).[4] This would be woven into our work together. Hilary agreed to this.

In EMDR people are encouraged to experience images, thoughts (or cognitions), feelings or sensations associated with traumatic situations while they maintain awareness of a 'bilateral stimulus'—something presented by the therapist that moves regularly and repeatedly for a number of short periods. People are often asked to watch the therapist's hand as it moves backwards and forwards, to be aware of the

---

4. See Shapiro, F. (2001). *Eye Movement Desensitization and Reprocessing*. New York: Guilford Press; Mollon, P. (2005). *EMDR and the energy therapies*. London: Karnac.

therapist's tapping on their hands, or to hear a sound as it moves from ear to ear on a set of headphones. As the person maintains awareness of the traumatic material as well as of the stimulus, the therapist—in this case me—is looking for 'clinical change': signs that the traumatic material, which may not have been fully processed in the mind, has been moved on and properly integrated into memory. Often one sign of this is that the person's interpretation of what has happened in their lives has changed. As is always the case with EMDR I explained the procedure to Hilary, also mentioning that previous, apparently forgotten material might surface during it. This is a common effect of EMDR, as associations between memories are uncovered and made clear as the traumatic material is processed.

We discussed which aspect of her traumatic memories Hilary would like to address first. She felt that the image of seeing David lying there was most pressing, with her feeling that he could easily live or die and the sense that she was helpless to do anything to save him. Hilary rated this image and the feelings associated with it as nine out of ten on a scale of perceived distress known as the 'subjective units of disturbance' (or 'SUDs'). Hilary focused on that image and the thought of being helpless, and maintained awareness of any bodily sensations that were coming up. I turned on my light bar, which presented her with the bilateral stimulus at a comfortable speed. I allowed twenty-four sweeps of the light. As is usual in EMDR and in any other type of therapy, I watched her reactions carefully; and when the light stopped, I said:

'Take a deep breath and let it go. What were you getting?'

'I could see David's eyes. It was after he was stabbed. I'm right there with him.'

We took that image, and those feelings, for ten further sweeps of the light. I could see the agitation in Hilary; she was shifting around uncomfortably in her chair, with her face showing a frown as her eyes moved.

'What are you getting now?'

'I'm trying to help, trying desperately to organize the others. If only someone would just call an ambulance.'

The image was moving and I sensed clinical change. We continued with further sweeps of the light, a little longer now that Hilary was feeling more confident with the technique. Tears had begun to well up in her eyes. In EMDR, though it may seem strange, we continue to process the emotion until it passes.

'I can see him going. I'm taking his pulse. His breathing is getting lighter, the colour fading from his cheeks. I'm looking around at the others there. I can see their faces, the shock on their faces.'

'Go with it.'

'Powerless.'

'Go with that.'

More sweeps of the light. I watched Hilary's face and body carefully for signs of change. Her tears had ceased for now, but she seemed to be lost in memory. Where was she now?

'Something strange happened there. I just had a memory that I hadn't had for years, decades. I was a young girl, about seven, and for a short time, a very short time, my mother was ill. She had to go away for a couple of days, and I had to go to my aunt's. I didn't know why.'

Very often in EMDR, people make associations and links to earlier memories, sometimes from decades before, that they had previously been unaware of.

'How did you feel then?'

'The same. Helpless. As though there was nothing I could do.'

'OK. Go with that.'

Then, as also quite often happens in EMDR, Hilary felt frightened as the memories came up. Though it doesn't feel good at the time—I've had strong feelings of panic myself from EMDR, and it can be scary—these feelings are often a good, healthy sign: a sign that the traumatic material is being processed and worked through. I watched on empathically as Hilary went through the feelings of anxiety and panic again, which she had first experienced when she was young. Further sweeps of the light.

'I'm feeling so frightened. I don't know where Mama has gone, and I don't know why I was in this new place. No one said anything. I was—I am—really afraid.'

Where did she feel that in her body?

'In my legs.'

We went with that. With a few further sweeps of the light, Hilary's anxiety was visibly beginning to ease; she looked firmer, more confident, and her voice reflected that.

'After a few days, Mama and Papa came to pick us up. I was so happy to see her. I felt so safe then: so different from what went before.'

Hilary's non-verbal behaviour reflected this; there was a smile of acknowledgement on her face. We were approaching the end of the session for the day, and so closed the session safely. By this time, Hilary rated her SUDs at the initial image of David lying there at three out of ten. When an SUDs score is more than one out of ten, there is often still work to do.

At the next session Hilary felt that she still found the idea of David's betrayal highly disturbing, and said that she wanted to work with that. Often in EMDR one channel of memories is addressed and resolved before moving on to look at further channels; but here it seemed to us that a close link between these events might exist. So we used the image of the problematic conversation, and the sense of helplessness that remained. It was experienced as very highly distressing, at ten out of ten. We did a few sweeps of the light.

'The image changed, but the feeling stayed the same. I'm back at my auntie's. I was seeing things in my mind's eye that I haven't thought about for years—the floor in her kitchen; the wallpaper in her living room, peeling at the corners. And the feeling of helplessness, of being out of control, was the same.'

'Go with it.'

'In my legs again.'

We went with that, and did more light sweeps.

'That was it. For that short time as a young girl, I felt so helpless and out of control when we had to go to my aunt's. I'd been so close to my mother, but there was no explanation. I felt as though it was the end of the world.'

We went with that. More sweeps of the light. I watched again, as Hilary's face and body gradually relaxed. Her face lightened and she settled back more in her chair.

'The phone call was like being taken to my aunt's. Both times it was like the end of the world; but I see that it's not. I was a helpless little girl then.'

We went with that adult recognition of her position as a child. And now?

'I see a connection now that I've never seen before. After the aunt thing, that's why I valued so much—or maybe overvalued—trust in everything I did. I was terrified of being abandoned again, and left like that young girl.'

Again, we went with that. We did three more sets of sweeps with the light.

'I see myself giving the younger me what I needed: the reassurance that Mama was coming back, that she was going to be all right, that everything could be OK.'

More sweeps of the light.

'I see that everything can be OK. I can be safe now. It was a difficult situation, but I did my best for David, and that's all I can do. Just because he wants to criticize me—that's his problem. I did my best, and that's all I can do.'

More sweeps of the light. It clearly felt to me that we were moving towards a good resolution of the issues. Hilary's following comments confirmed my feeling.

'I can make it now; I can be safe now. I'm not that little girl any more. I love her very much, and she was loved. But I can be safe now.'

I knew, when I heard these words, that we had moved towards the end of the EMDR reprocessing that we were doing and, indeed, the work that we needed to do together.

It had been a session of strong feelings. Certainly for Hilary as, making use of EMDR, she moved through and made connections between experiences in ways that she had never done before; but it was also moving for me to watch her do this and to help her through this process, as she made new, spontaneous realizations. EMDR is always satisfying for me to perform, too, because it confirms what I have always felt within me since I was a troubled young man—it is people's earlier experiences that, by a chain of learned associations, prepare the way for their later psychological issues. That connecting, and resolving of the difficulties in the presence of another, caring person, can have a powerful healing effect.

Together, after we had stopped doing EMDR Hilary and I reflected together on what had come out of our work. I wondered how she was seeing the whole set of traumatic events now.

'Much more connected. To begin with, my memories of the stabbing, and also of David's betrayal were in pieces—like a mirror that had been shattered. But in EMDR, everything seemed to be so much more of a *whole*; I remembered the whole sequence of events much more clearly than before—from hearing about the fight for the first time, to seeing David go off to hospital. But at the same time, it all seems so much less frightening now.'

This all fitted well with what is known about the effects of EMDR. It is often the case that people in EMDR find themselves recalling previously forgotten details of traumatic events much more clearly than previously. I also wondered how, in retrospect,

Hilary viewed the connection with the early memories that had resurfaced, to her surprise.

'It made it all much clearer to me; doing the mindfulness helped in that, too. I feel that since that time I've always made a big thing of trust with others, and felt trust to be particularly important. I'm very cagey with people when I first get to meet them, for example; that's also at least part of the reason why I always felt trust to be very important at work. It felt to me as though if I didn't set things up like that to begin with—as I did for David for many years—then things could really get out of control, and I would feel terrible. That's how it felt.'

Then, of course, things *did* get out of control on the day of the stabbing.

'And that's why it was so hard for me. It felt, as I said, as if my world was falling apart.'

'How does it feel now?'

'It feels as though I'm safer than I thought I was. I have a slightly different perspective now. I can see that the world is a complicated place, and people do leave us and betray us sometimes.'

They may not mean to, but they do. To do an extra check on her symptoms we checked her disturbance ratings for all potentially difficult areas—the stabbing, the phone call, and the initial sense of abandonment in childhood. In each case the SUDs were zero or one, which is a sign that the memory has been worked through using EMDR and is unlikely to cause future problems. Hilary and I were both happy with that.

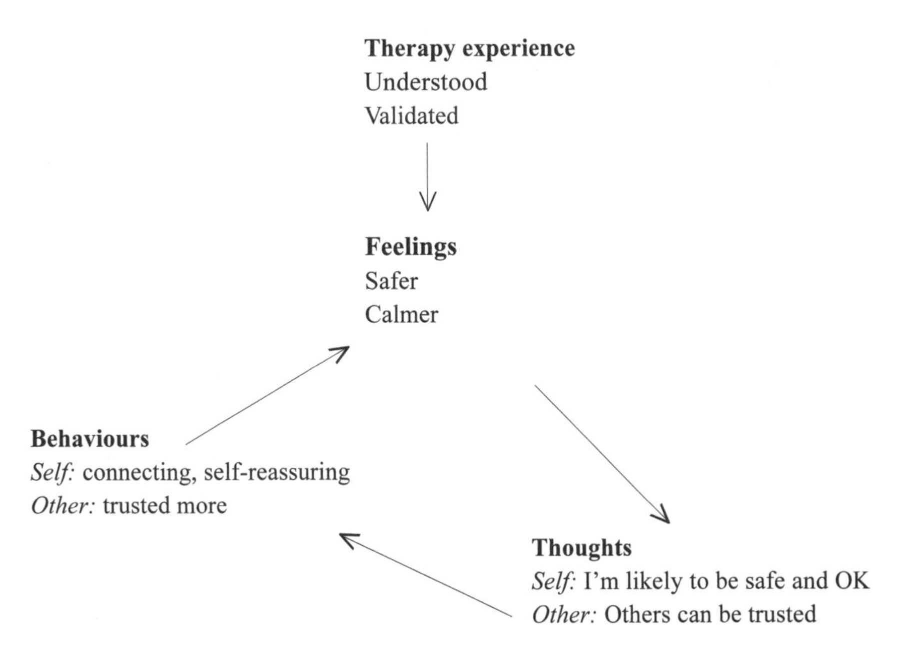

Figure 7.4 Hilary's formulation after therapy

By this time in our work—and we were well into the last of our sessions—Hilary was feeling so much better that she was considering a return to work. As often happens with EMDR after a one-off trauma in a previously psychologically healthy person, her symptoms—the feelings of anxiety and depression, as well as intrusive thoughts, feelings of threat, and nightmares—had lifted. Our work, together with the mindfulness that she was still doing on a daily basis, had helped to restore normal life again for Hilary by and large, and we were both glad about that—but perhaps not surprised.

Finding a Centre: Emotional management difficulties in Catherine, a 33-year-old woman – 18 sessions

Catherine wasn't the type of person that people generally associate with having psychological issues. She was a trim, impressive figure in her business suit when I met her for the first time. She spoke in clipped, carefully measured words which made me, as a reaction to her, feel more than usually careful and controlled about what I was saying and doing myself. However, soon after she started to talk her composure broke, leading quickly to tears.

'I've been in this state, or in and out of it, for years. Nothing's really helped me, and no one's really listened. I'm really not sure any more if life's worth living; I live a kind of half-life. I know what I'm missing, but I can't get there. I just don't get it.'

I felt moved by Catherine's distress and interested in how she shifted quite quickly between moods—being quite controlled and controlling one minute, followed by being tearful and very upset the next. Catherine said that these moods had been with her since she was growing up. As with many people, they changed according to the amount of stress she was under; at times when she felt stressed, or threatened, the feelings were experienced as being less controllable.

'I hate it when it's like that, but there's nothing I can do about it.'

I wondered if this were true. I also wondered whether Catherine's symptoms had taken any other forms over the years. She smiled.

'You're joking, aren't you? I've had everything I can.'

I wasn't joking, not least since I'd experienced myself at least some of the issues that had been affecting her. Could we make a kind of list?

'Well, when I was around 13 I became anorexic. That lasted for about three years, until they took me into hospital for it. I was on drips. For a while they said it was unsure whether I'd live or die; I was hovering in and out of consciousness. After that it seemed too risky to carry on, so I became bulimic, bingeing every two days or so. It ruined my teeth, of course, but no one knows that I wear the plate.'

OK. And after that?

'Since then I've always been underweight, but my diet has been acceptable most of the time. I decided to put most of my energy into studying. I got a business degree, and an MBA. While I was doing all that I got a great kick from it, and from the work that followed. Working, getting on, having more responsibility, helped me to fight off the bad feelings. For a long time they disappeared altogether, and I pushed them to the back of my mind. No one else at work would know that there was any kind of problem.'

'But underneath, there was.'

'Yes.'

We had been talking for only a short while—a few minutes—and already it was clear that Catherine had undergone at least three shifts in her emotional state. She had begun the session in quite an emotionally contained, dominant way. She then progressed to feeling tearful, and now she was in a more quiet, reflective state in which she was able to step back from herself and consider what was happening. All this made me wonder about her early life experiences. Often such rapid changes originate in early relationships that are such that we do not feel securely cared for, and in which the care received feels unreliable to us. Catherine fitted this description.

'My father could have been the best. I say "could have" because, while he had so much to offer—he was a bright, strong man at work and at home—he was not there much. He worked for an oil company, and had to travel. We only saw him every few weeks, and even then our time with him was short. We knew, my brother and I, that he loved us—but at a distance. It felt as though what he gave us wasn't enough.'

Mother? Catherine laughed a hollow laugh.

'Well, you could say that it was the opposite: we saw too much of her. She was an unreliable woman. She had married young— too young: it was a shotgun wedding after she had my brother when she was 17. She'd had a dreadful relationship with her own mother, who had kicked her out entirely when she was 12, so she was hardly ready to be a mother herself. Looking back, I think she had post-natal depression after having me; for years, I remember, when I was growing up you never knew where you were with her. She was unaffectionate—hardly ever touching us or hugging us. She also had a vicious temper. You never knew where you stood. One minute she'd be your best friend, smiling into your eyes; the next, apparently without warning, she'd shout and scream at us. All that went on until I left home to go to university.'

Catherine's memories of this were clearly still painful, and as she talked there were tears streaming down her cheeks.

'It sounds as though, growing up as a girl and young woman, you had a lonely time of it.'

Catherine shed more tears. It felt, she said, as though she'd been left to cope alone throughout her life so far. She explained that she had met various men in her work, where she was well respected and good at her job.

'But I have difficulties letting anyone in. There have been people in my life, yes, but I've never let anyone stay around. I've always pushed them away. The thought of having other people too close to me is unbearable.'

Why was that?

'Because it feels to me that they might be like my father or mother. If they're like my father, they might not be there when I need them. If they're like my mother, they might hurt me deep down, and that would feel unbearable. So you see, I keep my distance.'

I could see that. I wondered if I could also see Catherine trying to keep her

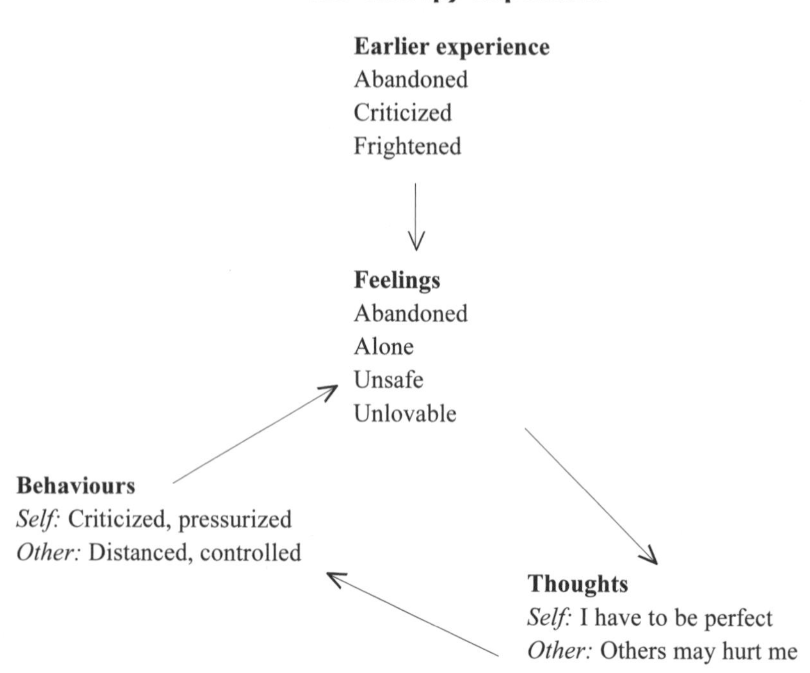

Figure 7.5 Catherine's formulation

distance from me now. It was almost as though she was saying: 'Don't try to come near me; I can't be helped, and I'm not worth helping.'

Catherine's difficulties showed at least some of the signs of what some people call a borderline personality disorder[5]—an unpleasant phrase, used mostly by people who have little or no idea about how some of the feelings actually feel. Perhaps because I've experienced some of the feelings myself, I prefer the term 'emotional management difficulty'—not least because that's what seems to be happening for such people. After experiencing early care (like Catherine's) during which their emotional needs are not met, or are only partly met by psychologically absent parents, such people do not learn the skills—often shown to us by parents as we are developing—that many of us have for managing our emotional states. Without such help these people can be prone to strong emotions, particularly when under stress, and this can lead to their feeling overwhelmed. It is quite commonly the case that at difficult times such people can feel desperate, empty and hopeless, in a way that others of us, who have perhaps had a better psychological start in life, can find hard to understand.

Also, at stressful times particularly, such people can tend to see others as more critical, abusive, punishing, rejecting or abandoning than they really are. The precise neuropsychological reasons for this are not clear, but poor early care is likely to be involved. It may be that key areas of the brain are sensitized early in life and, geared

5. For enlightening views of 'borderline personality disorder', including origins, research and treatment possibilities, see Ryle, A. (1997). *Cognitive Analytic Therapy and Borderline Personality Disorder: The model and the method.* Chichester: Wiley.

for survival at all costs, are predisposed to react, or overreact, to threat later on as we mature. These feelings can be difficult to explain to others but, if you've felt them they can seem very real. It's certainly my experience—having myself had less than ideal early care in some ways—that in my perception others can seem as if they don't really care much: why would they? part of my psyche says. Also I perceived that they're likely to be critical of me, when there's little objective reason for me to feel this. For instance, I have in my time transformed the kindest and most well-meaning group of nurses into a pack of human wolves, ready at any moment to strike, criticize or humiliate me. Yet they never did, and never would.

So when I heard Catherine talking about how she felt at difficult times, I felt I knew what she meant. I guess she sensed this too, because she kept returning for sessions. Our first task together, once the initial assessment was completed, was to work out which were the times when her feelings seemed to become most difficult and most unmanageable. We focused on two areas: her perfectionist behaviour at work, and her behaviour in her personal relationships. In both these cases, we agreed, she was busily trying to control herself, and her interactions with others, and her work. This had led her to work too hard, causing her to feel exhausted. I wondered what Catherine felt might happen if she ceased to do this. She had no doubts here, and answered immediately.

'I'd fall apart. I'd be vulnerable. People would see me for what I really am.'

What would that be?

'I'm despicable.'

Catherine's face reddened with the shame that she was feeling. 'They would leave me, and I'd be left alone to suffer.'

It felt to me as though this was a powerful moment—as though we had come close to core, underlying feelings in Catherine that had been present for most of her life. I wondered whether, just allowing her mind to float back, she connected these feelings with any particular time.

'I go back to when we lived in our second house, when I was growing up. Dad was away, as usual, and Mum must have been struggling to cope with me. I'd done something she didn't like, like breaking a couple of eggs on the floor. I have memories of her first shouting at me: "You bad, bad, girl. I hate you so much." Then, she used to pick me up and leave me to sit in the dining room, all alone. She said that I needed to think about what I had done and what sort of girl I was. She said that I'd have to sort myself out. Sort myself out. I'll have to sort myself out. That phrase has always stayed with me.'

In listening to this I was coming to feel something of Catherine's loneliness. I was getting a sense of how emotionally deprived she must have felt. What did she do?

'I'm not sure. But I think that being there, in the dining room—and for a few years it happened often —I absorbed the things she was saying. It was as though her hard voice stayed inside my mind, criticizing me, being hard on me.'

And also telling her to keep her distance from others—to try and 'sort herself out'. This might have been fine, except that it left her feeling at times very lonely.

Catherine acknowledged these feelings of loneliness in what she said, but I still had the feeling that because of what had happened, she was remaining at a distance from me. Often I felt that she would struggle very hard to cope throughout the work—living and working in hard-driving, perfectionistic ways—only to come and collapse in sessions with me. Ironically, her business was doing fantastically well at this time. Plans had been made to expand into Eastern Europe, and Catherine had been asked to take on more responsibility. But despite this apparently good news, she still felt depressed and internally fragile—not like the happy face she showed to people at work. In other words, the patterns of behaviour that had brought us to meet was largely continuing. I felt as though somehow we weren't quite able to connect emotionally, but I was content to wait, to trust my instincts, and to see what would happen between us.

Given that Catherine's internal world, following the treatment by her mother, appeared to be so harsh and had so little room for self-care, I wondered whether she might benefit from some mindfulness work. This was a particularly stressful time at work for her, so mindfulness, where the emphasis is on non-doing rather than doing, was appropriate. In doing mindfulness, Catherine had some interesting experiences. She decided to do it each day before going into work. Many people find it useful to do their mindfulness practice at that time, since it often helps them to start each day with a clear mind. A few weeks into her mindfulness practice, Catherine looked slightly different. She was a little more relaxed and her mood seemed more stable; she had been benefiting from the mindfulness. How? What had she been noticing?

'I've realized how quickly things had been moving internally. I knew about the patterns that we had talked about, but I really had no idea. Doing the breathing of the mindfulness, I became aware of the critical, pressuring voices inside my mind. When I'm under stress, and sometimes even when I'm not, they're constantly shouting at me.'

What were they saying?

'You're not good enough. It's not quick enough. It's not good enough. More, more, more; better, better, better. Or you'll fail.'

It sounded as though Catherine's internal space in her mind was very highly pressurized.

'And as soon as the tiniest thing goes wrong, or even looks like it might go wrong, the voice is there again: "Something terrible is going to happen. You won't be safe. You're really in danger."'

I wondered how those voices made her feel.

'Very upset; very threatened. No wonder I've struggled so much over the years.'

I could see that too. As is the case with many of us, Catherine had had little opportunity to develop a kind, compassionate, self-caring side to her personality. Because of the bad feelings that had been locked up inside her for these years, she treated herself badly—in ways in which she would not have treated others. I wondered how it felt for her, using mindfulness to begin to slow these psychological processes down.

'A little better. It's only a start, but I am coming to see how, driving myself on as I did, I was making life even harder for myself. Taking a little time for myself, even just a five-minute break here or there, can feel good.'

This was surely true. Just a small change in a person's habitual behaviour can begin to change how they feel. Catherine's use of the mindfulness also seemed to help increase the trust between us. She seemed to find it easier to be more open, more relaxed with me. I began to feel that compared with when she started work, and she would come and cry in sessions, we were there together, with views and feelings being exchanged between two *people*—rather than simply one person (me, the therapist) looking after another person (her, the client). In time the openness and trust between us grew to such an extent that we wondered whether Catherine might be further helped by using EMDR. I explained the possible benefits and, after giving the issue some consideration, Catherine agreed to try the technique. We wondered in particular whether EMDR might help unlock, and process, any early memories that were relevant to her later feelings. After gaining her consent and checking that she was not self-harming or dissociating, we began the next phase of our work together.

We decided to take as our initial focus Catherine's memory of when she was around six years old, and had been shouted at by her mother and told to sit in the dining room, alone. The feeling that Catherine noticed with regard to this was feeling 'empty'—something she felt quite often in her day-to-day life. The associated thought that seemed to sum up the situation best was that 'I'm a bad person'. We started there, with a few short sets of eye movements using the light bar. At first, there was no sign of change; nothing seemed to be happening at this time.

But with the fourth set of eye movements, I could see Catherine beginning to blush—a sign that we were beginning to move into an area of emotional material. What was Catherine noticing there?

'First of all I was sitting in the dining room, feeling sad and empty. That image stayed with me, and it felt bad to be there. But then I was soon aware of my mother's face.'

How did it look?

'She was really close up to me. She was angry. I was feeling terrified.'

Catherine's voice was quivering with fear as she said this. While it might seem somehow cruel, in EMDR it is the re-experiencing and reprocessing of the emotional material that is important for change to occur. For that reason we continued with the next set of eye movements, focusing on Catherine's mother's angry face.

I watched, attentively and sympathetically, as Catherine's anxiety level clearly continued to climb over the next sets of eye movements. She became breathless and flushed; the pupils of her eyes dilated. She was showing the signs of a high anxiety state. To an outsider that might well seem to be a cause for concern, but in EMDR work such states are expected as part of the work, as the person processes the necessary material. As I mentioned to Catherine, I was quite confident that her level of anxiety was likely to rise at first, and then eventually fall.

In the event, Catherine's anxiety dropped a little before the end of the session, rather than being fully resolved at that time. To complete that session safely we did some mindfulness work together, after which Catherine felt ready to leave.

In the next session Catherine reported that she had had some bad dreams, which were unusual for her; one key theme of these dreams had been strong arguments between her and her mother. I wondered whether these had been resolved either way, but they had not. Sometimes EMDR can trigger further processing in the form of dreams, and we wondered together if these were a sign that something within Catherine's mind had shifted. After the last, quite emotional session, and having felt fine afterwards with the help of some mindfulness work daily, Catherine said that she wanted to continue with EMDR. We picked up where we had left off, with the image of Catherine's mother's face, the feelings of terror and the lingering thought of Catherine's that 'I'm a bad person.'

This time, perhaps feeling a little more confident, Catherine was able to quickly access the feelings of terror, which again rose to a peak of high intensity. She reported feeling almost able to smell her mother's breath as she shouted at her daughter and intimidated her. Between quite long sets of eye movements, Catherine felt that she was getting a clear view of what happened between her and her mother. Previously the images had seemed to be fragmented; now they seemed to tell a clearer story. I wondered what kind of story was emerging for Catherine.

'I realized that one reason she used to shout at me was that I'd nag at her. I just wanted her to notice me, that's all. I felt unloved.'

This feeling was enough to cause more eye movements. Soon after we began them, Catherine's expression again began to change—but this time, rather than showing terror, she began to sob.

'I can see it now. There I was, a very young girl. I felt unloved: really neither our mother nor our father was there enough for us. I felt so lonely, unlovable and miserable, just sitting there all alone trying to "sort myself out".'

We did more eye movements on this. After that I wondered what, looking back at that time, Catherine really needed. Tears were again streaming down her face and I offered her a tissue. Without hesitation she said this:

'I can see that I needed to be loved. I needed to be held, to feel safe.'

This was a powerful moment for both of us. Shortly afterwards, we did some eye movements focusing on this feeling of neediness. Now there were no tears, and I wondered what Catherine had noticed during this set.

'It was strange. I could see myself there, in the dining room, the "little me". But I, the adult me, was there too. It was as though I could see myself from high up, as I am now; and I felt this strong urge to come into the room, swoop down and pick up that little girl. I could feel she wanted protection, and I wanted to give it to her. It felt good to do that.'

I could really understand that it did. Catherine had undergone something that often happens in EMDR—a quite sudden switch in perspective, a spontaneous reattribution, so that the person comes to have sympathy with their damaged selves, and to take care of those selves. Previously Catherine had, in effect, turned away from her younger self and her inner self, because of the feelings that came with the memories; but it felt as though by using EMDR we had been able to connect quite directly with these aspects of her personality.

According to Catherine, partly as a result of these central sessions of EMDR coupled with daily mindfulness practice, she came to feel calmer. She felt that she was less liable to feel emotionally unstable and to move quickly between different and sometimes quite extreme mood states. People had also noticed a positive change in her at work. Regarding her eating patterns, Catherine also felt that she was less controlling now of her food intake. Perhaps because of our connection with her real, underlying feelings of distress from her troubled development, she felt as though she was eating more as a way of taking care of herself, rather than using food as a tool of control or punishment. As a result of all this, she was looking well.

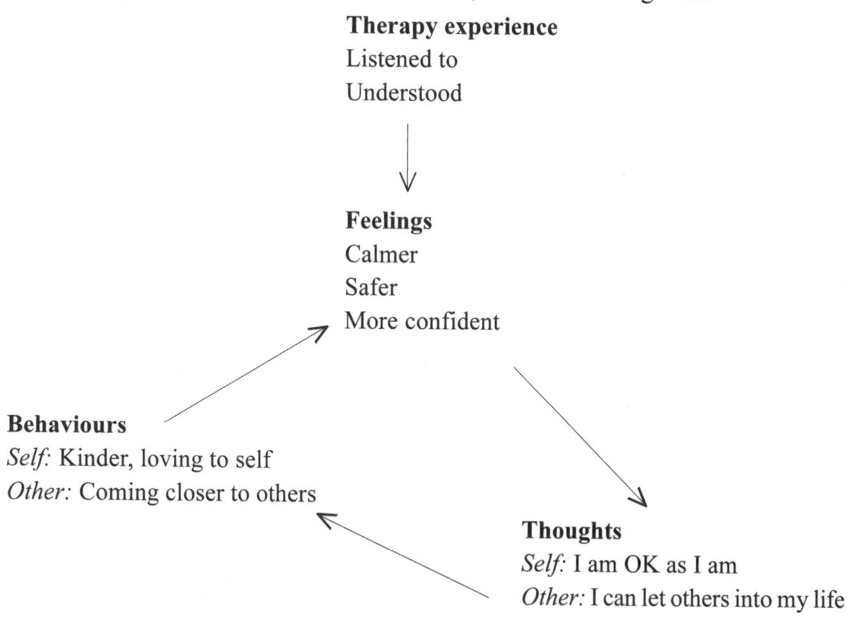

Figure 7.6 Catherine's formulation at the end of therapy

By the time our sessions had been completed, Catherine's level of emotional instability had markedly reduced. She had also, however, changed with respect to her presence in the room with me. At the first meeting, she had seemed difficult to get close to, defensive and attacking, for reasons that were not clear. But now, after we had addressed some of her early frightening experiences and provided her with some tools for self-management, she seemed much warmer and more relaxed—more mellow. She had arrived, some weeks before, in an imposing business suit. She left in trainers—and with a smile. Her psychological recovery towards being an autonomous, carefree, happy woman was under way.

Hearing what the voices have to say: Feelings of depression and psychosis in Andy, a 25-year-old man – 16 sessions

When it is identified by health services, psychosis can be, and often is, a highly destructive psychological problem. Until the last few decades, people who experienced psychosis most often struggled to find adequate care. With their symptoms badly understood, they often lived lives of fear, humiliation and shame. For this and other reasons people with psychosis sometimes committed suicide, seeing no other way of coping with their issues.

Recently, though, therapies for people with psychosis have improved and good information is available for the people concerned.[6] Medications, while still imperfect, offer some respite from the worst symptoms; and after very real progress over the last decade or so, psychological therapies are also now known to be useful for helping people cope with psychotic symptoms.[7] Very often—and contrary to what might be the public perception about psychosis—it is impossible to tell that someone is suffering in this way, unless they actually tell us. We can't read their minds. This was true of Andy when we first met.

As soon as Andy opened his mouth to talk, I began to find him likeable. He had been referred by his GP for help with quite strong feelings of anxiety and depression. Very calmly, Andy said that for over a year he had been feeling low—so much so that he could barely get to work and cope in his job as a printer. The low feelings made him feel like hiding himself away from other people, which he did often when he wasn't at work, and indeed even when he was. He kept in some contact with others, though, mainly through his friend at work, Brian. When he was feeling low, had he noticed any recurring patterns of thought?

'I'm rubbish. Everyone is looking at me, and they can see I'm rubbish. If I go out, it'll go wrong and I'll be ashamed.'

These are quite normal thoughts for anyone who is socially anxious; they are self-critical, but very common among the population. I wondered how Andy's feelings about himself had come about from his early experience. I was taken aback by the answer.

'My dad used to treat me badly. I was so young that I can't remember when it started, but it went on until I left home.'

'OK. What's the first thing that you remember?'

'Dad shouting at me when I was about six. Then, after that, him kicking me down the stairs.'

I jumped on hearing this. Unfortunately, such treatment of children by adults is, despite our expectations, quite common. All too often we do not treat each other well. Andy had been treated terribly at some points in his life. As he talked, I could see this a little more clearly in his face, and hear it in his voice now. He had a delicacy, a fragility, about him. I also felt strong empathy for his younger self. Here he was, a sensitive and very likeable young man, talking about his sensitive young child self being abused by his own father. How did that leave him feeling?

'I was always sensitive. I always felt on the outside of things, I suppose. It was like that through school. I was bullied, but only a bit. I had a couple of friends, but I lost touch with them soon after we left.'

This sounded like quite a lonely, unhappy life. What had happened then?

---

6. See e.g. De Hert, M., Magiels, G. & Thys, E. (2003). *The Secret of the Brain Chip: A self-help guide for people experiencing psychosis: 3rd edn.* Antwerp: EPO / Janssen-Cilag.
7. Bentall, R.P. (2003). *Madness Explained: Psychosis and human nature.* London: Penguin/Allen Lane. 504–509.

'Well, when I left school I drifted for a bit, not knowing what I could do. I thought about college, but school had been so hard that I didn't see the point. Eventually I found the job I have now. I don't like it, but I've been doing it ever since.'

Was there anything that made life a little easier, a little better?

'Talking to Brian about it all can be a weight off my mind.'

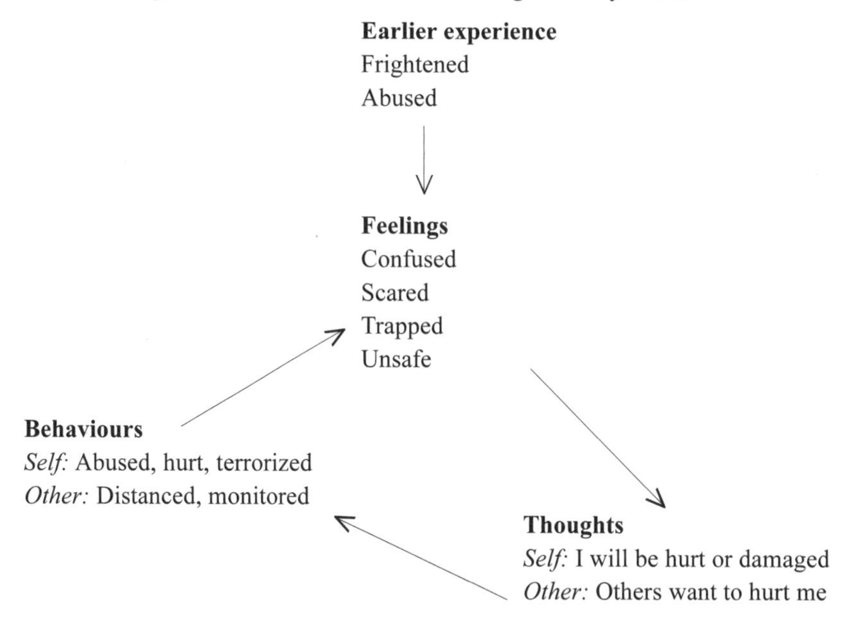

Figure 7.7 Andy's formulation

As yet, I had missed a key part of Andy's experience by not asking about it. At the beginning of our second session together, he said he had something to say. He said he had never told anyone before, but felt that it needed to be 'out in the open'. I was curious as to what the issue might be. Understandably, Andy seemed hesitant; he seemed to be finding it harder to make eye-contact than previously. I wondered if something that felt shameful for Andy was about to be said. He whispered now.

'I hear voices. They keep on at me.'

Andy's gaze dropped still lower; I wondered whether this indicated also a sense of hopelessness. It is well established that hearing voices, while being much more common among the population than we expect, can be (but isn't always) very distressing for people who experience them[8]—so I was very concerned to show Andy, even at this early point in our work, acceptance, acknowledgement and warmth. That's why I said the following:

'It's very common for people to hear voices. Many people hear voices, and don't ever worry about it; it seems to be part of their normal experience. But at difficult periods, when there's upset or stress around in our lives, the voices can often be worse.'

8. Bentall, R.P. (2003). *Madness Explained: Psychosis and human nature.* London: Penguin/Allen Lane: 96–101.

Andy showed interest in this and his face softened a little, whereas previously, feeling frightened and ashamed of himself, he had kept the voices secret. This had the benefit, as many people find, of keeping the problem quiet, but at the risk of increasing the sense of isolation. After this important disclosure by Andy we spent quite some time just talking about what it was like to say he had been hearing voices—how it felt. Understandably, he found acknowledging the presence of the voices hard: but we were able to take the work slowly, as is often needed.

Around this time one of our first steps, with the help of expert medical personnel—the relevant psychiatrist—was to find an appropriate antipsychotic medication for Andy.[9] If used correctly and as prescribed, such medications can be very effective in helping to address psychotic symptoms. Despite the possible side effects, Andy was keen to try the medication because of the possible benefits.

Then, while medication was being used by Andy, over time and moving very deliberately, gently and slowly—as is fitting with a person who has experienced psychosis—we were able to develop a picture of the voices, and of their effects on Andy's life. With difficulty, Andy said that he felt it was a mysterious figure he thought was called 'the Cardinal' who was doing the talking to him—someone who was plotting against him for much of the time. Like many people who experience psychosis, Andy said that the voice was powerfully negative and felt very strong to him. This sometimes led him to feel trapped by the voice, particularly at night, if Brian was out or busy and he was alone. These were the times when the voice felt most depressing: when the voice—the Cardinal, as Andy saw it—would shout at him, often swearing and talking in abusive language.

As anyone would, Andy found this distressing and frightening, especially because the voice seemed absolutely real to him. I felt for Andy as he was saying this. I've never yet myself experienced a psychotic-style voice, but I know from painful experience that a harsh, negative, critical internal voice can be very hard to live with. I struggle to imagine how it must be if one hears such a voice that seems to be real. Andy felt that the voice, when it came on most days, had made him withdraw from some of the things that he liked to do. It made work very difficult for him, and was interfering with that. The harsh negative comments, like 'You're useless, you idiot', made it almost impossible to concentrate. But Andy said that the most difficult thing of all was that the Cardinal's voice, as he saw it, made him withdraw from all social contact other than Brian—who was finding things difficult. The voice said such nasty words that Andy felt too ashamed, bad in himself, to be around others. While he had some colleagues who were normally friendly at work, he had always avoided going out with them; the Cardinal, he said, had been telling him that 'They'll see you for what you are, you dirty piece of filth.' Understandably, and feeling underconfident anyway, Andy had taken the voice's advice and avoided such social contact, which was a pity, since a good form of social support and psychological well-being for Andy was for the moment going unused.

---

9. For more information on anti-psychotic medications and their side effects, see: Healy, D. (2001). *Psychiatric Drugs Explained: 3rd edn.* Edinburgh: Churchill Livingstone.

The other important effect of the Cardinal's voice, as Andy saw it, was to make him hurt himself. These were probably Andy's times of deepest suffering. At those times when he was alone, in the evenings or at night, the voice would become so intense, so strong, that it would seem to Andy to be irresistible in force. The voice would say, repeatedly, 'Cut yourself, you worthless scum': and eventually Andy would cut and make superficial wounds, most of the time, just as the voice said. He explained that it was the only thing he seemed to be able to do to make the voice calmer, and himself less tense. At this point, Andy's situation sounded like a nightmare scenario to me. He had described being trapped with a powerful, vicious voice, bellowing instructions to hurt himself, and with no clear means of escape. As I said to Andy, it was understandable that he felt the need to do what the voice said; I, or anyone else, would have done the same.

In this way Andy and I gradually came to understand the kind of negative effects the voice had on the different parts of his life, which had temporarily been made very hard by the recent impact of the voice; but Andy had taken a first, good step in being able to tell us about it. To begin with, he had been worried about this. Some people with psychosis have the feeling that they cannot go against their voices, or defy them, because of the vengeance that the voice may take; but Andy found that he could talk frankly in our sessions about his experiences, without retribution from the voice. This made him a little more confident in talking in even more detail about what was happening in his life.

As we did this joint work of understanding, I think the bond between us deepened. To begin with we had been a little wary of each other; in particular Andy said that he had been worried that the Cardinal had somehow been in charge of me—perhaps directing *me* against him. That was hardly surprising, given that Andy had come into therapy with a frightening experience of psychosis, carrying a heavy psychological burden more or less alone and taking no helpful medication. But by this point in our work we shared a good working bond; we felt more comfortable with each other, and this prepared us for the next stage of the work.

Gradually we were able to make tentative connections between what the Cardinal had been saying to Andy, and psychologically important earlier life experiences of his. Until recently it was imagined by many people involved in the treatment of psychosis that the 'delusions' experienced by people like Andy were essentially trash, devoid of meaning and content.[10] This view has been replaced by the more common-sense and humane position that there is *always at least some truth* in the words of a psychotic person. The meaning of the words needs to be teased out since, like everyone, people with psychosis and its 'delusions' and 'hallucinations' are concerned with friendships, status, love and loss—all our usual, everyday concerns. With these matters in mind, we explored the Cardinal's punishing words. It was clear that they were often abusive, harshly dismissive of Andy. Talking about this together, we wondered whether there might be a clear link with Andy's father's negative voice, which he had heard from a very young age. To begin with, Andy felt that this simply *could not* be true.

10. See, e.g. Berrios, G. (1991). Delusions as 'wrong beliefs': A conceptual history. *British Journal of Psychiatry, 159* (suppl.), 6–13.

'It was the Cardinal. Simple as that. How could it be anything else?'

But when we reflected on this over a number of sessions, we realized together that the two voices—that of the father, and later the Cardinal, were in fact similar. Both were highly abusive of Andy and, like that of the Cardinal, Andy's father's voice had been extremely powerful when Andy was much younger. His father had also been strictly religious, and had forced his beliefs on the rest of the family. This, we thought, might help to explain the dark and distressing figure of the 'Cardinal'. Andy wept as he recalled feeling devastated, as a boy of about six, by his father's inexplicable raging anger towards him; and together we tentatively wondered if the voice of the Cardinal was not the Cardinal after all. It certainly *seemed* like an important Cardinal might—being strong-sounding, and viciously abusive—but Andy felt sure that he had never seen the Cardinal. We agreed to keep an open mind on this; there was no need for us to be certain either way. Such pushing for complete certainty probably wouldn't have helped, and could have made things worse if we had pushed for agreement in this delicate work.[11] It was notable, though, that around this time of our work, Andy said that he was generally feeling a little less stressed than he had been originally, and was finding the voice a little less troubling. He felt—and I felt, observing him—that its power over him was beginning to weaken, even if only slightly. This change, a benefit derived from medication and psychotherapy together—an effective combination, as research has shown[12]—gave him a greater sense of well-being.

We went on exploring Andy's experience of the voice, which continued, despite our knowledge about its possible origins in Andy's life as a young boy. As well as considering who the Cardinal might actually be, we also talked about the power of the voice: how it made Andy feel, and what could be done to help. At this time in our work we experimented with the voice, both in the sessions and between sessions, when Andy was at home. Like many people who hear voices, Andy found that even just a short period (a few minutes) of thinking about something stressful, like the verbal abuse from his father, could make the voice seem stronger; but we also found that its strength would often be reduced significantly if Andy really focused his attention on something other than the voice. We also tried mindfulness work for a week, but Andy, unlike some people experiencing psychosis, didn't find that at all useful. If anything, the inner space opened up by the mindfulness made things worse for Andy, so we stopped that part of the work. However, when he was at home he found listening in his headphones to loud music was quite helpful, while talking to others when outside the home had a similar effect. So here, too, a slight but important shift occurred in Andy's experience of the voice. At the beginning of our work we had a sense that the voice seemed, for the most part, to be uncontrollable and unpredictable, but by this time Andy did not feel so much that he was at its mercy. To a small extent at least, there were things that he could do to have a bit more control over it.

---

11. Rector, N.A. (2004). Cognitive theory and therapy of schizophrenia. In: R. Leahey (ed.). *Contemporary Cognitive Therapy: Theory, research & practice*. New York: Guilford Press, 245–268.
12. Rector, N.A. & Beck, A.T. (2001). Cognitive behavioural therapy for schizophrenia: An empirical review. *Journal of Nervous and Mental Disease, 189(5),* 278–287.

Finally, building on this work, we were able to look together at one of the most sensitive areas for Andy—his ideas that the Cardinal was plotting against him, and was sending out religious spies to look at him and what he was doing. He took as evidence of this people who had recently been calling around to his house, as well as a group of phone calls when the caller had hung up. Naturally all this had made Andy feel more cautious and defensive, not wanting to leave the house except when he could not avoid it.

Such thoughts and feelings of persecution are quite common in people who are experiencing psychosis; one reason is that the thinking of such people may be prone to thought-biases (as described in Chapter 2), in a similar way to people experiencing anxiety or depression. However, to take three examples: people with psychosis may be more prone than the average person to see even irrelevant events as being self-relevant; they may also be more prone to attribute harmful intent to the behaviour of others; and finally, there is good evidence to suggest that people experiencing psychosis may have a neuropsychological tendency to make over-rapid and confident judgements based on little evidence. This last tendency may be even clearer in stressful situations,[13] making life still more difficult for the person.

In view of some of these possible tendencies we looked, very gently, at some of the evidence for what seemed to be happening in Andy's life. Taking a little time to do so, we actually weighed up the evidence for the idea that the Cardinal was in charge of what seemed to be happening. We all acknowledged that some of the house calls and phone calls seemed to be happening close to one another—even on the same day; but despite what the voice had been saying about the Cardinal being involved, there was also some evidence to suggest a rather different conclusion. Andy agreed that when we thought about it, there was actually *no visible sign* that the callers to the house were anything to do with the Cardinal. They could have been businesspeople who were cold-calling in the neighbourhood. Similarly the telephone calls, while potentially worrying, had no clear, direct links to the Cardinal. We were all relieved to be able to tentatively reach such conclusions, since Andy had been so worried about these matters earlier on.

Towards the end of our therapeutic work, while Andy was still learning to cope with the aftermath of his psychotic experience—including a lasting but slowly reducing sense of shame and shock, and a potential drop in social status, at least in the eyes of some—he had also taken some steps forward. As well as encouraging him to take appropriate medication and to keep taking it, we had had quite a close look together at some of the things that concerned him. As well as tracing the possible origins of his fears to his difficult relationship with his father, which understandably made him sad, we had also looked at the evidence for some of his greatest concerns, and possible ways to help control the voices when they came—which they still did.

One sign of Andy's gradual psychological progress was that he felt able to go back to work, as part of a very sensibly phased return over a number of months.

---

13. Rector, N.A. (2004). Cognitive theory and therapy of schizophrenia. In: R. Leahey (ed.). *Contemporary Cognitive Therapy: Theory, research, & practice*. New York: Guilford Press, 245–268.

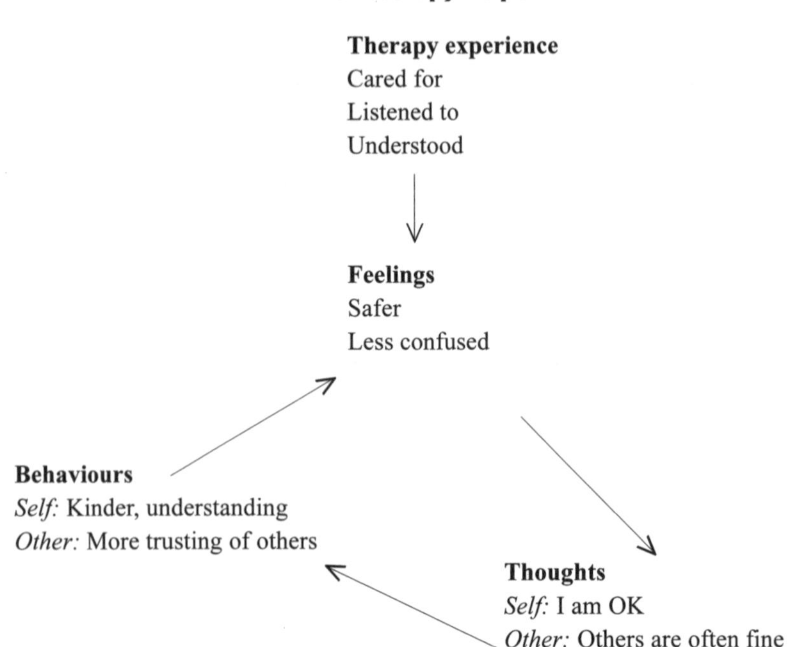

Figure 7.8 Andy's formulation after therapy

Previously, like many people with psychosis, he had avoided possible situations in which he would feel socially vulnerable or threatened. But feeling a little firmer now, on suitable medication and with some psychological tools for use at difficult times that he might encounter over future years, Andy was ready to leave therapy. He kept sporadically in touch with other members of the helping professions, but I didn't see him again. I later gathered, though, that his life was gradually moving in a direction that he liked.

* * *

No matter where we are or at which stage we are in our adult lives, we may experience any of a range of psychological issues, from relatively mild feelings of anxiety to more severe symptoms, including those of psychosis. Despite the fact that they can feel very distressing when they are with us, all these feelings are part of our collective human existence. At such times our experiences can be very different from what we might expect in our usual adult life. If at such times we then have the courage to acknowledge the difficulties, and to make contact with a person or people who can help, then our feelings can very often begin to change.

As I have said in this chapter, it is often the case that even where quite severe psychological symptoms are present in adult men and women, significant gains—and sometimes even startling gains—can be made. Through psychotherapy, with or without the practice of mindfulness, a person can sometimes be fully 'cured' of their problems. At other times the person's progress is less dramatic, but important to them nonetheless.

Most often, though, competent treatment with a psychotherapist gives an improvement in the level of hope and well-being in the adult, even where complex psychological problems are involved. Again, that is telling; with appropriate help, it is most often the case that people make a move towards recovery. For someone who has always been deprived of care—and I meet people who have *never* experienced being loved—just a little encouragement can have a powerful healing effect. I have worked with many people who, having felt very firmly that they had come to the end of the road, with a little psychological talk found another way forward. This is one benefit of the bonds between us as people, whoever we are. We can give each other new life, and help each other find new ways to be.

In other words, for the adult as for the child, kind psychological treatment can do much to undo the harm caused by earlier problems. In this way the adult's trust—often previously broken—in themselves, others and life itself can be at least partly restored. The adult person can then make a return, gradual or otherwise and to as great a degree as is possible, to the kind of autonomous, free and independent adult life that befits us all.

8

Mindful Treatment of the Person in Later Life

Whatever else life may be, it is good.
Goethe

Being an older person in the West is still hard. Despite rising living standards, better healthcare and the increasing human lifespan in affluent countries, older people routinely suffer poverty, are discriminated against in and out of work, are more likely to feel loneliness with increasing age and to be at a greater social distance from younger members of the population, who often take little interest in their elders.[1] While evolutionary mechanisms of the kind described in Chapter 2 may help partly to explain this situation, it remains outrageous.

In keeping with this neglect in society at large, until the last few decades older people experiencing psychological issues were also often effectively written off by doctors and staff caring for them. A century ago Freud himself took a misguided, negative view of the possibility of helping the older people in Western society. Fortunately such attitudes are now outmoded,[2] and there is much specialist interest and research in the psychology of older human life. Consequently older people have begun to benefit from recently developed psychological treatments that, like those for children and adults, put the older person's own experiences of, and feelings about, their life and the world first.

Above all, we now know more about the process of growing older as a human being, physically and psychologically.[3] On the one hand, it is well understood that the ageing process brings certain inevitable physical and psychological changes in the individual, which are affected by a person's genes and life circumstances (such as

---

1. See the website of Help the Aged: http://www.helptheaged.org.uk.
2. Kitwood, T. (1997). *Dementia Reconsidered.* Milton Keynes: Open University Press.
3. See, e.g. Cabeza, R., Nyberg, L. & Park, D. (eds.). (2005). *Cognitive Neuroscience of Aging: Linking cognitive and cerebral aging.* Oxford: Oxford University Press; Whalley, L. (2004). *The Ageing Brain.* London: Phoenix.

diet). Regarding physical health, it is well known that the body's organs decline in efficiency with time. Muscle tone, for example, decreases steadily after the age of thirty. The same is also true, in some ways, of neurological and psychological health. Certain memory functions—our short-term memory, for instance—can reduce in power as we grow older. On the other hand, it is also recognized that certain psychological capacities can often improve with age and experience. Older people, owing to their experience in specific situations (in business, say), find it easier to grasp the 'bigger picture' than the young. Our ability to manage our emotions can also increase with age. As we mature into older adults, we may be able to see matters more fully in the round, be less prey to powerful feelings and more likely to be able to keep our emotional equilibrium. At least that's what I'm hoping for. And, as our commitments to others––perhaps our children, or our colleagues at work—are reduced, we may also have more time for ourselves; consequently older people in the West are presented with more possibilities to enjoy life than previously. With the decline of traditional moralities in many Western countries, more freedom for personal action and choice is available, particularly for older people with financial resources. However, in order to be able to take these opportunities, older people, like children and adults, require the awareness, kindness and respect of others in the population to flourish.

Typically, the kindness of others is slowly withdrawn as people age in the West—leaving the lonely individual to suffer; but where kindness and psychological understanding are available, quality of life can increase. Healthy older people can often benefit from psychological care; but even where serious neurological problems occur—as in the case of a form of dementia—kindness and understanding can provide improvements, however small, in a person's feelings and situation, and those of their family.

In some ways the psychological issues facing an older person differ from those facing younger people.[4] Most importantly, perhaps, the matter of loss often cannot be avoided. In other central ways, though, the issue is the same: the welfare of the person, their relationship to others and themselves, and how this shapes their experience in life. This is where the practice of kindness in mindfully aware psychotherapy—embracing what has passed, is passing and is to come—can be useful, as I will explain.

Past Fears: Strong feelings of anxiety and depression in Miriam, a 76-year-old woman – 12 sessions

I met Miriam shortly after she had been at her lowest ebb. She looked very pale and tired, with her silver-white hair in quite an unkempt state. This made me wonder whether she was finding it difficult to look after herself—and whether, perhaps, she hadn't been looked after much at some time in her life before that. She spoke quickly, in a pressured way.

---

4. Knight, B.G. (2004). *Psychotherapy with Adults: 3rd edn.* Thousand Oaks, CA: Sage; Hepple, J. & Sutton, L. (2004). *Cognitive Analytic Therapy and Later Life.* Hove: Brunner-Routledge.

'I'm *so* pleased to see you; I've been *desperate*. I've had the most desperate time.' Miriam leant forward, almost into me, as she talked. This left me in no doubt about her insistence on being helped. I wondered what her problems were, how she saw them.

'Where do I start? I've been ill for almost a year now. When it was at its worst I had to take to my bed. I just felt so tired, I couldn't do anything I normally enjoy—the gardening, playing with our grandchild. I didn't speak to any of my friends; I just couldn't bother them, the way I was. I couldn't even go out, in the garden or anywhere else. The feelings were so terrible, so terrible.'

Miriam looked pained as she said this, and I wasn't surprised. I knew it felt bad at such times—but I was also feeling a bit breathless after the intensity of Miriam's talking. I felt we needed to slow matters down a little. I wondered what had appeared around a year ago to trigger the issues. No doubt about that, it emerged. She spoke forcefully.

'I'd had an operation on my hand, which I broke in my forties and which didn't heal properly then. It was only a minor procedure, but I had a general anaesthetic. I never really recovered after it. The hospital said that I needed a week or two off from what I usually do, then my energy levels would start to lift. I'd also lost one of my younger sisters to cancer eighteen months before. I loved her dearly. I thought I'd got over it; somehow, though, it went deeper than that. In the weeks and months after the operation, I just got lower and lower. For a few days I was able to be up and active in the house, but I soon succumbed, and my mood dipped.'

How?

'I was feeling frightened. Really frightened. I thought I was going *absolutely mad*. I was in London for the day. I was due to meet my old friend Julia by the London Eye. But as I was walking along the Thames, I don't know what happened, anxiety, panic, whatever it was, but I was feeling worse and worse and worse. I was feeling dizzy, and had to find a bench to sit down on. I just felt—it's hard to describe the feeling—that my soul had left my body. It was, on that horrible grey day, as though there was nothing left inside me, like I'd been emptied out. I panicked. I felt like jumping in the Thames, but I made it back home. Luckily, Julia understood.'

Though she wasn't crying, Miriam's eyes were filling up with tears.

'It felt as though I was being sucked down and down, ever deeper into a black hole from which there'd be no escape. I struggled and struggled, but it did no good. I felt so helpless. Completely helpless.'

This is a common experience of many people with strong feelings of anxiety and depression. I knew that almost everyone who experiences this feeling of terror survives intact—but Miriam, not being a clinical psychologist who is concerned to understand, and help to change, human behaviour did not know this. What did she do?

'I leant so much on Anthony. He's been my lighthouse while I've been tossed about on the sea: my light in the darkness. When I've needed him, he's been there for me. He's held my hand, read to me in bed, even *fed* me in bed. Sometimes, you see, I felt I needed that.'

'I'm sure you did. And it was fortunate that you had someone there like Anthony to take such care of you'.

Like many older people who come for psychotherapy, the couple had had long and interesting lives, both together and apart. This seemed like a good time to find out about the history of their relationship.

'We were very, very lucky to find each other. But we almost never did! I grew up in Kent; I'd spent a fabulous year in Milan as a student doing languages, and I was back in London seeing my boyfriend at the time. One day I was going to stay with a girlfriend in Manchester when my train had been cancelled because of a strike. I had to go the day after, by a different route, and it was on that train that we met!'

Of course, that's how it happens, the formation of relationships by chance, and it was good to hear.

'We've been together ever since. We've had our ups and downs, like everyone does, but we've had happy lives. We've a son and a daughter, both in their late twenties. We have one granddaughter, and we'd like more. But it's not about what we want, is it?'

That seemed right, and I said so.

'We moved around quite a lot over the years, mostly because of Anthony's work. When you work as a pilot, there are only so many places you can do what you need to do. But one way or another, we always managed. Even when I wasn't feeling good, we managed.'

Miriam's tone changed.

'Until *this* time. This time, it all just fell apart, and I still feel as though I'm broken, in pieces, scattered over the floor. Can you put me back together?'

When people ask me this question or a variant of it, as they often do, I never know for certain that we'll be able to do this completely; but in my experience I don't think I've ever met anyone who felt significantly *worse* after a completed course of appropriate, good-quality psychological treatment. So I said what I always say at such times: I don't know—but we'll try.

When we talked about how the psychological issues affected Miriam, it was striking that she sometimes had to spend time in bed, but also withdrew from social contact—or, more accurately, from her caring contact with others. It emerged that she had an older aunt, then in her nineties, living in the north of England and usually Miriam spent a lot of her time speaking to her aunt (at least three times a week). When we talked about this woman, Miriam groaned. She felt as though it was her duty to look after this lady, who had been there for Miriam herself at difficult times of her life.

'I just feel,' said Miriam, 'that I owe her so much. I want to give her something back.'

So what was the issue?

'She tires me out so when she rings up. Part of me wants to speak to her, but she's so demanding that I shake quite violently when the phone rings, and I end up getting Anthony to answer it and say that I'm not in. But that makes me feel so *guilty*. I should be able to do so much more for her. I don't know what my mother would have said about it; I can be so selfish.'

And there were other people Miriam cared for similarly: friends who had problems with their partners, friends who had been ill. In each case the pattern was similar: Miriam, when she was well, had been putting others' needs before her own—and still felt guilty, even when she was ill herself. This recurring pattern of giving care to others that we had noticed is a common one for many people. It also made me wonder about Miriam's life when she had been young. It was clear that she was fortunate enough to be in a very happy relationship with Anthony, but I felt that it might have been quite different from her psychological start in life. When I asked about the kind of care that Miriam experienced when she was developing as a young person, she laughed loudly.

'Ah, that's a story! You see my parents, while they were together, were what you might call 'characters'. I loved them dearly—still do—but they were not, shall we say, the best-qualified people to be responsible parents.'

She went on to explain.

'My mother, as everyone said, was a beautiful young woman; from a young age she had men falling at her feet wanting to be with her. But when she was eighteen, she met my father. He was in his late twenties and making a name for himself as a barrister. For a few months they were together, and my mother always said she had the time of her life. They travelled, and danced and loved. That's how she put it. It sounded blissful.'

It did sound good.

'But then it all went wrong for them; Mother fell pregnant with me. Of course, they were unmarried and in those days—this is the 1930s, remember—it wasn't the done thing just to get rid of the baby, or split up, or whatever people do now. They decided they had to stay together. It was the worst thing they could have done.'

Why?

'They just weren't suited to each other. Father was much older, for one thing; he was happy pottering around, living a quiet country life. Mother, though, really wanted to be the belle of the ball, in London, I think. I remember her as being frustrated: bitter, even. I remember her saying to me often: "Miriam, you must take your chances when they come, or life will simply pass you by." That's how she felt.'

They stayed together?

'Well, you could call it that. What happened was rather sad. Mother, who was still beautiful, attracted a lot of attention in the community and began to have affairs. Naturally Father, who worked away for much of the week on the legal circuit, hated that. Absolutely hated it. Anyone would, of course. He drank. Then they argued. Both flew into wild rages.'

The tears in Miriam's eyes suggested that it had been a difficult time for her—yes?

'It was. It was a really difficult time. After the rows, which were terrible, Mother used to regularly disappear for days on end: two or three days at a time.'

But where did that leave the children? As we were saying this, it felt as though we were getting where we needed to go.

'We—me and my two younger sisters, Isabelle and Margaret—had to fend for ourselves. When she went, and Father was away at work, I took over at home. Did the washing and cleaning, made sure we were all able to get to school.'

I wondered how old Miriam had been when this was all happening. It sounded like a lot for a girl to be coping with.

'I was about ten. But I thought nothing of it at the time; I certainly didn't know any different. "Oh, there we are; there's been some sort of rumpus, Father's been drinking again, and Mother's gone off ." We just had to survive, I suppose. I just had to survive.'

Naturally, that was true: but how had it all left Miriam feeling about what was happening at home, all those years ago? About herself, life, other people? It was now that Miriam came to show her feelings. She wiped her tears from her cheeks as she spoke.

'I've always tried not to think about those times. It was very difficult and frightening. I was so young—and for her to go off like that, with me looking after her children. I've never really forgiven her for it; I feel she let us down so badly. They both did. It might have been better if they had divorced much earlier, but you didn't do that sort of thing then.'

I was interested in hearing how it was for Miriam, particularly at the times when her mother had left her in charge of the young family. Again, Miriam's eyes welled up with tears.

'It was *terrifying*; a terrifying responsibility for a girl of that age. I had to learn to wash and to cook, and to get the others and myself to school. Father was often away at those times, so we were self-sufficient. Of course, it meant that all three of us children grew very close.'

I wondered, though, whether the experience of physical and emotional abandonment by her mother had left Miriam with at least two issues that are common among people who have experienced poor early care.

First, I wondered whether Miriam's taking care of others had originated in these experiences. Like many people, she may have learned to put other people's needs first and not to have a very well-developed sense of *her own* needs. In many people, such a pattern of caregiving can lead eventually to exhaustion. Second, I wondered if these early experiences of insecurity may have left Miriam feeling *very* shaken internally – perhaps leaving her with a sense that her life and her relationships were quite fragile, and could have been taken away almost at any time. As I was talking, she nodded.

'I think that's it, or close to it. At some level, I've always felt like—and have never been able to escape from—that little ten-year-old girl whose mother had walked out. I felt so vulnerable then. I really needed my mother to be there for us—but she wasn't. When we needed her, she wasn't there.'

I felt moved, hearing this. For a few moments, it felt as though we had the feeling that we were there with the lonely young Miriam, feeling desperate as she found out that, yet again, her mother had gone and the children had been left alone.

That was an important time in our work together: the recognition of powerful feelings from Miriam's past that had never been fully talked about or resolved. It seemed that Miriam's terrible feelings and fears recently were very like some of the feelings she had had as a child. Even though, rationally, she knew Anthony was still

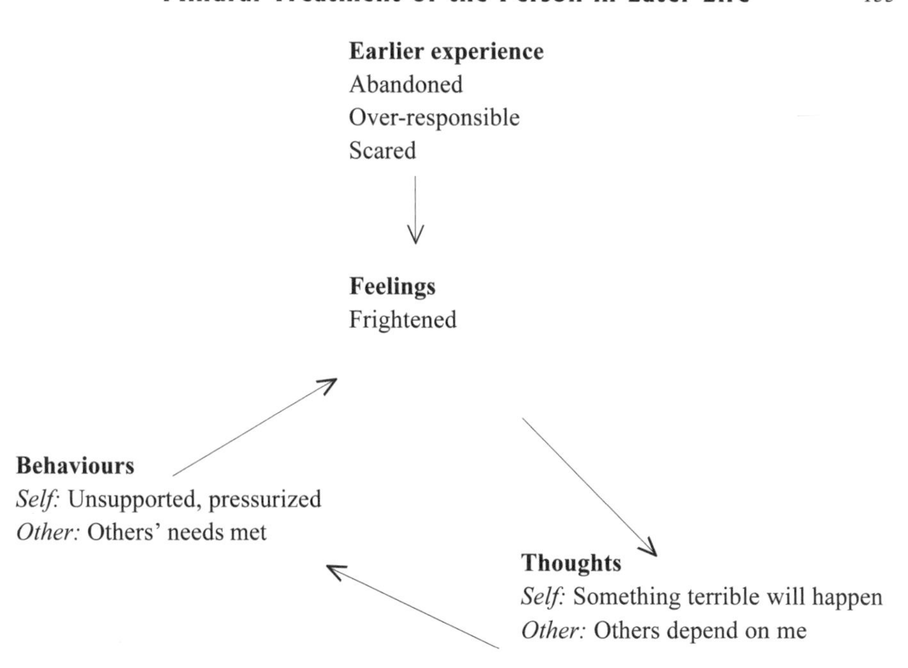

Figure 8.1 Miriam's formulation

there, she felt the same, wrenching feeling of abandonment from her youth. Making this link was important to our work; with this recognition of the difficulties' origin, psychological movement in a healthy direction began to be made.

One sign of this was that Miriam came to feel a little less guilty when she didn't want to talk on the phone to people who really wanted her to care for them, and who weren't really interested in how *she* was. After some discussion about this, she came to feel that she had needs too. If she were to continue looking after others when she herself needed to be taken care of, this was only likely to continue to lead to her feeling exhausted. On the other hand, when she experimented with doing things a little differently, putting herself first, Miriam seemed to benefit from this by feeling better.

'I could get used to this!'

I could see what she meant; it seemed to feel good to her to be putting *her* needs first. Of course, this was done within reason. I was interested to hear that she and Anthony continued to be kind and considerate towards each other, as they generally had always been. The people affected were those outside the immediate family who had placed, and had been allowed to place, quite intolerable demands on Miriam.

Also, looking back together and reflecting psychologically on what had happened decades before, but which had had a powerful shaping effect on Miriam's life and behaviour, she was able to realize that she also felt great anger towards her parents.

'I feel that what they did was so wrong. Anything could have happened to us. If it hadn't been for me picking up the pieces of their marriage, it probably would have. I'm furious with her, especially: furious.'

I was pleased to hear this too, since I felt it was another sign that Miriam was getting in touch with her own feelings about what had happened to her. Anger can be a healthy feeling that protects us; as she had never before considered what had happened with regard to her parents and the legacy she had been left with, the feeling of anger seemed to be protective for Miriam, who was now well into her seventies. It seemed to breathe still more new life into her.

To some people it might seem curious that our relationships when we are growing up as young children can affect us throughout adult life, and into and throughout older age; but very often it is the case. Because of this, and as with Miriam, psychotherapy can provide a particularly interesting experience. With the benefit of great and long hindsight, older people can be encouraged to survey their lives, making connections between different life-stages and gradually coming to appreciate the impact of one event upon another, and the impact of events on the development of personality. If we are fortunate and have had a broadly secure start in life, this work can be quite easy; but if we have had significant disruptions throughout our psychological lives—perhaps through insecurities, losses and trauma—the work can be more difficult and more painful. Most often, however, when their stories have been heard and they themselves have been listened to and acknowledged, people gradually achieve some sense of peace and serenity.

This was the case with Miriam. She had arrived for therapy feeling awful, terrorized by feelings that she could not explain alone and that left her a virtual prisoner in her own house for months. Working together, though, we had made a little more sense of her life story as a woman who, having had rather too little care during her early development, had devoted herself partly to the care of others—but at considerable cost to herself. Our work had been about finding out what Miriam's needs were for security, space and time. We realized that she needed more of those things, and she felt better once she had them. The feelings of terror, put into their historical context as products of a fearful past, came to be less threatening to Miriam.

We did some mindfulness work, too, both in the sessions themselves and individually. We found over a number of weeks that this allowed Miriam to come into contact more with her own needs and feelings, just to be aware of them. That was the start of it; but also to realize that even when they were at their worst, these difficult thoughts and feelings could not hurt her. From the mindfulness perspective, they were just 'stuff'.

As is often the case in such work, there were important matters that we did not cover in detail. The loss from cancer of her younger sister Margaret had helped to prompt the recent problems in the first place, but that issue was left virtually untouched. My feeling was that once Miriam was feeling a little stronger in herself, she was in a better position to fully grieve her loss, rather than avoiding her feelings or being terrorized by them. That was work she could do naturally, after the therapy and without formal psychological help .

Over the weeks, as our understanding of Miriam and her life deepened, she came, as she put it, 'back to life again'.

'I'm feeling much more sociable, much more. I'm not back to my old self again, but I feel as though I'm getting much closer to it. I realize what I was doing to myself before. Now I'm much kinder to myself. It's good for me, and it's good for Anthony. I've begun to get my life back, and Anthony's got his wife back.'

Miriam's eyes welled up now, but for different, reasons.

'I never thought it would happen. I thought that was it.'

I could see that. Miriam then laughed, with a twinkle in her eye.

'But now I know that I wasn't seeing things quite right, back then, don't I?'

In Miriam's recovery from anxiety and depression there were, as with anyone, brighter days and darker days; but we treated the darker ones, mindfully, as temporary feelings and most often they passed, with more pleasant feelings coming to take their place. Over time and with Anthony's help, she regained her strength. She had some colour in her face. Against her original expectations of being 'finished', Miriam became much freer to enjoy some of what life in older age had to offer. She came to take pleasure, once more, in her garden. She and Anthony spent time together again and could enjoy it; she had made a plan with Julia not just to go to London, but to go on the Eye; she was playing like crazy, when she got the chance, with Joseph their grandchild, on days when his parents were at work; and she was looking forward before too long to becoming a grandmother for the second time.

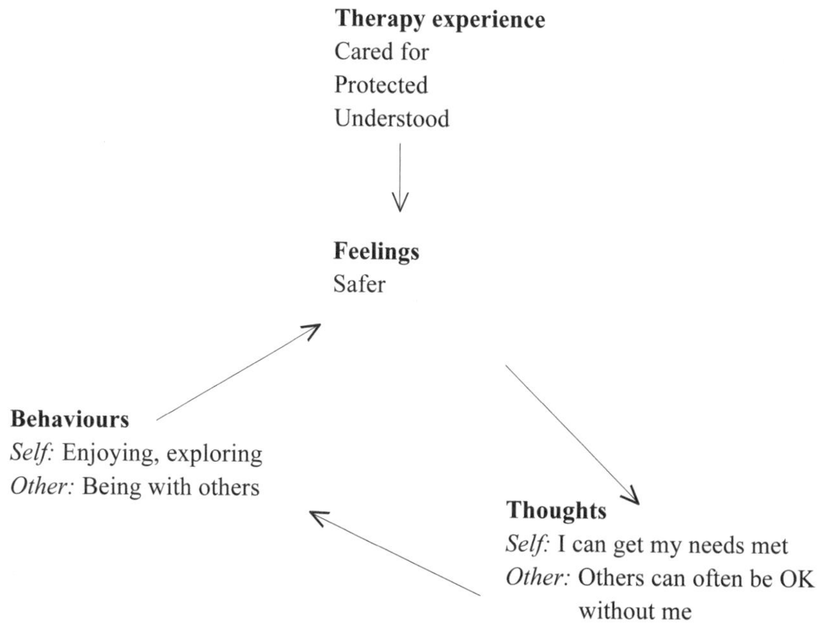

Figure 8.2 Miriam's formulation at the end of therapy

While during psychotherapy Miriam had come to see that she could do too much for others, like many of us do she kept some aspects of her previous behaviour. This meant that despite our work she continued to have an air of gentleness, even grace, about her. I missed her when she left for the last time. I've sometimes wondered about sending her a postcard asking how she is, how her recovery's going: but then I stop myself. She doesn't need me to do that. That's just a therapist's fantasy and wouldn't help anyone.

Memory Processes: Alzheimer's disease in David, a 75-year-old man – 20 sessions

On seeing David initially there was very little to suggest that anything was wrong. He seemed to be a well-kept, proud, upstanding man. Dressed in a smart jacket and tie, complete with a tie-pin, he had a certain dignity about him. He had been referred to me by his GP, who was concerned about David's memory. The GP said he had become rather more absent-minded over the last few months, as well as more moody at home. I was interested to hear what David himself thought. He was not impressed.

'I don't see that there's anything wrong with me; I don't want to be wasting your time.'

I reassured him that he was not wasting my time at all, and that I enjoyed doing this work. That didn't help much.

'Well, put it this way. My wife thinks there's something up with my memory. I'll admit that it might not be quite as good as it was, but that's quite normal, isn't it? My father had dementia in his old age, but I don't quite think I'm ready for that, do you?'

He winked at me, which made me wonder. Though it was hard to have him do it, and he resisted a great deal, David admitted that actually he had been having problems over the last few months in various areas. He was having a number of 'senior moments', as he put it, around the house—quite often forgetting what he was meant to be doing even from one minute to the next. He had begun to have trouble remembering longer and more difficult words. Formerly he had had a good vocabulary when talking; now he noticed this was becoming more difficult and also he had found it more difficult to recall the names of old friends. Finally, he was sometimes experiencing apparently inexplicable bleak moods, when he just felt 'terrible'. Taken together these things might, depending on their level of severity, be nothing but a sign of growing older; some deterioration in the functioning of our minds is to be expected with time. But such symptoms, I realized, could also have been early signs of a serious degenerative problem,[5] so for this reason I suggested to David that we assess the functioning of his memory. Predictably, he didn't like the idea at all. I tried to explain that if something was wrong, it would help all of us to know more accurately what it was.

'You're the doctor,' he growled. 'All right, then.'

Various psychological assessments exist that can show how well and reliably many parts of our conscious minds are working, including our memory. Some methods are quicker than others. In view of the symptoms that David had noted, I did a full cognitive assessment on him; the results showed what I had suspected, and feared. While there were parts of David's intellectual functioning that were still in good order—his visual memory, for example—there were other areas that were performing at a significantly lower level than might have been predicted. For a man of his ability (a retired company manager), his short-term verbal memory was showing deficits and David was finding it very difficult to remember the verbal material that was

5. On psychotherapy with older people with dementia, see Knight, B.G. (2004). *Psychotherapy with Older Adults: 3rd edn.* Thousand Oaks, CA: Sage: 187–203.

presented to him; in fact in the assessments that we did, he recalled very little. For a man like him this would have been a highly improbable result if his mind had been fully healthy; it appeared to me very likely that David was showing signs of Alzheimer's disease. Since it is impossible to test people's brains directly in order to check for such a problem, diagnosis is often made as the most likely explanation for the noted pattern of symptoms.[6] A brain scan added to the information available, since it showed some thinning of the cerebral cortex in both the parietal and temporal lobes, typical of Alzheimer's disease. In David's case, the data suggested that Alzheimer's was the best fit for the available data.

It is always extremely painful to have to tell someone, and the people who care about them, that such a problem as Alzheimer's is likely to be present. Sorrow and the utmost compassion are appropriate. If such a diagnosis is correct, great losses are likely to occur. Dreams that we have about ending our lives peacefully, often far away in the sun, may have to be revised, and for some people the dreams can be hard to let go of. Parts of our identity are also likely to change; the impact on those close to us may be enormous, and there may be much fear to cope with for all concerned. For these reasons, I asked David to bring his wife Maria to our next session.

David and Maria reacted with some shock when I told them what I felt to be the problem. As I explained to them, there wasn't another explanation that made as much sense. David's level of anxiety and depression, for example, was not so high as to be interfering with his memory functioning as strongly as the results of our assessments suggested. David spoke first.

'I'm obviously sorry about this. But at least we know now, don't we?'

He looked at Maria, who was holding back her tears; the moment was a sad one for all of us. We then spent a little time before they left talking about some of the possibilities for care that the couple could receive. We agreed to continue meeting for the time being; Maria, particularly, was keen for psychological contact.

By the time of our next session it was clear that Maria and David were actually finding it quite difficult to get on, in a way that hadn't been clear before. Maria wished to speak to me at more length, and David was happy to allow that. Maria was experiencing some of the feelings commonly suffered by the partners of people who have a degenerative problem like Alzheimer's, which often affects the working of the wider family. Even though the David she knew was still *physically* with her, she felt as though the bright, fun-loving husband and father she had loved throughout her married life had gone months before.

'He was such a witty man—enjoyable to be around. We had so many lovely times. But he's changed so much now.'

How?

'Well, obviously his mind is being affected, but it's also his behaviour. It's very unlike him—or unlike how he was all his life until now. Lately he's been getting grouchy.'

---

6. See: Whalley, L. (2001). *The Ageing Brain.* London: Phoenix: 125–136.

I wondered if there was anything more to this that Maria hadn't yet mentioned. Did he get very angry with her sometimes?

'Yes.'

I explained to Maria that such strong emotional states are common in Alzheimer's sufferers. As well as there being strong feelings of uncertainty, driven by worries about the illness, the gradual decline in memory and intellectual functioning can leave sufferers feeling confused. People with dementia may also be affected by emotional reactions from others, and become distressed themselves. At such times they may be more likely to hit out hurtfully at others, either verbally or physically, or both. This can be shocking and very difficult to cope with for other family members, especially to begin with. Often the person suffering from the problem is unaware of any triggers for these feelings themselves, but they can be helped by paying attention to other members of the family. Maria, David and I looked at the problem a little more closely together.

The couple kept a check over a week of the times when David's mood dropped, and when he felt most annoyed. Examining the week in the next session, it seemed that most of the difficult times seemed to be started by arguments about Maria going out by herself. She would plan to do some shopping, as she always had, but David would plead with her to take him too. The problem emerged because if David did go along, he found it 'so, so boring' and would become so upsetting, and upset, that the couple would have to return home anyway, with the shopping not done. I was interested in why being alone, when it had never apparently been a problem before, seemed to be such a worry for David now. His long-term memory was still functioning well, and he supplied important material here.

'I should think it's something to do with my parents, and what they did or didn't do. It was during World War Two. We were living in Nottingham; father was away in Burma, and there was apparently a danger of us being bombed. I was about four years old. One day mother took me to see what she called an 'aunt' in the countryside near Exeter; we went by train. It seemed to be a marvellous day out to begin with; but when we had got there and met my aunt, my mother said something about staying with her while she went to the lavatory—but she went to the lavatory and didn't come back. I didn't see her, or my father, for the next two years.'

'So you were abandoned by your mother, then?'

'Well, not exactly. I could see, looking back, that she had done it for my safety what with the war—no one knew what was going to happen. But abandonment: that's exactly how it felt at the time.'

I wondered, then, if this early experience had something to do with these recent problems when Maria was trying to leave the house. Did it feel to David as though he was being abandoned all over again? He spoke first.

'I never would have thought of that, or the connection there. It seems such a long time ago, my childhood; a lifetime ago. But now you put the two things together, it makes sense.'

Maria joined in.

'And when you think about it, David, you never *did* really like it when we were apart before, did you? You just tolerated it, but sometimes it was too much. Do you remember when we were in India and I got stuck in a lift in that shop? You were frantic, Sweetie, weren't you?'

That idea made sense to all three of us. Owing to some anxiety-provoking incidents in his youth, coupled with the effects of Alzheimer's now, David was sometimes prone to become confused and frightened about where Maria was. Without the balance to these feelings provided by a healthy memory and mind, David was becoming upset more easily about the situations he found himself in. So by the time

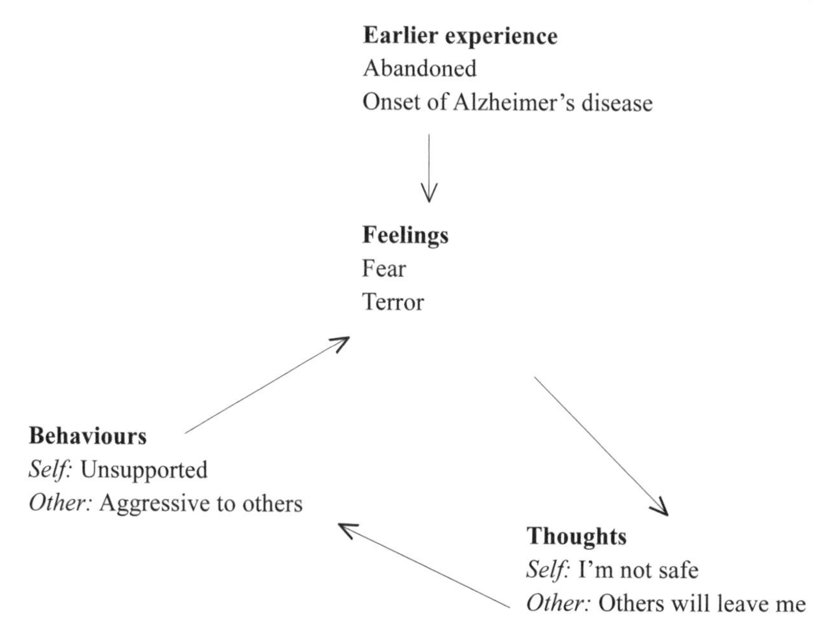

Figure 8.3 David's formulation

Maria returned from an outing, for example, he could be feeling very agitated indeed. Often, in the case of degenerative problems like Alzheimer's, a relatively small psychological change in the system can have benefits for the person with the problem and for other family members, including those who care for the sufferer. In this case, we decided together to do two different things at this point. First, we ensured that wherever Maria was going, David was clear about where it was and when she would be back. Odd though it felt to her to begin with, this meant Maria repeating quite often exactly what her plans were, in very clear terms. A clear and straightforward use of language is often very important as Alzheimer's progresses over the years, because the person with the problem can find it increasingly difficult to grasp complex ideas. Also, before she left Maria wrote down where she was going to be and how soon she was likely to return. This provided David, who didn't feel comfortable with the difficulty of using the telephone any more, with a clear reminder. Finally, we ensured that when Maria was out David had a large picture of her nearby. There were plenty of these to choose from, given the couple's long and happy history together. The picture, a simple face-on view of Maria on a summer's day, was enough to provide

David with a feeling of reassurance that he would not be abandoned and that Maria would come back to him.

As part of the care package the couple also had regular contact with the multidisciplinary team, which includes a psychiatrist, nurses, a physiotherapist, an occupational therapist and a social worker. This helped both David, and more particularly Maria, to feel supported.

I met the couple every few months over the next two years. The psychological measures above, and the contact with the multidisciplinary team, seemed to help a little. David was less agitated at times when Maria was out, and Maria gained more of the freedom that was important for her physical and psychological well-being. Life as a full-time carer can be highly stressful, and we took special note of Maria's feelings as part of this work.

During this time, as would be expected as part of Alzheimer's, David's condition continued to deteriorate. His particular form of Alzheimer's was quite aggressive, so the changes in him over the two-year period were quite obvious; his memory function and ability to communicate continued to decline quite steadily, as repeated neuropsychological assessments confirmed. While that was happening Maria was undergoing her own psychological changes, which we discussed in a session between me and her that David had agreed to.

Maria felt that she was well into a grieving process for the David she had known and loved, while still living with the David who had changed so much. She explained: 'It feels as though he's a completely different person now. Not the man I married—not at all. It feels as though his soul has already passed on; but physically, there he still is. And in a curious way, he needs me more than ever. When I step back sometimes and look at his face—just for a moment—there is a spark, and the man I loved so much for so long is still there; but then it's gone, and we're back to the harsh reality of our life. Is that strange?'

Those mixed feelings, which can be so strong as to include even love and hate—are quite normal for someone in Maria's position. I reassured her of this.

'And sometimes when he is lying there, asleep and at rest, there is such sadness in me. I wish, ever so, that this could only have been different, that—God forgive me—it could have been someone else other than him. He seems so fit and healthy and we had so much planned; we wanted to do so much together. But now he's like a ship drifting off into dark waters.'

Maria, so understandably, was upset now.

'And there's nothing anyone can do. Who is there to go with him?'

In some ways she was right, but in other ways she was already doing what she would need to do to prepare for life after the loss of David. She was grieving for him and she was already beginning to let him go together with the cherished ideas about their future together. This letting go of another, cherished person can be very painful for us to do—perhaps the most painful thing that any of us can face. I tried my best to listen as Maria described the loss of David as the man and the loss of the spirit she had known; though I did not witness it at first hand, I know that Maria's private process of grieving continued for months after this talk.

I met David and Maria again over a year later to reassess the situation. David's condition had continued to worsen; he found it much more difficult to talk clearly than he had done, and was now more obviously confused about where he was and who he was with. He was unsure, for example, about who I was, and had only a slight recollection that we had met before. Maria said that he often forgot her name now. She found that difficult, but reminded herself that it was the Alzheimer's that was affecting David's ability to think and remember. Sometimes the carers of people with Alzheimer's can feel that the person with dementia is being deliberately difficult or obstructive, and so may get into arguments with them; most often, though, the sufferers are trying their best to cope—and it is the dementia that is affecting their abilities.

At this time David was well into the middle stage of dementia. He was struggling with all but the simplest tasks at home, and needed much care from Maria. This, she explained, often meant getting up in the night to help him back to bed if he was feeling confused about where he was, or what time of day it was. It was exhausting work in itself—but caring work that Maria was coping with very well and with great fortitude. She was also benefiting from the involvement of social services and the practical help they were able to provide, which included some respite care for her.

'I can deal with it—just. I have good days and bad days. Sometimes I feel OK; at other times, like earlier this week, I feel as though I just can't take any more—as though I'm all completely exhausted, washed up, and it will never end.'

Was there any particular part of the caring that seemed to be the most difficult, the most wearing?

'Most of the time, as I say, I can cope; but when I think about it, there are periods when David just seems to be so, so upset. Don't you, David?'

David looked distractedly at her.

'Yes.'

We explored these times a little, together. They sounded a little like the feelings that we had discussed when we first met—perhaps a sense, somehow, of overwhelming distress on David's part. Unlike that time, though, there didn't seem to be any identifiable pattern to the strong feelings—or at least none we could easily identify from the available information.

Sometimes such seemingly unprompted, unprovoked feelings emerge in people with Alzheimer's, and can be distressing to all concerned. When we stood back a little and reflected on the matter, it was obvious that David was feeling a high level of distress and that he needed to be comforted somehow. One technique that is sometimes useful in such situations is that of a positive distraction, which can take the person away from the difficult and troubling feelings and perceptions. Since with middle-to-late stage dementia people find it difficult to remember what has recently been in their minds, helping them to consider less distressing material can sometimes be helpful, even if the effect is temporary. We decided to try such a strategy. Maria agreed to try to switch David's attention at difficult times, when the feelings of distress were beginning, towards something that he enjoyed. We were aware that there was a particular television comedy that he had loved in the past, so we tried a strategy of either reminding David of that (if the feelings were not too strong), or of actually putting on a video of the show for him.

When we next met, Maria said that the attention-switching strategy had *sometimes* been helpful. On occasion it had not worked at all and she had had to wait, with great patience, for his mood to change. However at other times, for reasons that were unclear to her, David had been helped to move from feelings of anger, upset or worry towards comfort, relief or good humour. It was only a small thing that we could do for David, but it was something that helped to reduce the couple's distress.

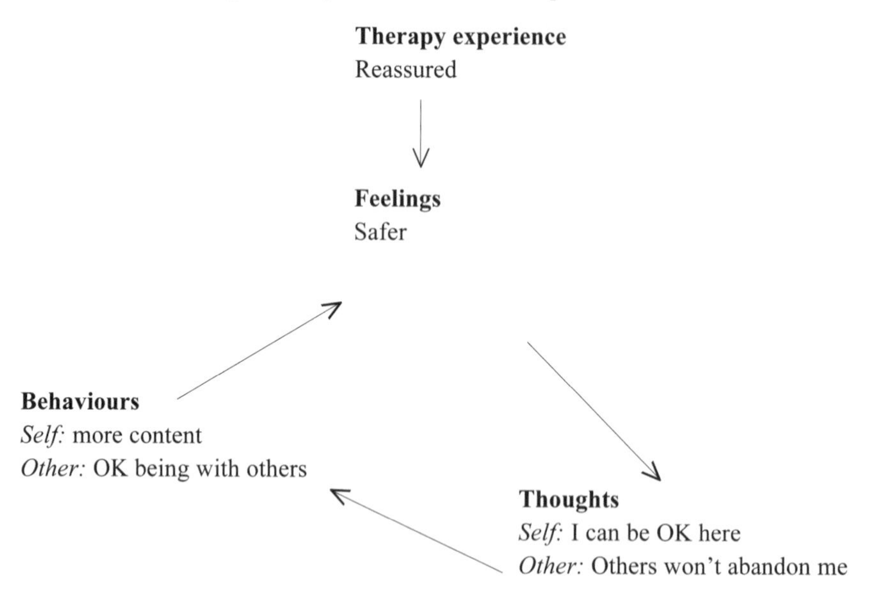

Figure 8.4 David's formulation during therapy

Over the next two years or so I had sporadic contact with David and Maria. As we all do to differing degrees, they travelled through patches of darkness and light. It was clear from David's functioning in the house that his condition was slowly declining; but Maria, still supported by contact with social services, continued to devote herself to his care, day and night. I wondered how she summoned the strength, night after night, to lead David back upstairs, to change the bedding, and to gently stroke his hair as he drifted off back to sleep.

'While I have the strength, my love will always make me stand by him.'

I found Maria's devotion to her husband remarkable. Eventually David's Alzheimer's was moving towards its late stage, by which time the functioning of his brain had been severely affected by the disease. He could no longer talk coherently, recognize Maria or other family members, or take care of himself. Maria called because she felt, very understandably, that she had reached the limits of her capacity to care for David at home, even with the input of social services. Indeed, to continue to care for him might have put her own health at significant risk—which of course David would never have wanted. She had found a possible care home for him, and he had settled in over the previous few weeks. Maria was concerned that the home should be right for him, and asked for my view—which was justifiable, since homes for people with degenerative disorders differ greatly in quality. I met Maria outside the home one afternoon later that week.

Maria was actually looking well now. Her eyes were clear, her voice firm, her movements lively—all more so compared with the last time we had met. I wondered to myself whether perhaps things were shifting psychologically for her—whether some of the grief's weight had begun to lift ever so slightly. As we walked up the drive together my first impressions of the place were good. It was clearly well kept, and the manager was friendly and happy to see us (I would have been concerned if that wasn't so). I had wondered whether David might be quite disturbed by the change of environment he had undergone, but, Maria explained, that had not been the case. She had been careful to pack some reminders of her, and of home, which might ease the transition. Nevertheless, I was still concerned that David's deeper insecurities, stemming from his early life, might be reawakened.

As we approached one of the living rooms downstairs through a corridor, we could hear a commotion. Someone was calling out confusedly, and the noise was affecting other people around them, who were in turn becoming more agitated. The confused person, we could see, was David. We stopped where we were, just to observe. In a place where care is not good, distress of this kind among residents is often left. Such people's needs can often be ignored by staff, so that the people's level of stress increases and their general level of health and well-being decreases.

But as Maria and I stood and waited, something else happened. A young female member of staff who had been in the room previously came into view. She leant down towards David, still there, dignified, in his chair, and put her hand on his forearm. It looked as though she was really making an effort to connect with him; then in a caring, quiet yet firm voice she said:

'It's OK, Mr Thompson. It's OK, Mr Thompson. Mrs Thompson is coming to see you. It's going to be OK.'

The young woman looked at David as she was saying this; she smiled, and quite quickly, David calmed down a little. Feeling distressed, he had been calling out, instinctively wanting care and wanting help. Wanting something, in any case—some human contact: and, as Maria and I watched, that is exactly what he got, as he responded accordingly. David hadn't asked for much, yet it had been given by this young woman, who can't have known him well and certainly hadn't known him when he had been in his prime. Maria and I gave each other a knowing look. Perhaps we both realized that at least part of our question about the choice of this new home for her beloved husband had already been answered, simply by this air of genuine concern for him by a virtual stranger.

Both sensing this, we went over to speak to David, who put out his arms to touch Maria. The young woman and I looked on as this happened. David's intellectual capacities may have been severely reduced by that point; but any impartial observer, watching how David reached out to his wife in the twilight, might easily have thought that deep down, at some level beneath the conscious and for ever hidden to us all, he knew well who was standing there before him.

Reconciliations: Feelings of loss and physical illness in Helen, an 84-year-old woman – 16 sessions

On meeting Helen it was quickly evident that something, somewhere in her life, felt sad for her. Her movements and her speech were slow. She smiled little. Her shoulders drooped. And when she talked, she struggled to make eye contact, as though she was ashamed of either herself or what she was saying—or both. When she was talking, though, it was clear that she was a sensitive, thoughtful woman and I was interested in what had been happening in her life. She took her time in speaking, as I listened and observed.

'I don't think you'll be able to help me; nothing's helped me until now. I've just been feeling so incredibly, incredibly tired. The feeling is with me more or less all the time. Mostly, I can get done what I need to do, but sometimes it's so bad that the only place for me to go is to bed. That can help a little to get my strength back.'

That was understandable, and I was glad that it seemed to help. I wondered how long the feelings of tiredness had been around. How had they begun?

'It's been so long that it's difficult to say. It's certainly years rather than months; and I wish that I didn't feel like this, I really do.'

I wondered if Helen could try to be just a little clearer with regard to the beginning of the problems.

'All right, then—so long as you don't mind my going back a bit. We had been living in France for a long time, my husband Gerry and me. He'd worked hard as an accountant and saved carefully, so he could retire early—when we were both fifty. We'd been looking forward to it so much; our two children were already at university, and things were set fair for us. We found a little flat in the south of France and had the most wonderful fifteen years. We relaxed, we had a good social circle. It was a super time.'

Helen looked more animated as she said this. It was obvious that it had been a happy and memorable period of her life.

'But Gerry became ill. At first we thought that it was a cough, going on a bit longer than usual: but it went on, and there were investigations. It turned out to be lung cancer. Gerry had always dreaded the idea—but never enough to stop him smoking. He was always the optimist. When they did a proper check the cancer was already well advanced, and spreading. Two weeks after we went to the doctor, it was clear there was nothing we could do. We just had to wait for the end.'

In telling her story, Helen seemed curiously neutral. Though it was a difficult question to ask, I was interested in how she had experienced Gerry's death. I was wondering if this was still affecting her mood even at the time we talked. Helen spoke, but with little clear emotion.

'It was a very hard time. Gerry died in 12 weeks flat. The doctors—the French doctors, who were excellent—explained that the best we could do was to make things as painless for Gerry as possible. That's what they did; and before long, he slipped away.'

I understood all this, but Helen's account struck me as over-short, and lacking in real emotion. What had happened then, after such a drastic change? How had she coped?

'Well, I think I just *had* to cope. Our son Michael came over to help me for a week. We sorted things out, sold the flat. Something told me that it was time to come home, so I followed my instinct.'

Helen had had a difficult situation to face, one that confronts many of us, particularly in later life.

'So there I was, home again. I went back to where we had lived—we'd rented out the house all the time we'd been away—but obviously things were different. Many people had died, or moved on; it seemed like a different place entirely. I tried to make the best of it, and for about a year I did quite well, pottering about the house, making myself busy. I was quite getting used to that.'

It sounded as though something else difficult had happened.

'That's right. Well, there were two things, one after another more or less. The first was that my dear friend Annette, whom I'd known since we'd had our children together, moved away. We'd always kept in quite close touch, by letter, by telephone. She and her husband had finally retired—they went in the opposite direction, to live in Spain. That was shock number one.'

Again, Helen maintained her composure completely when she was retelling this part of her life. I wondered how she might be feeling about this deep down, but was prepared to wait to find out.

'And then there was shock number two. About four months after Annette left, I was diagnosed with breast cancer. After a debate among the doctors, it seemed that the only option was a mastectomy. This was difficult for me to take; but I had no choice, you see.'

As I write this, and as Helen was saying it, I felt a strong feeling of empathy with her—even though her feelings did not seem to surface easily within her for some reason. While she seemed curiously cut off from her feelings, I felt quite strongly moved for her. In a short space of time Helen had lost her beloved husband, a very good friend had moved away, and she herself had undergone major, body-altering surgery. I wondered whether her feelings of tiredness had begun around this time.

'It's difficult to be precise, looking back. Having chemotherapy was very draining, certainly; but yes, that's when the tiredness really set in. And while it's come and gone up to a point, it's always been there since. I'm not sure if you can do anything about that. It may be just the way I am—you know, slowing down a little, getting older and so forth. I suppose it might be nature's way of telling me something?'

As I explained to Helen, many people—including older people themselves—imagine that it is 'normal' to feel low, sad, tired or depressed with age, but there is no reason why this should be so. Many older people lead very happy and contented lives, often free of the psychological baggage that they carried during earlier stages of life. To take Helen as an example, when there are persistent feelings of tiredness in an older person, as with any other, there are often key psychological reasons for it and they need to be discovered. In particular, I was interested in how Helen had grieved for these important life-changes—or rather, to be more precise, how and why she had avoided grieving. This was an important question. When we truly grieve what we have lost, we begin to let go; and once we have let go of what we so cherished, we can begin to move on. I wondered if grieving felt difficult, somehow, for some reason, for Helen.

'Perhaps it did. There certainly wasn't much time for it, and there wasn't really anyone around to listen to me. I did what I was used to. I suppose I put it all to the back of my mind, where it seemed to belong.'

I was interested in this account by Helen. It is usual for some of us, sometimes those of us who are older, not to give vent to our emotions—particularly if they are difficult or 'negative' emotions. But it seemed to me that with Helen, this effect had been taken to quite a high level. I was interested, in particular, in helping her to explore what it was that had helped to block her grieving.

'I can't think what it is. Aren't most people like that?'

It was a good question from Helen, but it did feel to me that beyond the limits to emotional expression set by her cultural background as an older, white, British person there was something else that we had missed up to that point. I wondered tentatively whether there had been other events earlier in adulthood that had been difficult for her: an abortion, or a miscarriage perhaps?—something that emotionally had simply gone quite deep within her, and not emerged until now?

'Not that I know of. But when I think back before that, our family—I mean the one I grew up in—never spent any time with things like sadness. It just wasn't the done thing.'

I needed to hear more about this so that we could understand what had happened psychologically.

'My childhood was safe and secure. I've always thought I was lucky in many ways; I never suffered some of the things that other people went through. Mama and Papa were always around and we all knew that they were around and that they loved us. They put real effort into being there for us, because that's what Mama had had so little of when she herself was younger.'

Again, this was leading us to where we needed to be.

'We never knew the full story, but what Mama did explain, particularly in the years before she died, was that her own mother had been a drinker. It was never much talked about in those days, of course—this was the early 1900s. My grandmother and grandfather had a rocky relationship. He had been a very spoilt child, and struggled to cope with responsibilities like work; she grew frustrated and depressed with him, but couldn't leave—so she drank. From the little Mama said, she used to get so drunk that she would scream at the children.'

I wondered how this had affected Helen, when she had been developing.

'Well, you see, when I was growing up the thing was that feelings were not what it was about in our family. You might have felt them, but they weren't shown. I think, looking back, that Mama—because of her own mother—was frightened of showing too much feeling. So in a way, she squashed the feelings in herself, and she squashed them in us. All of us four children learned very well how to control ourselves.'

But perhaps, from a psychological point of view, a little *too* well. As I explained to Helen, it had become clear to me that her tiredness, which may have been connected to her inability to grieve her recent losses, was linked to her way of dealing with feelings, including sadness. This in turn had been learned, in part at least, during her childhood; so our next task was to help Helen see that it was OK to consider her feelings and to begin to get in touch with them.

Like many people who have had relatively little experience of 'feeling their feelings' —and up to the age of 21 or so I was certainly one of them myself—she felt that if she got too close to the feelings, something terrible or catastrophic might happen.

'I might never be able to control them, if they start!'

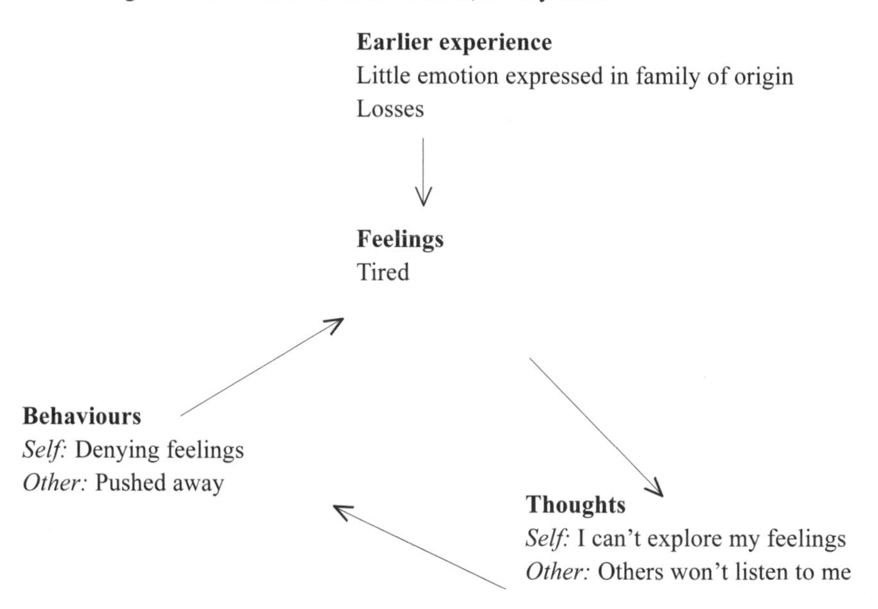

Figure 8.5 Helen's formulation

I reassured her about this. Feelings are natural. They are our way of coping with the world we live in; often or even always, we can trust them to guide us. This is what I gradually tried to help Helen to see. We tested this out by talking to begin with about times in her life that had been joyous and wonderful: her wedding, for example. We noted that when she thought about that she was filled with joy, with her feelings calmed soon afterwards. We wondered whether the same might be true of her sad feelings, too; there was no reason why this shouldn't have been so.

From this gentle starting point, we moved towards the difficult things that had happened more recently to Helen. We shifted backwards and forwards, as required, between the matters of Gerry, the loss of Annette, and her mastectomy. In grief work, it is usual to shift in this way between the stages including denial, sadness, anger and resolution. The cycles may be repeated numerous times.

With me gently leading Helen, we discovered in our discussions that in fact she had a very deep well of untapped feelings about these three things. As we talked over the weeks, she experimented with letting go of her self-control. At first, her eyes were sometimes moist as she talked; at those times, and as we reflected, she was coming to see that it was safe to experience emotions quite fully. This gave her more confidence to go to emotional places, seemingly faraway places that were very different from where she came from: places that she had never visited before.

Helen also did some mindfulness work. Over a number of weeks of practice—since persistence is often very important—Helen came to feel more at home with her own feelings, closer to them, happier to have them and own them. Previously, virtually without thinking, they would have been split off and denied; now, partly as a result of her mindfulness work, she was experiencing them much more richly.

When we were doing this work the atmosphere in our sessions was changing. At the beginning of our sessions the feeling between us had been warm, yes, but controlled, formal and stiff. As we approached the central part of our work—the body of feelings about the losses—the interactions between Helen and me became more fluid, more flexible. As is usual in this type of work I encouraged Helen to talk in detail about her losses, from various different viewpoints, and as she did so she did what I hoped she would do. She sobbed.

As she talked about how much in love she had been with Gerry, how much they had meant to each other, and—feeling this strongly for the first time, she said—how she felt she had lost her dream of their future together, Helen sobbed like a child. For minutes at a time when she talked, she became desperately upset. I witnessed this with compassion; but perhaps against what might have been expected, I didn't step in to rescue Helen from these feelings. This was because I knew they were in the process of setting her free. In psychological work of this kind, it is the repeated experiencing of the feelings that allows them to be emptied out, and the person to begin to change.[7] So Helen's grief would touch on her sadness about Gerry; then there would be a pause before she would come to consider the changes in her own body after her mastectomy. She felt this, too, to be a drastic step for her, about which she had had no choice. We discussed how, since being a young girl, she had always valued her feminine appearance and taken real care of it. Losing her breast felt like a great blow to her, and one that she felt had affected her confidence as a woman. We realized that it had made it more difficult for her to be sociable around others.

'I'm sure, stepping back, nobody knew: but I did. I just wasn't feeling whole any more.'

With the matter of this change, as with Helen's loss of Gerry, we needed to talk about the problem from various perspectives and, above all, to allow Helen to feel the feelings for the first time. Unquestionably this was painful for her to do, because it meant considering great losses that were so close to her heart.

While this work of grieving was difficult and sad for both of us, even during it there were small signs of positive change. At first, towards the end of an emotional session Helen simply often wondered out loud about some of the things that she could do, in future, if she ever came to feel better again. But as the sessions continued, and as she continued to practise her mindfulness, she felt as though she did actually want to

---

7. Knight, B.G. (2004). *Psychotherapy with Older Adults: 3rd edn.* Thousand Oaks, CA: Sage: 145.

make some small plans. I had wondered if we might see some signs of her returning to be with others; now it had gradually started to happen. Together we wondered what might be possible, and what she might enjoy. Helen felt that she'd like to meet someone—not for dinner, or anything so serious as that—but just for a cup of tea during the day; but with the loss of Annette, was there anyone to do that with?

'Well, I haven't seen her for years, but there is another friend of mine, Sheila. I always thought it had been too long for me to ring her, but needs must. Perhaps it might be all right after all. She might even be thinking the same thing!'

I agreed with Helen, of course. It was quite possible—even if we often feel as though it's too late to rekindle old friendships. I was also glad because Helen's attention had begun to shift a little from what was dark and difficult to what might be possible; in other words, hope had begun to be restored. This was an early sign of recovery.

For the next few sessions the structure of our work remained similar. We considered together, and with strong feeling sometimes, what the life-changes Helen had been through would mean for her. Prominent here was the understandable and frequently experienced feeling that it was strange for her to be without Gerry, and to be thinking of a life without him. She had never thought of herself as being 'single' again—and it had been decades since she had been in that position.

'I was a 22 year-old girl; that's over six decades ago!'

It did feel very odd to Helen that she was alone without Gerry now. As part of that feeling there was also some guilt that she had been left behind; but there was also another feeling accompanying it. It was the realization that things had changed, and that things had to change—and she with them. The world turns and moves on—not because it wants to; because it must. Helen allowed this view into her mind: and soon there were fewer tears.

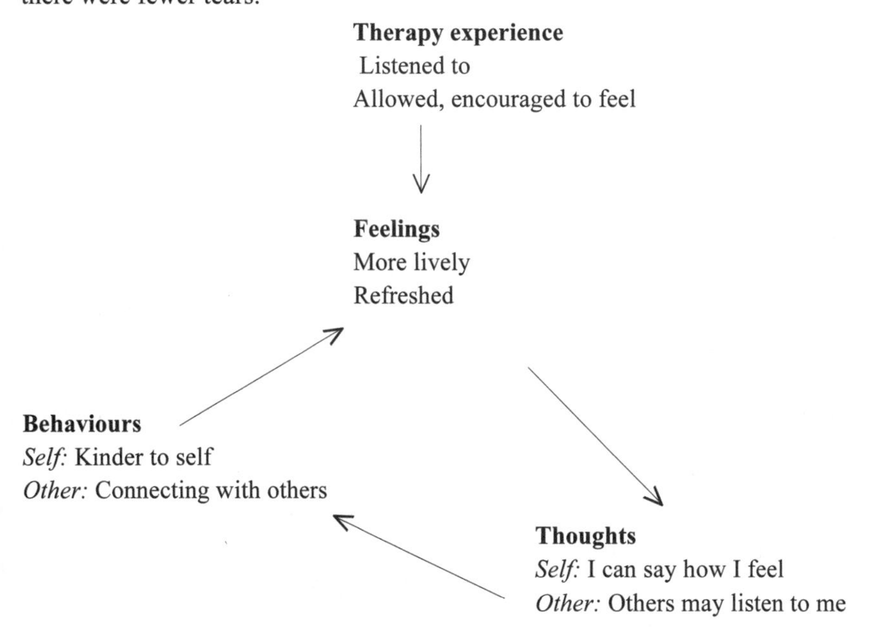

Figure 8.6 Helen's formulation at the end of therapy

Session by session, Helen also came to say how she had been out with her friend Sheila for cups of tea. An opportunity had also arisen for joining others, friends of Sheila's, for a whist drive. Helen didn't feel quite ready for this re-entry into society, but did feel that it was a kind offer, one that she might take up in later months. It felt to me as though we were gently moving towards the conclusion of our work together. Now there were no tears. Unlike before, Helen was wearing make-up and going regularly to the hairdresser, a little luxury that she enjoyed. One thing we did need to discuss was her level of energy, as when we first met Helen had felt so tired that she was unable to do most of the things that she wanted. Perhaps because our talks had been about many other things, she was taken aback.

'Do you know, I'd quite forgotten how tired I had been. Hmm. When I stop to think about it, I am doing much more than I did, aren't I?'

That was right.

'Well, I'm certainly not feeling like doing the Marathon next year, but I might be up to getting out into the garden.'

That seemed to me to be a sign that some change had taken place. By gently and compassionately talking about the changes that had occurred in Helen's life, by letting out some—though not all—of the grief associated with them, she had become more free to reconnect with the life and possibilities that she still had. She was able to see this clearly.

'There's still time for me to live, for myself, in my own way. Gerry's gone, people have gone; I've changed too—but there are still things I want to do, people I want to see. Even little things, like the blossom on the cherry tree in the garden, can give me pleasure, make me come alive.'

On hearing that, I felt that Helen was right. For the most part, for her, the long, dark winter was over. Spring was surely not far behind.

Invasion of Tranquillity: Feelings of post-traumatic stress and depression in Geoffrey, an 85-year-old man – 10 sessions

Everyone, including Geoffrey himself, had been puzzled by his symptoms. They seemed to come on quite suddenly. Over about a two-month period, his GP said in his letter, Geoffrey had changed significantly from being an outgoing, sprightly 85-year-old man to one who struggled hard to make it through each day. He hadn't specifically gone to the GP for help, but had begun to talk about how he was feeling during a routine blood-pressure check (the pressure was normal). Geoffrey's description of what he had been feeling encouraged the doctor to send Geoffrey to me—or rather, me to Geoffrey, since our first meeting was at his home.

As I approached Geoffrey's house in his suburban street, I noticed that the garden had become a little unkempt. I made an internal note of this, since it is sometimes the case that people's gardens offer an indication of their psychological health. A state of complete garden disrepair can indicate problems.

Geoffrey took some time to answer the door. While he was tidily dressed, with his silver-white hair neatly brushed, he looked rather tired and drawn. He showed me into the living room, where his wife was pouring some tea. She was the first to talk.

'Well, doctor, we're very glad to see you. Geoffrey hasn't been himself at all over the last little while. You've been acting in a rather peculiar way, darling, haven't you?'

'If you say so, dear.' Geoffrey did not sound convinced.

'It's true, though, darling, isn't it? You see, doctor, everything was fine before. We've been retired for many years now, and we've had a happy life here. Our children bring the grandchildren over most weeks—we're very lucky in that respect. But at the moment, something seems to be wrong with my husband, and I'm really not sure what.'

I wondered how Geoffrey saw the situation. He sighed heavily.

'She's right, I suppose. I have been feeling a bit odd, shall we say, over the last couple of months. I'm not sure why myself.'

I wondered what Geoffrey meant by 'feeling a bit odd'. What exactly was happening now that was not happening before?

'Well, that at least is an easy one to answer. I started to feel a bit down in the dumps, quite quickly. Also, little things began to worry me more than they normally would. Like paying the bills, keeping the garden in good condition. Those things I usually wouldn't have any problem with.'

That sounded to me like possible symptoms of anxiety and depression. Interesting: but was there anything else that Geoffrey or Glenda had noticed?

'As a matter of fact, there is. I've been having terrible nightmares. Around three times a week, I would say. Often I can't get back to sleep afterwards, and I get up feeling awful. No way to spend a night, is it?'

Bad dreams are sometimes a sign of low mood or depression, but I needed to check out a little about the content of the nightmares, if Geoffrey was able to recall it.

'Well, they differ. Last night, for example, I was being chased by a gang of men, all of them armed. They backed me into a corner and were about to set on me; then I woke up, sweating badly, my heart pumping. The nightmares are often like that, with me feeling pursued, or trapped, with a feeling of no escape.'

By this time I was beginning to wonder whether something psychologically significant had happened to Geoffrey in some way, at some time. Were there any other changes or symptoms that he had noticed?

'I'm just—what's the best way to put it?—just feeling on edge a lot of the time.'

I asked him to expand on that.

'I just feel that somehow it's probably not safe to relax: that if I let my guard down, something could happen to me or Glenda. And I don't want anything to happen.'

Of course he didn't; he wanted both of them to be safe. I wondered whether Geoffrey was having any strong intrusive thoughts, or actual flashbacks, at any time. He seemed surprised to be asked the question.

'Actually, I think I am, you know.'

What was he getting?

'Now you ask, I keep on having these thoughts of how things used to be. It seems such a long time ago, I can't think why the thoughts should be there now.'

What were the powerful thoughts of? Geoffrey's eyes fell, and he looked embarrassed.

'I've never actually told anyone this before: not even you, Glenda. I've never thought that I ought to trouble anyone with it. It seemed like a private thing, and that it should stay that way.'

I could understand that. It's normal, and quite often happens, for older men to find it hard to talk about what's happening psychologically in their lives. For this reason, I was pleased that Geoffrey was being as open as he was now.

'All right. There's no point in pussyfooting around, is there? Quite often nowadays, I find myself back where I was as a young man in the mid-1940s. That's what comes into my mind, and I have a devil of a job getting rid of it.'

We needed to be still clearer about what had happened. It felt as if we were almost there.

'As a young man, I was called up to fight in the war. For me, like for lots of others, parts of the whole thing were good—like a boys' own adventure. But there were parts of it that were, shall we say, very grim indeed.'

And those parts are were Geoffrey had been remembering?

'Yes'.

It sounded as though Geoffrey had symptoms of post-traumatic stress. This would make sense of his intrusive thoughts, flashbacks, nightmares and poor sleep. But I wondered how long he had been feeling these things; it can be very exhausting suffering from such symptoms.

'I'm not sure that it's been so long. A few weeks, perhaps.'

Glenda interrupted.

'Oh, come on, Geoffrey, its been longer than that, hasn't it? I think I can remember when it started. It was the anniversary celebrations of D-Day a few months ago. That's when it all started, dear. '

Geoffrey looked rather sheepish as he nodded in acknowledgement. It was a difficult thing for him to admit, and I wanted to make it as easy and acceptable as possible for him to say what he needed to. At this point, his eyes welled up with tears. He wasn't crying, but he was close to it.

'Yes. It was something about that day, you see. We saw the whole parade on television—and they were all there, those of us who survived, and who are still alive now. Somehow, d'you know, it brought it all back. I'd buried the whole damn show, the whole thing, for so long, with very few problems. But that day in particular, it brought it all flooding back into my mind, and it felt as though there was nothing I could do to stop it. It had happened a few times before, but then I'd managed to keep a lid on it. This time, it all carried on.'

Glenda was surprised at this. Like many Western men, because of the feeling of shame about 'not coping' emotionally, Geoffrey had not told even the person closest to him how he was feeling, but instead had remained silent about the truth of his emotional state.

'It sounds,' I said, 'as though you've really been having a difficult time.'

Geoffrey smiled. 'I fear you may be right, young man.'

Geoffrey's feelings and symptoms were beginning to make clear sense to me now, as I explained to him and Glenda. He had had some traumatic experience during the latter stages of World War Two when fighting against the German Army. Like many men who fight in a war, Geoffrey had picked up very understandable emotional scars that had lasted right up to the present—a period of over half a century. Most of the time—again like many of us—he had been able to distract himself from his suffering, often by simply keeping busy; but, perhaps with more time on his hands and with a powerful reminder in a significant anniversary of the D-Day landings, the feelings had returned to trouble him, day and night. Both Geoffrey and Glenda said they were surprised that what had happened so long ago could be so relevant now, but they felt that the explanation made psychological sense.

'The thing is, now, doctor, what can we do about it?'

This was a good question. I explained that we had two options open to us. The first was to try to use eye movement desensitization and reprocessing (EMDR) to help Geoffrey fully process and integrate what had happened to him. This option promised to be possibly the quickest means of doing the relevant work: but there was an obstacle. Geoffrey, like many people, had a heart condition that might have made it risky for us to attempt EMDR, because of the high levels of emotion sometimes involved. The second option was to use a gentler method, trauma-focused cognitive behaviour therapy (TF-CBT), to address the issues.[8] We agreed together that this approach would be the best to try.

To prepare for this work, I passed on some skills of mindfulness meditation to Geoffrey over a couple of sessions. Mindfulness was new to him, as it is to many people who come for psychotherapy. We practised in-session, and it took Geoffrey some daily practice over weeks to build his ability to be aware of what was in his mind. At first it seemed strange to him; he felt odd 'not doing anything' and simply observing his psychological processes—his thoughts, feelings and memories—whatever they were. But gradually he felt as though he was getting used to this 'non-doing', and was even beginning to enjoy it.

Once Geoffrey had begun to develop his skills of mindfulness, we began to look in more detail at the traumatic events that he had been part of. He had, he explained, been a young man when the D-Day landings were going on.

'After joining the army I worked in munitions distribution in England, being responsible for sending weaponry to troops as and when it was needed. Mathematics had always been my strong point when I was at school, and I used my scientific skills when we were working out who was likely to need what, what was needed where, and the logical side of how to get the stuff there. Most of the time, I'm proud to say, we managed very well—even when money and time were very tight—but towards the end of the war I was getting itchy feet. I had friends who had been fighting on the Continent and, while they weren't exactly enjoying it, had a real sense of achievement.

8.See Clark, D.M. & Ehlers, A. (2004). Post-traumatic stress disorder: from cognitive theory to therapy. In: R.L. Leahey (ed.). *Contemporary Cognitive Therapy: Theory, research, and practice.* New York: Guilford Press: 141–160.

I suppose, looking back, that I wanted a share of that.'

So he went away?

'I did. It was a difficult decision, because Glenda and I had just met, but I felt that apart from anything else, my country needed me, as we used to say. So I left munitions, and it wasn't long before preparations started for D-Day. It was exciting and frightening at the same time. But however we felt about it, we had to do it; there wasn't really a choice.'

It was a different world back then, for most young men.

'For the first few days everything went well; there were no major hitches. We were making large gains in territory—more than we had expected, but then my battalion was called in to deal with a situation in a French village. We got a message somehow that some German soldiers were holed up there. Six of us went in to investigate.'

How was he feeling at that point?

'Fine—but we'd had other situations like it and everything had been all right, without any problems. This time, as soon as we reached the barn where they were all meant to be, it was different. There were locals gathered around, hiding as best they could. We waited outside the barn, while one of the American fellows shouted to the Germans inside. The situation was worse than we thought. We worked out that there were six German soldiers in there, but they were demanding free passage out of the village and back towards their lot. This wouldn't normally have been a problem, because we would have gone in quickly and sorted them out. The issue was that they had taken two French women as hostages.'

'I see.'

'We waited for hours. It was like a siege, with each side waiting for the others to act; but eventually something had to give. We decided that the only thing for it was to storm the place by night.'

Had Geoffrey been heavily involved?

'Yes. We staked out the place, and two of us clambered up into the back of the barn through the drainage system—a struggle, I can tell you. We were making our way quietly, as planned, towards the front area of the barn when a horse must have seen us and whinnied. All hell broke loose. The Germans began firing at us. We returned their fire, and three of them were killed quickly. The others looked as if they had minor injuries, but they still had hold of the two French women, who were terrified, quite naturally. I can still see the looks on their faces; it was awful. We were having to think fast, and make good decisions although we were exhausted. For another half an hour or so—but it seemed like a month, it went so slowly—there was another stand-off. But one of their men was injured and bleeding; he was looking and sounding more and more desperate. He was saying that unless we left the building immediately, the two women would be punished. We knew what he meant. While all this was going on, another one of the Americans, a sniper, had taken up a position now with a view onto what was happening. We were content, for now, to try and talk to the Germans—but the sniper must have had a clear view, or a rush of blood to the head, or both, because he started firing, hitting one of the Germans. It was terrible now. The German soldier with the women shot one, who fell to the floor. I could see what was happening and tried to rush in. I wanted to take him down safely, but it was impossible. I shot him, but before I did so he had already taken care of the other woman with his pistol. The other two German soldiers surrendered, but the last woman—she was a girl, can't have been more than twenty— died in my arms. So there I was. I'd volunteered for this operation to begin with: but I was stood in a French barn in the middle of nowhere, with the dead and the dying around me, with life ebbing away from them as I stood there. It was the blood of the innocents, as well as the guilty. Carnage. The French women had never hurt anyone, and still they died. It was pointless. All of it, so pointless.'

I wondered whether it changed how Geoffrey saw the war, or himself, after that.

'Of course, of course. It couldn't have been otherwise. I felt, and still feel, such guilt at what happened on that farm. It had been partly me, encouraging the others to go in gung-ho and sort out the German soldiers. If it hadn't been for me, those women would probably have lived. In a way, it feels to me as though it was I who killed them. Sometimes they're there, in the daytime or in my nightmares, pleading with me. Not in French: in English. Pleading, just pleading to be saved: but then dying.'

Geoffrey was very upset by this point. We had, I felt, found the issues that had been troubling him. After such a strenuous session of explanation of his most difficult time, we agreed that he would need a good rest before we continued our work in the next session.

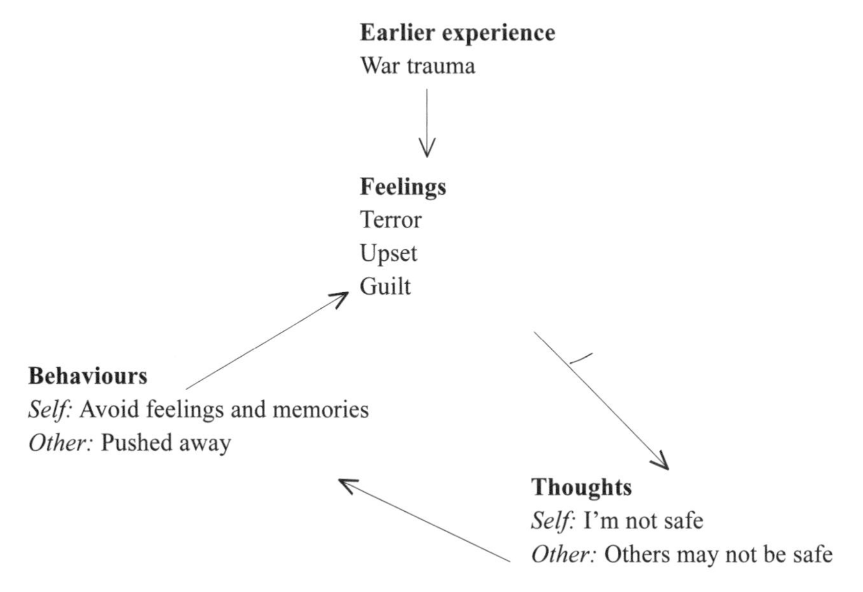

Figure 8.7 Geoffrey's formulation

As a basis for our remaining work, Geoffrey continued to use mindfulness meditation, which helped him feel more stable. Working daily he gradually found, like many people, that mindfulness offered him a slight respite from, and a different perspective on, his trauma-related thoughts and feelings. When we had first met he had often felt completely overwhelmed by the memories of what had happened, as well as by the feelings of anxiety and stress that were triggered. Now, Geoffrey began to find that while the flashbacks and the images came just about as frequently as they had when things had been at their worst, his level of distress when this was happening had begun to fall slightly. By about ten per cent, he estimated.

I asked Geoffrey to continue his mindfulness work, something that he had never tried before, throughout the remainder of our therapy. Given Geoffrey's heart condition, it did not make sense to try EMDR with him, so we focused on a more traditional method of helping him to accept, acknowledge and psychologically integrate what had occurred well over half a century ago. To do so, we needed to focus on the particular meanings the trauma had had for him, and to help him work through them. As part of this aspect of the therapy we focused on any 'hot spots' of the trauma that he was aware of—the parts of it that he found most distressing. Some people are able to identify numerous such hot spots to work on in therapy, but Geoffrey felt that he had just one. Which was that?

'It's the point when the shooting has finished and I'm holding the young French girl in my arms. And'—there were tears in his eyes again—'she's dying as I look at her.'

I wondered what Geoffrey saw then.

'I'm looking at her. Her eyes are open but there's blood coming out of her dress. Pouring out. She's opening her mouth to say something, but she can't talk because her voice won't work. And I'm there thinking to myself: I killed you, woman, I killed you. I want to save you now, but there's *nothing I can do* and it feels as if it's *all my fault*.'

We did two things here, Geoffrey and I, over the next ten sessions or so. We spent much time talking about the incident, the trauma, moving backwards and forwards over it. We did this in ever-increasing detail, so that the parts of the memory that were most disturbing to Geoffrey were often brought to mind. This had the effect of gradually helping him to 'habituate' to the trauma. Like animals, if we are presented once or twice with a frightening, traumatizing event, we are likely to be fearful; but when presented with the same event numerous times, our level of arousal tends to drop. In time we can come to see the same events as less frightening or threatening. Sometimes in psychological work this can be done either by having a person write, and then rewrite many times, the story of the troubling event; or by having them record their telling of the story on audiotape, and then playing it daily over a number of consecutive days until their level of arousal diminishes. This is what Geoffrey chose to do between sessions, because it felt like less hard work to him, and of course his days of hard work were over: now was the time in his life to relax.

The other thing that Geoffrey and I did was to consider more precisely just how guilty and responsible for what happened he really was. While he had begun by feeling that the deaths of the women were 'all my fault', with a little help from me he began to shift his position on this. We began to change his distortions about what happened and who was responsible. We looked at how he had got involved in the war in the first place. In fact, he had had no choice: he had been conscripted. We looked at whether he knew what he was letting himself in for by moving from the munitions operation. Geoffrey acknowledged feelings of guilt about this for his thoughtlessness, but on reflection we realized that there were many young men at the time, British, American and German, doing exactly the same—each of whom was unsure about the consequences of the adventure they were setting out on and none of whom, Geoffrey included, would have been able to say when they began the war what was likely to happen. Finally, and perhaps most importantly, we looked at Geoffrey's strong feelings of guilt about being directly involved in the deaths of the innocent women. We were able to consider these feelings in some depth. It was clear to both of us that, as soldiers, Geoffrey and his colleagues bore *some* responsibility for what happened to them; but it was also true that Geoffrey had not meant the women any harm. He had not killed them, and indeed to the best of his ability he had tried to save them. These ideas were not immediately clear to Geoffrey when we were beginning this work, but emerged gradually during our hours of discussion.

All this work also went on as, over the weeks, Geoffrey was doing his mindfulness meditation work. He found, as many of us do, that mindfulness began to weaken, slightly but still significantly, the strength of his original feelings and thoughts about what happened. This was certainly the case towards the end of our work. He came with Glenda to my office.

'I never thought I would be saying this to you, but my views on the whole thing have changed rather a lot. I still get the thoughts about what happened that day; they come quite often, but something, somewhere, has changed inside here.' He tapped the side of his head. 'I just don't feel so guilty any more. What happened was terrible—but we were all caught up in the war, all of us. We had no control over where we were sent, or what we were going to find when we got there. There were many difficult, impossible times. There were things that we couldn't prevent, even when we tried. But whatever else we did, we did our best.'

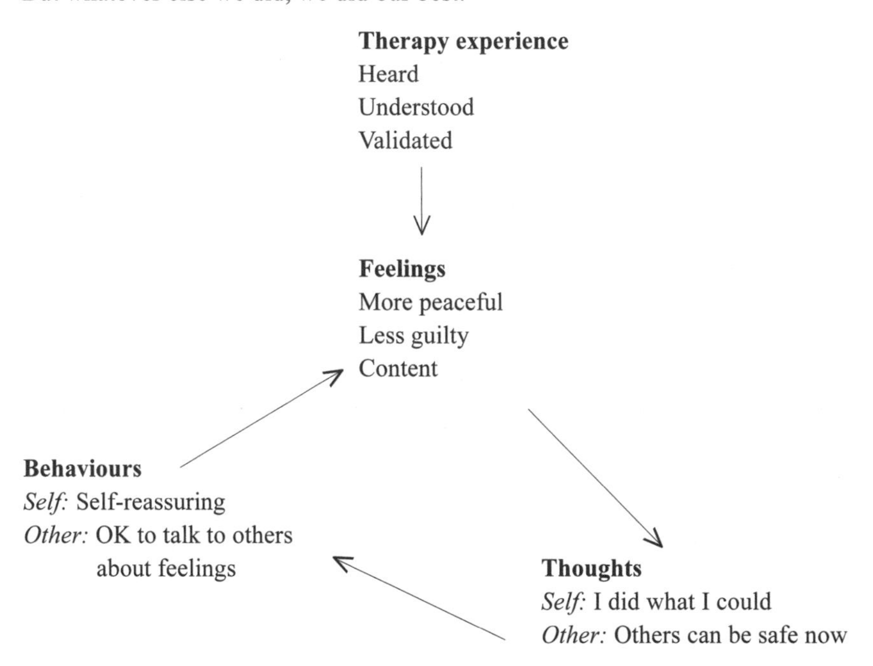

Figure 8.8 Geoffrey's formulation at the end of therapy

This was a big shift for Geoffrey. Like many psychological changes, it hadn't been sudden and it wasn't complete, but it was enough of a change to allow Geoffrey to feel more at peace with himself I felt at the time that there was no need for a dignified gentleman who had bravely served his country in the cause of freedom to experience such psychological suffering. Like much psychotherapy, our work had been slow and painstaking, but it had been worthwhile.

I met Geoffrey and Glenda some months later for a follow-up appointment. They both seemed very well. Glenda explained.

'He's very much back to his old self. There are some days when he's a little off-colour, but for the most part he's as he was, pottering about the garden, up in the allotment—even back on his bicycle. It feels as though the ghosts of the past have finally started to disappear.'

Geoffrey was clearly about to talk: but he looked so well now that I was able to guess, quite accurately, what he was going to say.

* * *

It is very easy for many of us in the population, including older people themselves, to feel that they can't be helped by psychotherapy, and that a natural part of growing older is to decline inevitably into misery, burdened by the losses that they see around them. Worse still, for various reasons the young very often treat older people with disregard, all too often acting as though the older person is not there.

Yet the people in later life are there, if we will take time to look. They do exist, and if we younger people will allow it, they might have much to teach us. Above all, psychologically speaking though, *the older people are people too*. We all share psychological histories, developed out of our relationships with others, that if we are unfortunate earlier in our lives can leave us fragile and troubled for much of our lives. Regardless of age, we need the presence of others to sustain us within the human community; and where psychological problems do arise for older people, just as for younger people, they need care, kindness and love to help nurture and replenish them—to help them enjoy their days and sleep peacefully during the nights. It takes only a little reflection on our part to remember this. What kind of treatment would we prefer, if we were them now? The warmth of kindness, mindfulness for one another—or cold indifference?

Psychologically we all seem so similar in this. Take the youngest infant, take an adult, take an older person in the latter stages of their life: all three, if they are smiled at, will be very likely to smile back. If pain is caused to them, they will be hurt and will show that they have been hurt; but if we treat them mindfully, with kindness, they will respond and will show kindness in return. Could this be telling us something about how we might try to interact with people in later life? And how they might begin to feel, if we did?

9

Hope

> Never above you. Never below you. Always beside you.
> Walter Winchell

We affect each other. Directly or indirectly, and whether we remember it or not during the different times of our days and lives, *we affect each other*. In their slightly different ways, the Buddha and Christ—and other figures with similar messages from other religions—were right to emphasize that how we live with each other is important for all of us. Psychological science has shown that to be so beyond reasonable doubt. With this knowledge, I wonder if we can begin to imagine some slightly different possibilities for ourselves?[1]

From what we do or say to one another, we leave our own imprint on our fellow humans. Just as the parent or caregiver shapes the emotional experience of each sensitive child, each of us can, whatever our age, class or social position, shape the emotional experience of any others, regardless of who they are. We can ruin each other's existences if we try hard enough, and behave abusively, mindlessly or unkindly enough; or we can, psychologically speaking, give each other new life.

We can do it. As I've said in the previous chapters, the psychological problems experienced by people most often have much, or even everything, to do with other people. These others, even if they have not directly caused the problem, have usually contributed significantly to it. Since we are largely designed, after millions of years of evolution, to look out for and take care of *ourselves* first and foremost, we may sometimes need to make a special effort to really appreciate, understand and be mindful of the feelings and perspective of others—and then, perhaps, to act a little differently towards them.

Making such an effort can be very difficult to do, but it is usually worth it and repays all concerned. In each of the cases discussed in this book, with people that I have known and worked with and also in my own life, a simple pattern has recurred.

1. Phillips, A. (2005). *Going Sane*. London: Faber: 12.

People need help after harsh or unfair treatment from others. They may show all manner of psychological and physical feelings and symptoms that are connected, sometimes in quite hidden ways, but when that person comes into contact with kind, positive human help—often regardless of the specific type of psychotherapy involved—something vital changes. At a human-to-human level, a shift occurs. When someone shows in an appropriate way that they care about us somehow, that they are mindful of us, remember us and think about us, new light illuminates the problem. The darker the previous history, the more clear the light becomes. We are given new life by such human companionship, and with it the shamed can begin, slowly, to come out of hiding. The frightened find a new reserve of courage. The desperate may find some comfort. From each one of us, hope may be offered to others; and then, as I say, there can be new psychological life, as the person naturally begins to grow again. Someone who has previously had only dark dreams in which they were terrorized, threatened and trapped, after kindly contact from other human beings can start to dream of compassionate, understanding and warm figures. Such feelings of hope after kindness is offered, which start to emerge like bluebells after the showers of spring, can be an early sign of recovery. That is the story I have tried to tell here.

Such changes would require us to become more mindful of ourselves, and of each other. As I have tried to show, this could mean allowing ourselves and others, for once, enough space to breathe psychologically, to begin to explore where we actually are—as opposed to where we might like to be—in relation to ourselves and our lives, perhaps for the first time. By doing this we can give our natural emotional intelligence the best possible chance to heal ourselves, and to help heal others.

We could begin with ourselves, and with those who are closest to us; it is often they who need us most to be there for them. But clear changes can occur when we live more mindfully, and begin to treat ourselves and others even just a little differently. In the first years of the twentieth century the novelist Tolstoy, by then in his seventies and having emerged from a spiritual crisis, put it directly:

> Why and for what purpose do you torment yourselves and all the others with whom you come into contact in this world? [...] Begin to live by seeing the purpose and well-being of your life in [...] the increasing perfection of love. Just begin to do this, and from the first day, from the first hour, you will experience a new and joyous sensation of the awareness of complete freedom and well-being flowing ever increasingly into your soul.[2]

I think we would all have to admit that this does sound good, at least in theory. Could we give it a go?

Like many people in the cash-rich West, though, I slip so, so easily into habits of comfort, mindlessness and selfishness. This human failing can take us away from the importance of showing kindness to others. It is one of the easiest, and in some ways—

---

2. Tolstoy, L. (1905; trans. & repr. 1987). The law of love and the law of violence. In: J. Kentish (ed.). *A Confession, and Other Writings*. Harmondsworth: Penguin: 151–227.

for some of us who feel that we could stand to lose what we most value (like, perhaps, a little of our comfort or wealth)—one of the most pleasurable things in our lives to remain distant from others: other people who may seem very different from us; we criticize them, sneer at them, refuse even to try to understand them. Doing these things can feel good, or even better, fantastic sometimes; for example, I've enjoyed delicious, seductive fantasies of revenge against some people—nurturing them, keeping the fantasies alive. Undeniably that sometimes feels good, particularly when our own feelings have been badly hurt, or when we feel threatened by mindless treatment from others. However, when at work or at home I extend myself towards others and really try to understand them, good things reliably seem to happen; new, different and life-giving psychological cycles begin to be set up. By this deliberate, mindful human contact, seemingly impossible problems turn out to have solutions that, until two people look carefully together, one person alone has understandably not been able to see. It has taken me, as a materially spoilt, only child who had too much his own way—but who has also had to struggle in other, psychologically definable ways—many years and much painful experience to realize that we can and perhaps even should help each other to a great degree, in ways that we often do not appreciate, or appreciate but then forget.

Yet still mistakes will be made by us as people, wherever we are, and will inevitably continue to be made by us. Even great people—the apparently assertive, the creative, the intelligent, the supposed 'strong'—make terrible decisions, form false opinions and act in terrible ways that cause the suffering and even the violation of others. We have plenty of psychological evidence to suggest that we see ourselves, others and our world in very biased ways—and that, tragically, we often act according to these biases. What are we to make of this, our all-too-human fallibility? I wonder whether, somehow, we might begin to use our proven fallibility as a reminder of our need for others, and them for us. Where we make mistakes, even cause damage, others offer us hope of correction and repair; the favours we have received from them, we might eventually return, either to them or to other people. This fact of our dependence on others, and our awareness of it, might bring us closer together. Whatever else we can do, and however much we might try to fool ourselves into thinking otherwise, we just can't make it alone at any stage of our lives.

Isn't this awareness of others, and being mindful of their needs, all a bit old-fashioned? There are many parts of modern life—not least the images, lifestyles and messages of the media—that if we take them at face value, mindlessly, can lead us towards pushing ourselves forward at the expense of others, and towards more or less unbridled self-assertion. I've known this type of greed for *more* of this, or that, or whatever, in myself and in my own life. We may be led to crave and obtain what is materially new rather than what is human and real. I have also said that, as evolved animals, we may be partly designed to assert ourselves before others. We know from experience where such processes can lead our communities, locally, nationally and globally. While some individuals and groups—the highly educated, the intelligent, the wealthy—are more likely to prosper, as history shows, other people suffer. If and when we have forced our way mindlessly to the top, we may find that there's nothing there—and the time of our lives has slipped like sand through our grasping hands.

Around a century ago the philosopher Nietzsche, drawing on aspects of Darwinism, said that 'self-overcoming' was important for Western people. We were, Nietzsche said, to override the 'weaker' parts of ourselves and our societies, and drive onward to success, and damn the consequences. The destructive results of such a self-centred approach, though, were obvious during the mass slaughter of innocents during the wars of the twentieth century, and it is now clear that a different kind of self-overcoming is required that is the humane opposite of Nietzsche. What may be needed is the gradual awareness of our own tendencies toward selfishness and self-assertion, and awareness of how this self-seeking might be reduced. Mindfulness, in other words. We have, as James Lovelock recently said: 'the capacity for disastrous destruction, but also the potential to found a magnificent civilization.'[3] Mindfulness, widely practised and reflected upon, might help us to release this vast potential.

Perhaps too, if we were to choose to go a little further down this track for a while, we might also change how we feel about ourselves. Being more mindful, maybe we might be less likely to think in fixed ways of ourselves and others, whoever they may be—young or old, black or white, Eastern or Western. By such a route or routes, we might individually and collectively discover newer, lighter ways to be, and slightly different, more flexible identities. We might learn to tell different, more life-giving stories about ourselves and others, from the wealth of stories we know of;[4] and if we were able to provide support for each other, there is experimental evidence that it might be easier for us to begin to accept our weaknesses.[5]

Of course, though, it cannot be denied that it isn't easy to be a little more aware of the psychological needs of others—to be mindful. However, by knowing a little more about how we can affect the psychological lives of others, as I have shown in this book, perhaps—just perhaps—we might be tempted to stop ourselves, and wonder. In the same situation, if I were that person before me, or about whom I was thinking—*actually, how would I feel if I were that person?* Maybe we don't do this too much today. This, of course, is what Christ was suggesting with the idea that we should do unto others as we would wish them to do unto us. The difference is that now we know, beyond reasonable and scientific doubt, what can happen between us when there is no care, where there is mindlessness and no respect. People can get hurt and can suffer, sometimes for almost all of their conscious and unconscious lives.

But aren't these people just being rather oversensitive, and shouldn't they just get on with life in what is sometimes inevitably (as we often, ordinarily think in these isles)[6] a hard, harsh world? It is true that many aspects of our lives with each other are fast-moving and unpredictable. It is also correct to say that different people react in

---

3. Lovelock, J. (2006). *The Revenge of Gaia: Why the earth is fighting back—and how we can still save humanity.* London: Penguin/Allen Lane: 6.
4. Booker, C. (2004). *The Seven Basic Plots: Why we tell stories.* London & New York: Continuum.
5. For a summary of evidence here, see Sedikedes, C. (2005). Close relationships—what's in it for us? *The Psychologist, 18(8),* 490–493.
6. Fox, K. (2004). *Watching the English: The hidden rules of English behaviour.* London: Hodder & Stoughton.

different ways to the same events, including the same treatment by others. Some individuals may have, for instance, a slight genetic predisposition to becoming depressed when faced with appropriate life-stresses. All this is true: but these are not strong enough reasons for us to simply forget each other and act as though we don't need to respect our fellow people, male or female, whatever their age or culture. In any case, I have met many people who, though clearly very psychologically strong in themselves, have still suffered lasting damage from disgraceful abuse from their parents. One such person I can think of, who is otherwise healthy and strong and doing their best to cope independently with all the normal issues of adult life, when they were a young child had their faces pushed into animal faeces by their parents as a 'punishment' for 'bad behaviour'. A child, acting like a child—and being hurt for it? No.

What is required is just a little more awareness of how we feel in a given situation, and how someone else might feel. What's our incentive for doing this, for being so mindful of what is happening, for deliberately slowing our psychological processes down and observing them in action? Others will be grateful if we treat them with mindful respect if they are suffering; and one day it might be us—given the human tendency to grow older, fall ill, then die. One day we will need compassion to be shown to us. too.

We can do it. I have seen many people struck down psychologically for years of their lives by mindless cruelty, prejudice and injustice. One person psychologically affects another. Yet I have also seen many such people move back to health and take steps towards personal liberty, by virtue of their, and our, human intelligence, resourcefulness and, above all else, human kindness and mindfulness. When we offer our hand to someone they will, noticing our action and even without conscious thought, often take it. There is hope. It may be distant, but there is hope on the horizon. We can do it. Can you see?

Index

The Therapy Experience:
How human kindness heals

Why do people hurt each other so much?

What use is psychotherapy?

How can mindfulness help?

In *The Therapy Experience,* Dr Roger Kingerlee, a practising clinical psychologist, draws on his personal and professional experience of psychological issues, as well as current clinical psychological science, to argue that there are excellent reasons to treat each other, and ourselves, respectfully—as happens in good psychotherapy. This is because each one of us sets the psychological climate in which others live, no matter what our age, gender or cultural background.

Given our tendency to treat ourselves and others mindlessly, Kingerlee says, in this part-self-help book, part-confession, part-polemic for compassion, it may be wise for us to take a step back and to be mindful of how we lead our lives and, in particular, *what we do to each other*. Everyone of us needs psychologically respectful treatment in our day-to-day life if we are to lead fulfilling lives. This is why people respond so well to good psychotherapy at every life-stage, as numerous case studies show. Gradually becoming more mindful of our own and others' psychological needs might take us to an altogether different, more enjoyable, more humane, life-giving and respectful place. If, as Kingerlee believes, human mindlessness is the problem, the focused practice of human mindfulness may be the cure.

Dr Roger Kingerlee was educated at the Universities of Oxford, Berlin, Hamburg and East Anglia, and is now a practising chartered clinical psychologist in Norfolk. He helps people address their psychological issues using cognitive analytic therapy (CAT), cognitive behavioural therapy (CBT), eye movement desensitization and reprocessing (EMDR) and mindfulness meditation techniques.